W9-ADC-592

CORRUPTION IN CUBA

Corruption in Cuba

CASTRO AND BEYOND

Sergio Díaz-Briquets and Jorge Pérez-López

UNIVERSITY OF TEXAS PRESS
Austin

Copyright © 2006 by the University of Texas Press
All rights reserved
Printed in the United States of America
First edition, 2006

Requests for permission to reproduce material from this work should be sent to:
> Permissions
> University of Texas Press
> P.O. Box 7819
> Austin, TX 78713-7819
> www.utexas.edu/utpress/about/bpermission.html

∞ The paper used in this book meets the minimum requirements of ANSI/NISO Z39.48-1992 (R1997) (Permanence of Paper).

Library of Congress Cataloging-in-Publication Data
Díaz-Briquets, Sergio.
    Corruption in Cuba : Castro and beyond / Sergio Díaz-Briquets and Jorge Pérez-López.— 1st ed., 2006.
        p.   cm.
    Includes bibliographical references and index.
    ISBN-13: 978-0-292-71321-5 (cloth : alk. paper)
    ISBN-10: 0-292-71321-5 (alk. paper)
    ISBN-13: 978-0-292-71482-3 (pbk. : alk. paper)
    ISBN-10: 0-292-71482-3 (alk. paper)
    1. Political corruption—Cuba.   2. Corruption—Cuba.   I. Pérez-López, Jorge F.   II. Title.
    JL009.5.C6D52   2006
    364.1′323097291—dc22

                                                          2006005140

To Nicholas, Tanya, Anya, and Tonya for their contributions to closer Cuban (American) —Russian relations

Sunlight is said to be the best disinfectant; electric light the most efficient policeman.

—LOUIS BRANDEIS, 1914

I was telling you how the world was greatly in need of a vaccine against corruption. Fortunately, the Revolution, through its sense of morality, through its sense of responsibility, immunized the basic cadres against corruption.

—FIDEL CASTRO, SPEECH TO THE EIGHTH SCIENCE
AND TECHNOLOGY FORUM, 1993

I think that more important than a vaccine against cancer, even, would be a good vaccine against corruption.

—FIDEL CASTRO, RADIO SPEECH ON CORRUPTION, 1993

An old proverb teaches that "power corrupts, and absolute power corrupts absolutely." . . . If the first step to combat corruption is to identify it, the second step is to shine a light on it.

—"LA CORRUPCIÓN," EDITORIAL
IN *Revista Vitral,* 2004

CONTENTS

LIST OF TABLES AND FIGURE

PREFACE

Corruption has been a chronic problem for the Cuban nation. At crucial historical junctures, corruption became inextricably linked with political, economic, and social developments to set, in a perverse way, the future of the country. The documentary evidence we examine shows the corruption burden a newly independent Cuba inherited from centuries of colonial rule at the dawn of the twentieth century. It also shows how since the early days of the Republic, the promise of democratic governance was undermined by the unethical practices embraced by Cuba's rulers and many of its citizens. Such was the harm produced that it would not be far-fetched to claim that the country's history of corruption was one of the reasons Fidel Castro's 1959 Revolution was able to upset the existing political order with relative ease.

As often happens, a revolution born with the pledge to make corruption a thing of the past failed to live up to its commitments. By the time Fidel Castro declared Cuba a socialist state in 1961, new corruption modalities were emerging along the lines described by Milovan Djilas and other writers about the ruling elites of communist countries. As political power and control of the economy became increasingly concentrated in the hands of the totalitarian state, inevitable consumer-good shortages and inefficiencies in resource allocation led to black-market activities and the unsavory transactions they produce.

After three decades of socialist rule and with the promise of material prosperity dashed by the collapse of the socialist world in the early 1990s, petty corruption became ubiquitous, and more and more Cubans became adept at trading on the black market whatever they could steal from the state. As socialist Cuba opened its economy to the outside world as a survival strategy, absent former Soviet subsidies, many among the political and military elite turned into socialist managers and entrepreneurs and began to fathom new ways to protect and in many cases enhance their privileges by entering into shady deals presumably forbidden by socialist morality rules. Notwithstanding heavy doses of anti-corruption rhetoric from Castro and several anti-corruption campaigns—including the most recent, in the second half of 2005, when gas station attendants were dismissed from their jobs because they allegedly stole gasoline that was sold in the black market, and when there were crackdowns on agricultural markets—illegal activities involving the most basic consumer goods remain the rule.

There is some evidence that, in anticipation of inevitable changes toward market reforms and a more open political regime likely to follow Castro's eventual death, Cuba's ruling elite has begun to prepare the ground for a wholesale assault on the country's patrimony to safeguard its own economic well-being. And this is likely to be juxtaposed on an environment where petty corruption is widespread, as even the most rudimentary forms of social and administrative controls would be difficult to enforce during a transition. In this regard, what is likely to occur in a Cuba in transition will not be very different from what was observed in most former communist countries: the explosive appearance of grand-scale corruption as former high-ranking political operatives, often in connivance with unscrupulous private-sector interests, managed to bend or fashion emerging marketplace rules (particularly regarding privatization) as laws are somewhat in flux.

These concerns and the potential for corruption to severely compromise Cuba's future, together with our lifelong interest in the country's affairs, led us to undertake this exploration of the impact of corruption on the country's current and future development. We arrived at our joint analytical venture through different but converging paths. As students of the development process, we became increasingly aware of and sensitized to the enormous burden that corruption and mismanagement of resources exact on the development of nations. Our awareness was further enhanced by our international professional activities and by our growing appreciation of the significance of informality in Cuba's socialist economy.

Many colleagues and friends helped us appreciate and understand better many of the issues we discussed in this book. We are grateful to Damián Fernández, Richard Lotspeich, Olga Nazario, Matías Travieso-Díaz, Eduardo Gamarra, Jaime Suchlicki, Marifeli Pérez-Stable, and Ricardo Puerta for valuable insights and references to relevant literature. We also acknowledge the contributions made by members of the Association for the Study of the Cuban Economy (ASCE), where so many different issues about Cuba are regularly aired and where we had the opportunity to present some of the ideas included in the book. We benefited as well from very thoughtful comments from anonymous readers that led us to strengthen some of the arguments in the book. We are indebted to the University of Texas Press staff for their warm reception to our manuscript and their support in its publication. From our first contact with Editor-in-Chief Theresa May, to our collaboration over several months with editors Lynne Chapman and Tana Silva, as well as to our interactions with Lisa Tremaine, Nancy Bryan, and Casey Kittrell, we have been impressed with their professionalism and responsiveness.

CORRUPTION IN CUBA

One CORRUPTION
AND TRANSITIONS

The long-delayed transition in Cuba gives policy makers the opportunity to consider averting corruption an integral part of the overall transition strategy. Corruption imposed a heavy burden on the economic transition of the former Soviet Union and its East European allies, just as it did in post-Sandinista Nicaragua. Expectations for reconstituting these countries into modern nation-states with political and economic structures akin to those of the democratic, market-oriented West were in many cases dashed in no small part because of corruption.

As these former socialist countries started the transition, the priorities of policy makers were macroeconomic stabilization, liberalization of prices in product markets, privatization of state-owned property, creation of an institutional base to support the market, and establishment and nurturing of democratic institutions. As these economic and political transformations were being carried out, the potential for corruption to derail a successful transition was not understood. Only in hindsight have the enormous negative effects of corruption on the transition process been appreciated.

More than a decade into the transitions of the former Soviet Union and the socialist countries of Eastern Europe, a body of literature has emerged that assesses the strategies and outcomes of such transitions (e.g., Aslund 2002; Svejnar 2002; World Bank 2002). The consensus is that the transitions have been painful—more so than was initially envisioned—and resulted in deeper reductions in output than anticipated. Initial conditions (among them geography and natural resources, years spent under central planning, specific nature of socialist development) had a very significant influence on performance, particularly in the early stages of the transition. It is clear that politicians and economists underestimated the difficulty of the transition and that in some instances questionable policy choices were made. Although growth performance has varied greatly across reforming countries, those nations that made the most concentrated reform efforts recovered soonest and positioned themselves to make sustained economic gains and improve the standard of living of their citizens.

Svejnar (2002) concludes that differences across former socialist countries in the ability to carry out economic reforms successfully turned on two factors: the ability to collect taxes with which to finance public programs and the ability to minimize corruption and rent-seeking behavior.[1] Aslund (2002, 441) goes further, arguing that the main determinant of success in the transition was the extent to which a state was able to avoid the harmful effects of rent seeking on economic performance: states undergoing transition that succumbed to rent seeking got stuck in partial reform traps and lagged in economic performance.

A related insight is that the lack of a market-oriented legal structure was the Achilles' heel of the first dozen years of the transitions. Policy makers underestimated the importance of a well-functioning legal system or believed too readily that free markets would take care of any major problems (Svejnar 2002, 7). In the "no man's land" between a centrally planned economy and a market economy—as the "old" national institutions of totalitarianism were being torn down and decentralization, privatization, and the opening of these economies to international participation were taking place, while new institutions promoting good governance had not yet taken hold—uncertainty about property rights during privatization often allowed managers to tunnel assets from state-owned enterprises into spin-offs they controlled and to benefit from monopoly rents in a partially reformed economy.

In theory, these gains should have been short-term because as the transition progressed, the distortions that gave rise to them would disappear. The reality was that the short-term winners of reform—the so-called oligarchs—in many instances converted their gains into political influence to preserve the very distortions that generated the rents (World Bank 2002, 92). Architects of reforms seem not to have accounted adequately for the behavior of those in transition economies who did not desire a strong legal system because it was not in their interest and who contributed to the corruption of public officials (Svejnar 2002, 7).

THE NATURE AND DETERMINANTS OF CORRUPTION

What Is Corruption?

Social scientists define public-sector corruption as "the use of public office for private gain, when an official (the agent) entrusted with carrying out a task by the public (the principal) engages in some sort of malfeasance for private enrichment which is difficult to monitor by the principal" (Bardhan 2002, 1321). Corruption among private parties is equally pernicious, although the regulatory power of the state plays a significant role in limiting its incidence. Our focus in this book is public-sector corruption, as this is more relevant to policy in a Cuba in transition. However, throughout the book we will make reference to the private sector as an indispensable partner in many forms of public-sector corruption.

The potential for corruption exists whenever a public official has discretionary power over distribution to the private sector of a benefit or a cost (Rose-Ackerman 1997, 31). Private individuals or firms are willing to pay bribes to obtain benefits or avoid costs. Under certain circumstances, public officials—sometimes in collusion with private parties—bend the rules for their own enrichment.

Corruption is as old as government itself. Kautilya, chief minister to the king in ancient India, wrote in the fourth century BCE in his *Arthasastra:*

> Just as it is impossible not to take the honey (or the poison) that finds itself at the tip of the tongue, so it is impossible for a government servant not to eat up at least a bit of the King's revenue. Just as fish moving under water cannot possibly be found out either as drinking or not drinking water, so government servants employed in the government cannot be found out (while) taking money (for themselves). (Quoted in Bardhan 2002, 1320)

Moreover, corruption is not the province of countries with certain forms of governance structures or at certain levels of development. Virtually all countries have laws that proscribe corruption, and yet the practice exists everywhere. In developing and transition countries, private individuals or firms take advantage of fragmented rule of law and weak legal enforcement institutions to corrupt government officials in order to advance their interests. In developed countries, implementation of tax codes and government procurement practices often lend themselves to corruption (Schloss 2002, 18).

The ubiquitousness of government and the desire of individuals or firms to advance their own interests create the conditions for corruption to exist.

- National, state, and local governments buy and sell goods, distribute subsidies, organize privatization of firms, and provide concessions. Individuals or firms may choose to pay off government officials to have their names included on lists of bidders for projects, to be selected as winners of bidding competitions, to charge higher prices for delivering goods or services, or to deliver goods or services of a lower quality than paid for. Privatization of government-owned enterprises is conceptually similar to tendering for a large infrastructure project and therefore creates the same opportunities for corruption. Individuals or firms may also pay bribes to obtain goods sold by the state at lower prices or subject to more convenient delivery schedules, to gain access to credit or to foreign exchange, or to obtain a subsidy.

- National, state, and local governments also enforce rules and regulations, levy taxes, and enforce criminal laws. In performing these functions, governments can impose costs selectively and therefore affect the competitive positions of individuals or firms in an economy. Certain individuals or firms may be willing to pay bribes to get favorable interpretations of rules and regulations, pay lower taxes (e.g., through lower tax assessments), pay lower import duties (e.g., through undervaluation or deliberate misclassification of imports), or avoid application of criminal law (e.g., through bribes paid to inspectors to overlook violations).

- Government officials often have information that is very valuable to outsiders. Private individuals or firms may pay government officials to obtain information on bids tendered by competitors, on the locations of highways or other public works projects to be built in the future, or on the economic conditions of state-owned companies that may be candidates for privatization.

- Individuals and firms may also choose to pay bribes to influence the timing of government actions. In most instances, individuals and firms pay bribes to expedite government action, whether to obtain payment from the government more quickly for goods sold or services rendered, provision of services (installation of telephone or Internet service, for example), or issuance of the myriad permits and licenses that are required to operate businesses. In other instances, a bribe may be paid to delay an action that could favor a competitor until the payer of the bribe can bolster his or her bid. In still others, public officials may exact small bribes from individuals in exchange for overlooking alleged or actual law violations (such as a policeman demanding a bribe to overlook a traffic violation).

- Finally, individuals and firms may provide illicit contributions to politicians or political parties with the expectation that if elected to public office, the recipients will provide favorable treatment or even create rules that benefit the contributors.

The Determinants of Corruption

All else being equal, the size and structure of the state determine the demand for corrupt services, i.e., the supply of bribes. Klitgaard (1988, 75) has summarized the "basic ingredients of corruption" using the formula

$$\text{Corruption} = \text{Monopoly} + \text{Discretion} - \text{Accountability}$$

That is, the level of corruption depends on the degree of monopoly exercised by the state over the supply of a given good or service, the degree of discretion enjoyed by a government agency in making resource-allocation decisions, and the degree of accountability of the government (or its agents) to others.

MONOPOLY

The size of the government and the types of activity in which it engages are important indicators of potential government monopoly and degree of corruption. A positive correlation exists between the size of a government—as measured by its share of gross domestic product (GDP)—and the level of expected corruption: the larger the share of GDP that government controls, the greater the extent of corruption that will likely emerge. A large government share of GDP is consistent with high levels of regulation, bureaucracy, red tape, and opportunity for malfeasance (LaPalombara 1994, 338).

Types of government activity are as important as size of government: a government that operates monopolistic state-owned enterprises or limits competition through excessive regulation or trade restrictions creates economic rents and thus opportunities for corrupt rent-seeking behavior. Empirical research has shown a positive correlation between corruption and the share of state-owned enterprises in non-agricultural GDP and a negative correlation between corruption and the openness of economies measured by trade shares (Elliott 1997, 182–183).

DISCRETION

The greater the discretionary power of government officials, the larger the supply of benefits that may be subject to bribes. For example, government officials may be able to extract payoffs from a contractor by introducing delays in payments (that could be expedited with a bribe) or by adding regulatory hurdles not in the original contract. They could also implement regulations inconsistently, extracting payments for specific outcomes. They could channel public resources to projects that are more prone to corruption (large infrastructure construction projects, military procurement), regardless of the projects' relative contribution to national welfare. In privatization processes or in instances of natural-resource concessions (such as authorization to mine a certain ore or to build a resort hotel on a particular beach), government officials might be able to manipulate decision making to favor a particular bidder who is willing to pay a bribe to obtain the newly privatized firm or concession (Rose-Ackerman 1997, 39).

ACCOUNTABILITY

The accountability of the state and its agents to the public affects the degree of government monopoly and discretion and therefore the potential for corruption. At one extreme, total absence of accountability over the state's actions or inaction means that the state's monopoly power and discretion are unchecked and that the potential for corruption is high. Positive public accountability—in the form of transparency in government operations, including procurement activities, accounting and auditing standards, grievance and appeal procedures, media scrutiny, and disclosure of political party financing—inhibits monopoly, discretion, and corruption.

CORRUPTION AND SOCIALISM

One of the key features of socialist centrally planned economies (CPEs) was "the virtually all-encompassing public sector," which included not only the realm of high-level government officials, but also the dealings of shop clerks (Heidenheimer, Johnston, and Levine 1989, 443). Under this system, "there is no distinction between public and private purses, and government officials simply 'appropriate' state assets" (Rose-Ackerman 1997, 33).

In the idealized socialist CPE, the totality of production facilities of the nation would be under state ownership. In practice, the degree of state ownership across CPEs varied, but a common feature of each was state control over the preponderance of productive facilities, with the exception of agriculture.

Public ownership of productive facilities resulted in a lack of identifiable ownership and widespread misuse and theft of state resources. An analyst's assessment of the Soviet system applies to other CPEs as well: "most reliable sources agreed that theft of socialist (state) property is as wide-spread as state property itself" (Feldbrugge 1989, 318). Individuals in these societies tended to use state property as their own, with very little stigma attached to such practice.

The high degree of state ownership also meant that relatively little private activity was allowed. CPEs had myriad state regulations waiting to be broken by enterprising individuals with the connivance of corrupt government officials. The sheer size of the public sector, in combination with the web of regulations that circumscribed private activity, created opportunities for illegal behavior and for the use of state property for private gain.

Socialist systems such as the ones that were in power in the former Soviet Union and Eastern Europe and that remain in China, Vietnam, North Korea, and Cuba present a complex interplay of governmental and economic institutions, ideologies, and traditional political cultures that make them particularly prone to corruption (Heidenheimer, Johnston, and Levine 1989, 443–444). The overwhelming size of the public sector meant that the state employed an inordinately large number of workers. Therefore, the potential for corruption of government employees was very large. Central planning of hundreds of production enterprises, thousands of retail outlets, and tens of thousands of individual products and services required a huge bureaucratic apparatus. At every turn, production and distribution decisions were regulated by inflexible plans and allocation procedures; enterprise managers often had little choice but to use illicit influence to get around planning strictures to obtain labor or raw materials. And the ruling party itself was often the locus of corruption, as the top leadership was normally immune to exposés and reprisals from below and could engage in self-serving behavior.

In a study of corruption in communist societies, Holmes (1993, 77) gave the following definition of corruption:

> Actions or non-actions—by an individual or a small group of individuals occupying (an) official (party and/or state and/or legal and/or military and/or socially responsible) elected or appointed position(s)—that are perceived, at least by some criteria, to be improper or illegitimate in the particular sense of being seen simultaneously against the collective (societal) interest and in the official's (officials') individual (self-regarding) interests.

Based on this definition, Holmes developed a taxonomy of twenty forms of corruption in communist countries (Table 1.1). It should be noted that

TABLE I.I. TAXONOMY OF CORRUPTION IN SOCIALIST SOCIETIES

Deliberate Dereliction of Duties, Inaction, and Obstruction
1. Turning a blind eye
2. Refusing to investigate/charge and/or obstructing investigation
3. Avoiding specific procedures

Improper Filling of Office, Patronage
4. Nepotism
5. Cronyism
6. Conflict of interest

Deliberate Deception
7. False reporting—overstatement
8. False reporting—understatement
9. Deceiving supplicants
10. Forging documents

Other Interactive, Gain-based Forms of Corruption
11. Accepting bribes
12. Offering bribes
13. Extortion
14. Blackmail

Possibly Non-interactive, Gain-based Forms of Corruption
15. Not earning one's salary
16. Improper use of socialized property
17. Embezzlement
18. Speculation
19. Smuggling
20. Treason

Source: Adapted from Holmes 1993, 81–88

two or more forms of corruption may be involved in a single act; for example, an official may forge a document in return for a bribe, or an official
may refuse to investigate criminal activity carried out by a crony.

The very extensive and personalized power in the hands of government officials in socialist societies translated into wide discretion to act in
a corrupt manner: taking bribes, getting cuts or kickbacks, extorting graft.
Exploitation of the power of an office for personal gain was enhanced by
the dictatorial and secretive nature of the regime and mutual solidarity of
members of the political elite (Grossman 1979, 845).

One form of corruption that reached exceptionally high levels in CPES
was the system of perquisites and favors attendant to the ruling class or

political elite, what one analyst called the "new class" (Djilas 1957) and others the *nomenklatura* (e.g., Voslensky 1984). Djilas (1957, 152) described the "new class" of rulers of the Soviet Union as "those who have special privileges and economic preferences because of the administrative monopoly they hold." According to Voslensky (1984, 75), the *nomenklatura* was: a list of key positions with the government, appointments to which were made by the higher authority of the Communist Party; and a list of persons appointed to these positions or waiting to be placed in them. This group of government officials was fiercely protective of its status and privileges and suspicious of actions that might erode its position. Djilas (1957, 65) further explains:

> The new class instinctively feels that national goods are, in fact, its property, and that even the terms "socialist," "social" and "state" property denote a general fiction. The new class also feels that any breach of its totalitarian authority might imperil its ownership. Consequently, the new class opposes any type of freedom, ostensibly for the purpose of preserving "socialist" ownership. Criticism of the new class's monopolistic administration of property generates the fear of a possible loss of power. The new class is sensitive to those criticisms and demands depending on the extent to which they expose the manner in which it rules and holds power.

The privileged class of the former Soviet Union was able to draw on the resources of the state and to treat socialist property as its own: salary supplements; the best housing; special food allocations; access to restaurants, stores, and other facilities; vacation country villas (*dachas*). It also participated heavily in the system of taking bribes in return for doing favors such as appointing persons to prestigious posts, protection, promoting people up the bureaucratic ladder, and using influence to stop the government from taking actions (Simis 1982; Voslensky 1984).

Corruption and Transitions from Socialism

Examples of corruption in former socialist, centrally planned economies during the early stages of their transition to market-oriented economies in the early 1990s abound:

- Credit relations and the financial system generally suffered from widespread corruption in Hungary, including the exchange of loans for bribes, self-enrichment schemes, and manipulation of bankruptcies, state-initiated debt restructuring programs, and banking supervision processes ("How Hungary Escaped" 2001).

- Corruption was rampant in Romania: bribes were common for making reservations in hotels, renting real estate, or getting a grave in a cemetery. Moreover, the political leadership took over homes and other property in the early days of the transition and regularly sold favors for private gains (Mungiu-Pippidi 1997).

- In October 1994 the head of the Czech privatization agency was caught taking a large bribe in connection with the sale of a dairy (World Bank 2000, 32).

- In Russia, the process of *privatizatsia* ("privatization") was nicknamed *prikhvatizatsia* ("grabitization") to highlight the high degree of cor-ruption that it involved; it has been estimated that 61 percent of Russia's new rich were former Soviet managers who appropriated the industries they managed during privatization (Naím 1995, 253). With the loosening of the restraining hand of the KGB, the Soviet Union's once-illegal "shadow economy" came into its own as the *mafiya* (Malia 1995). Capitalizing on corrupt officials, organized crime in Russia—the *mafiya*—has acquired large holdings of state assets through criminal and violent methods and has broadened its reach to more than two dozen countries, including the United States, Canada, and Sweden.

Naím (1995, 251) points out that the transition from socialism and the deepening of democratization should have corruption-curbing effects. Why, then, did corruption run rampant in countries transitioning from authoritarian, centrally planned regimes to democratic, market economies?

One explanation for this phenomenon is that in the absence of strong institutions, democracy and free markets provide more—and more visible—opportunities for corruption than those present under authoritarian rule. Under authoritarian rule, corruption can be institutionalized, controlled, and predictable. Naím argues that a well-organized dictatorship can provide "one-stop shopping" for corruption services, where the right amount of money given to the right official will take care of all needed interventions. In such a system, bribe takers under the control of the authority (either the authoritarian leader or a political party) collude and keep their actions out of the public's view. Under a democratic system, in contrast, the central government's control over the providers of bribery services is diluted, and corrupt officials compete for bribes, resulting in a process that is more visible to the public than under authoritarianism.

Freedom of the press and independent civil society organizations also contribute to the perceived increase in corruption—whether or not it has really increased—as allegations of corruption that would have gone unreported under the authoritarian regime are openly aired by the media and discussed by the public and by civil society organizations.

Krastev (2004, 46–47, 63), based on the experiences of the former Soviet Union and Central Europe, explains the paradox of the perception of the rise in corruption in post-communist societies in terms of a shift from an economy of "favors" to an economy of "paid services." Individuals and businesses in communist societies depended on a generalized system of illegal "favors" (known as *blat* in the former Soviet Union, "connections" in Bulgaria) for survival for their families or the enterprises in which they worked, in an environment of state ownership of the means of production and centralized decision making. As we have discussed above, these practices were generalized and socially acceptable in part because they did not involve monetary exchanges and were perceived to increase social equality by redistributing goods and services under state control. The transition "marketized" these relationships and brought them into the open. Krastev (2004, 63) concludes that in societies undergoing transition, "*Blat* networks are re-organized on market principles. *Blat* networks are transformed into classical corruption networks involved in the redistribution of the state assets while other *blat* networks simply disappeared. Personal interests have become business interests."

Particularly during the early stages of transition, corruption can explode. Glynn, Kobrin, and Naím (1997, 10) suggest:

> Corruption in these emerging markets is doubly pernicious. First, it compromises the efficacy and efficiency of economic activity, making the transition to free market democracy more difficult. Second, and equally important, corruption distorts public perceptions of how—and how well—a proper market economy works. Under such circumstances it becomes all too easy for economically beleaguered publics to confuse democratization with the corruption and criminalization of the economy—creating fertile soil for an authoritarian backlash and engendering potentially hostile international behavior by these states in turn.

It is probably fair to argue, however, that democratic regimes, over the long run, engender more powerful antibodies against corruption than authoritarian systems under which political liberties are stifled (ibid., 11).

DECENTRALIZATION

The relaxation of the state's economic monopoly created novel opportunities for rent seeking by government officials. For example, the economic opening brought about by *perestroika* in the former Soviet Union legalized some secondary markets, and that translated into an increase in corruption and black-market activity as government officials diverted scarce (and low-priced) goods from the distribution system into secondary markets where they could gain rents from resale (Schuknecht 1990). Deregulation of areas that were formerly under the exclusive control of the state created opportunities for fraud until a regulatory structure was established.

PRIVATIZATION

Privatization, the transfer of state-owned property to private owners, provided manifold opportunities for rent seeking and other misconduct by government officials. The experience of reforming countries of the former Soviet Union and Eastern Europe undergoing massive privatization was an increase in corruption. As is discussed in more detail below, the connection between privatization and the rise of corruption has prompted some analysts to question whether corruption is the inevitable price to pay for privatization (Kaufmann and Siegelbaum 1997, 421).

OPENING TO INTERNATIONAL PARTICIPATION

Opening the economy to international participation—through increased international trade and investment—created opportunities for corruption, particularly in the form of "commissions" for issuing import and export permits and authorizations or allocating foreign exchange or for misclassifying goods to obtain more favorable tariff treatment. The approval process for foreign investment, particularly if it required a multitude of discretionary permits, was fertile ground for corruption.

MULTIPARTY POLITICAL SYSTEMS

The establishment of multiparty political systems opened the door for new forms of corruption as private parties attempted to influence the rules of governance through the political process in a setting where political power was not monopolized by a single party.

Aslund (2002, 3) argues that some of the former socialist countries lost the battle against corruption, becoming rent-seeking states where the dominant interest was not the economic welfare of the whole nation, but the redistribution of available resources through the budget and through regulations to benefit a privileged few oligarchs. These oligarchs were often the beneficiaries of one of the initial and most notorious manifestations of corruption in transition economies, widely known as "spontaneous privatization": the appropriation of state property by members of the *nomenklatura* through the paper reorganization of state-owned enterprises into "private" corporations of which *nomenklatura* members were owners or directors.[2] Spontaneous privatization took place during the early stages of the transition, when state socialism had weakened but while there were still legal gaps and uncertainties in property regulations (Agh 1993, 15). It is also observed that a full transition to democratic rule and the market is thwarted when former *nomenklatura* members retain power under several political guises, as has occurred in several African countries and in Cambodia. In the uncertainty that surrounded the start of the transition, "those possessing economic power carve out for themselves and their clients valuable pieces of the state-owned cake" (Sik 1992, 58).

Unbundling Corruption in Transition Economies

The World Bank (2000) has developed a typology that unbundles corruption in transition economies and recognizes that different forms of corruption have distinct origins and consequences. Differentiating patterns of corruption across transition economies is an essential step to developing specific policy recommendations tailored to them. The typology distinguishes between administrative corruption and state capture:

- *Administrative corruption,* akin to what social scientists traditionally define as corruption, refers to the intentional imposition of distortions in the prescribed implementation of existing laws, rules, and regulations to provide advantages either to state or nonstate actors as a result of the illicit and nontransparent provision of private gains to public officials. Examples of administrative corruption include bribes, "grease payments," and misuse of public property by state officials for their own benefit or that of their families.
- *State capture* refers to the activities of individuals, groups, or firms in both the public and private sectors to influence the formation of laws, decrees, regulations, and other government policies (i.e., the basic rules of the game) to their own advantage by means of an illicit and nontransparent payment to public officials. For example, an oligarch who heads a financial or industrial group could pay off legislators to get them to erect barriers to the entry of firms that

might provide competition to his group, or a political leader might be influenced to shape the framework of reforms to ensure that specific individuals control key resources (World Bank 2000, 1–2). Recent Russian Federation rules that ban foreign firms or consortiums of firms that are more than 50 percent foreign-owned from bidding on natural-resource projects are cited by analysts as an example of the work of oligarchs—whose firms would be unable to compete with the technology, efficiency, and cash flow of foreign firms—in limiting competition for their own gain (Stratfor 2005).

The main distinction between administrative corruption and state capture is the nature of the political relationship that underlies them: in administrative corruption, private parties seek individualized exceptions from rules or their favorable application, while in state capture they attempt to shape the rules to their own narrow advantage, which subsequently constrains the actions of others. That is, the main difference lies in how deep the corrupt transaction reaches into the operations and functions of the state and the extent to which the advantages of the corrupt transaction are institutionalized in the rules of the game (World Bank 2000, 2).

While state capture was most evident in several countries during the initial stages of the transition away from socialism, its principal features also can be found in other settings where transparency and government accountability are lacking. State capture occurs, to recapitulate, when firms attempt "to shape the laws, policies, and regulations of the state to their own advantage by providing illicit private gains to public officials" (Hellman and Kaufmann 2001, 1–2). What is meant by "firms," however, should be clarified. In privatization schemes, foreign firms could conspire with former or current corrupt bureaucrats to appropriate for themselves state-owned assets, or former or current bureaucrats could enter into a conspiracy to illicitly assume ownership of state-owned assets. This is not an inconsequential distinction since it has important implications for the manner and the timing at which misappropriation of government resources begins or is consummated.

Privatization processes in Eastern Europe and the former Soviet Union proved vulnerable to corruption, as government officials attempted to manipulate them to favor certain groups or individuals, including themselves. Among the methods of privatizing state-owned enterprises employed in these nations, often combining more than one technique, were assets sales (Hungary, East Germany), voucher-based mass privatization (Czech Republic, early Polish divestitures, Russia), share offerings (later Polish sales), management-employee buyouts, tenders, and insider privatization (Russia), and spontaneous privatization (Slovenia) (Meggison and Netter 2001).

Kaufmann and Siegelbaum (1997) analyzed the corruption potential of the privatization methods by assessing the extent to which each increased or reduced the exercise of control rights by politicians and bureaucrats, which was hypothesized to be associated with more or less corruption. They concluded that voucher-based mass privatization and liquidation were the least prone to corruption,[3] while management-employee buyouts and spontaneous privatization were highly conducive to corruption, principally due to their slow pace, high level of discretion on the part of administrators making decisions, and lack of transparency and public information. While spontaneous privatization stands above all others as the most corrupt form of privatization, Russian insider privatizations—particularly of oil and natural resource companies—that disproportionately benefited managers are also examples of privatization that resulted in grand corruption and the creation of oligarchs intent on state capture.

So outrageous have been the examples of corruption associated with privatizations that some have blamed privatization itself for giving rise to corruption. However, Aslund (2002, 265) argues quite convincingly that the corruption eruption in the socialist countries, just as the rise in crime, is a reflection of the weakening of the state rather than a consequence of privatization or any other individual reform measure. In this context, Aslund (2002, 266) writes,

> Regular privatization started one or two years after the demise of communism. By elementary logic, a cause cannot follow its effect and privatization appears more likely to have contributed to the abatement of corruption, as officials had less to sell. Like many other transitional events, corruption and privatizations occurred roughly in parallel and involved wealth transfer, but that is true of many other phenomena, and simultaneity must not be confused with causality.

Kaufmann and Siegelbaum (1997, 428) find that "while it is undeniable that, in the transition economies, an increase in corruption coincided with the process of privatization, it does not necessarily follow that this increase was actually caused by the privatization process."

Has there been a quantum increase in corruption around the world in recent times? In other words, has there been what Moisés Naím (1995) referred to in an influential article as a global "corruption eruption?"

The inherent difficulties in measuring corruption, either at a point in time or over time, make it impossible to assert unequivocally that corruption has been more or less prevalent in the post–Cold War period than before. However, Tanzi (2002, 22) posits that the recent interest in corruption probably reflects an expansion in the scope of the phenomenon—because of an increase in the role of governments in national economies in the post–World War II period, the growth of international trade and business that has created more situations for the payments of "commissions" (bribes), and privatization of state-owned property—rather than just a greater awareness of an age-old problem.

But more importantly, it is very clear that corruption is no longer a topic that is considered a cultural characteristic of a society and therefore taboo to international discussions and criticism. Today, corruption is openly recognized as a development issue. Thus, the more than 150 high-ranking public-sector officials and key leaders of civil society from sixty-three developing and formerly communist countries who responded to a survey conducted in 1996 by Kaufmann (1997, 125) identified public-sector corruption as their countries' most severe impediment to development and growth.

Corruption has also been recognized by the World Bank and the International Monetary Fund (IMF) as an impediment to development. The IMF's Guidelines on Governance (IMF 1997), for instance, reflect the consensus within that organization of the importance of good governance, including the elimination of corrupt practices, for economic efficiency and growth. In Chapter 2 we examine the literature that documents the costs of corruption on economic performance and the determinants of corruption in general and with respect to specific sectors or issues such as agriculture, the environment, education, public health, energy, the justice system, military spending, and the political system.

CORRUPTION IN SOCIALIST CUBA AND THE TRANSITION

The corruption problem that could be anticipated in a Cuba in transition will be a very complex one because of the confluence of several factors. First among these is the long history of administrative corruption in Cuba during the Republic (1902–1958) and even during the Spanish colonial rule (1492–1898) and U.S. intervention (1898–1902). As we will discuss in Chapter 3, corruption can be traced back to administrative and political institutions and practices during four centuries of Spanish colonial rule. We argue that at the advent of the Republic in 1902, Cuba was already burdened with a deeply ingrained tradition of corruption that rested on governance practices instituted by colonial administrations that placed a premium on the extraction of rents from public office, a management approach that encouraged the sale of official positions, nepotism, and poorly compensated officials.

With the establishment of the Republic and with opportunities for social and economic advancement limited by foreign domination of the economy, Cubans turned to the state to advance their economic situations and security. The state employed a very large pool of poorly paid civil servants, many of them susceptible to corruption or enjoying sinecures obtained through patronage. Many others protected their often meager labor, professional, or business interests through political lobbying, a process that often involved the payment of bribes. Few were the Cubans immune from a culture of corruption, as in one way or another they looked to the state to provide a modicum of security.

Second, the country must contend with the legacy of more than four decades of socialist rule. Since the early 1960s, Cuba's socialist government has actively worked to eliminate the market-oriented economic institutions that existed in republican Cuba and supplant them with institutions that support a centrally directed economy. As we discuss in Chapter 4, Cuba has excelled in adopting the institutions of socialism that are particularly prone to corruption, among them public ownership of the means of production, central planning and government control over most economic activities, absolute political control by the party, generalized privileges for the ruling class, and extremely limited government accountability as reflected in the lack of competitive elections, the limits on creation and operation of genuine civil society organizations, and the government control of media.

In this environment, the most basic anticorruption pillars have eroded. In most societies, moral and ethical guidelines traditionally act as deterrents against malfeasance. The residual effects of those moral and ethical deterrents are not likely to be significant in Cuba after nearly a half-century of socialist rule. The Cuban government's disregard for the rule of law regarding property rights began with its confiscation of privately owned assets in 1959 and the early 1960s.[4] This was followed in the 1960s by wholesale expropriations of property owned by foreigners and Cuban citizens. Throughout the entire revolutionary period, from 1959 to the present, routine expropriation of personal property of all permanent emigrants has been the rule. This latter development alone, it could be argued, has given rise to social attitudes that condone—in Cuba's environment of scarcity—taking advantage of someone else's misfortune and assets for personal benefit.

Third, notwithstanding Fidel Castro's assertion that "the Revolution, through its sense of morality, through its sense of responsibility, immunized the basic cadres against corruption" (Castro 1993a), we argue that corruption is rampant in contemporary Cuba. Although measures of corruption—imperfect as they may be—in contemporary Cuba are not available, in Chapter 5 we present a range of corrupt activities for which some concrete evidence is available from the national and international media as well as from insiders' reports; these include misappropriation of state resources, misuse of office, and special perquisites extracted by the Cuban *nomenklatura*. Such administrative corruption pervades Cuban society mainly because of the nature of the economic system and the scarcity of goods and services it has created. As in other former socialist countries, when given the opportunity, few citizens hesitate to steal from the government. Since the bulk of productive resources are owned and managed by the state and the vast majority of Cubans work for state-owned enterprises, these petty crimes are widespread.

The opening of the economy in the 1990s to foreign investment and the dollarization process created new opportunities for corruption to thrive. To keep a lid on administrative corruption, the Cuban government has taken several steps such as promulgating new anticorruption laws and a code of ethics for government officials, creating a Ministry of Audit and Control, and tightening accounting practices. Despite these efforts, corruption in state-run companies, particularly those that operate with hard currencies in the tourism sector, seems to be out of control. Among the corrupt practices that are alleged to be common in the tourism industry are accepting commissions from foreign businessmen, nepotism, selling jobs, and misuse of official cars, expense accounts, and travel. So widespread is corruption in the tourism sector that in early 2004, First Vice President and Defense Minister Raúl Castro assumed oversight of the industry and appointed military personnel to key industry posts. Raúl Castro has been quoted as stating that the corruption-laden tourism industry, Cuba's main earner of export revenue, is like "a tree born twisted that must be uprooted and planted anew" ("Tourists" 2004). In the second half of 2004, the Cuban government tightened control over enterprises, limiting their ability to engage in foreign trade and to hold foreign exchange balances. In February 2005 it issued draconian rules governing workers in the tourism sector that severely curtailed contacts with foreign visitors and banned acceptance of gifts and tips ("Cuba limita" 2005).

Fourth, there is evidence that the basis has already been set for the eventual occurrence of grand corruption in the form of state capture. We discuss in Chapter 5 the very worrisome factor that state-owned commercial ventures (for example, the tourism corporation Gaviota operated by the Cuban military) and joint ventures with foreign investors that have sprung up in recent years provide a foundation for appropriation of public property by influential bureaucrats once a formal transition gets under way. These same bureaucrats could be parties to state capture, shaping the transitory legal and regulatory framework to favor special interests, consequently undermining Cuba's economic recovery, laying the groundwork for decades of social and political discord, burdening Cuba's court system, and poisoning the country's international commercial transactions.

Averting Corruption in the Cuban Transition

Corruption thrives where there are opportunities for under-the-table deals and where government officials are not accountable to the public for their actions. Corruption abhors transparency, openness, and accountability. As U.S. Supreme Court Justice Louis Brandeis aptly noted in 1914—in a critique of large banks that were colluding with businessmen to create trusts in major U.S. industries—transparency is the best antidote against illegal dealings and corruption. The same view is echoed in an editorial in early 2004 in *Revista Vitral,* one of the very few limited-circulation publications from the island free of government control: "Transparency is the most effective weapon to fight corruption and to prevent corruption. Making public the business accounts and transactions of state enterprises, public agencies, and state government is the only way to shine a light on what is occurring within them" ("La corrupción" 2004).

Transparency International (TI), a nongovernmental organization at the forefront of the global fight against corruption, has proposed a model "National Integrity System" to encourage the development of transparency and accountability strategies needed by modern governments to promote the interest of the public rather than the interests of those in control (Pope 2000). Such a system is designed to promote transparency and accountability through the standard checks and balances of democratic societies and the operation of administrative and citizen-driven control mechanisms. The ultimate goal is to have all of the elements operate as part of a coherent whole. In a work published by TI Jeremy Pope (2000, 37) gives an example of the need for such cohesion: "What is the benefit of a sound and 'clean' Judiciary ready to uphold the Rule of Law, if there is corruption in the police, investigators, prosecutors or the legal profession? The Judges would simply not receive the cases they should hear; they would then sit in splendid isolation—honest, capable, yet able to achieve little."

Cuba's Transition Strategy and Corruption

The central thesis of this book is that averting corruption in the Cuban transition and beyond is critical for sustained economic growth and democracy in the nation. A rich inventory of policy initiatives has been found to be effective in combating corruption in other national contexts and may be relevant to a Cuba in transition—relevant to a transition government as well as to the international development community that will play a key role in Cuba's economic recovery. We posit that during the early stages of the transition, the lessons drawn from the experiences of former socialist countries would be most germane to combating corruption in Cuba, while in the longer term, the most relevant lessons might be those from elsewhere in Latin America and in developed countries. The strategy to avert corruption consists of a set of measures designed to stem the most harmful types of corruption by relying on effective policy levers. The proposed strategy encompasses short-, medium-, and long-term interventions to minimize the incidence of corruption during and after the transition.

What we propose in this book is unique: in no transition instance was averting corruption addressed as a policy priority. While we recognize that combating corruption cannot be the central policy objective of a Cuban transition strategy, we are also cognizant of the potential for rampant corruption to undermine the transition process itself. If unchecked, corruption could retard Cuba's economic growth, negatively impact the flow of foreign investment, lead to the sale of national assets at lower than market values, have a profound regressive effect on income distribution, and increase the costs of providing social services and improving the country's physical infrastructure. Corruption could erode political support for the transitional and subsequent governments and prevent the consolidation of emerging democratic governance institutions, thus potentially contributing to political instability and alienating citizens from the political process. Finally, corruption could also serve as the gateway to international organized crime, including drug trafficking and money laundering, and—due to Cuba's proximity to the United States—make Cuba a transshipment point for undocumented migrants. Because of its cross-cutting nature, we believe that corruption must be addressed as a policy priority in the design and implementation of every aspect of a transition strategy.

The most obvious problem when discussing the elements of a transition strategy that a future government in Cuba might want to consider is the array of unknowns, both primary and secondary. Most evident is the unpredictable form the transition will take (rapid or gradual, peaceful or violent) and when it will occur, nor do we know who would lead it (almost certainly officials in positions of authority in the country today). Equally unpredictable is the extent to which the leaders of a transitional Cuba would condone—or even willingly participate in—corrupt behavior instead of pursuing an honest and transparent political agenda to set the stage for a peaceful and prosperous future.

In Chapter 6 we discuss the conditions likely to shape the early stages of the transition and some of the economic policy levers that could dampen corruption in Cuba over the short term. During the early transition, then, the focus should be on initiatives to prevent the illegal appropriation of the national patrimony by corrupt bureaucrats or phony homegrown "businesses" with or without associated foreign cohorts, while limiting many forms of petty administrative corruption through gradually dismantling state controls over the economy. In Chapter 7 we address long-term policy initiatives, including those associated with institution building, that will be necessary if Cuba is to bring corruption under control. Over the long term, the incentives for administrative corruption should erode gradually as the role of the state in economic management is reduced. The key to controlling corruption lies with reforming the institutional setting that engenders corruption, rather than with sanctioning the corrupt (although it is necessary to do so as well). Klitgaard (1998, 6) has noted that solving the problem goes beyond putting a few corrupt officials in jail, creating one or two new government institutions, and passing a few laws: "combating corruption should focus on the reform of systems."

Hellman and Kaufmann (2001) posit that state capture is not only a symptom but also a fundamental cause of poor governance. The capture economy is trapped in a vicious circle in which the policy and institutional reforms necessary to improve governance are undermined by collusion between powerful firms and state officials who reap private gains from the continuation of weak governance. Influencing the legal, policy, and regulatory environment in which they operate constitutes a normal and indeed healthy process for firms and interest groups common to all countries. What is special in the capture economies is *exclusion:* some firms enjoy exclusive privileges to influence decisions of the state while others are systematically excluded, enabling state officials to make choices that concentrate benefits on those with access at a high cost to those who do not have such access. The prescription to break out of the vicious circle of state capture is to shape a virtuous cycle of competition, transparency, and accountability.

We cannot predict the future, but we are confident that Cuba will evolve toward a democracy with a market-oriented economy, probably with a significant role for the state in selected social sectors such as health and education. We can also predict with a high degree of confidence that unless forceful actions are taken, Cuba will confront an eruption of certain types of corruption as political and economic institutions are transformed. While it may never be possible to totally eradicate corruption in Cuba—or anywhere else, for that matter—the anticorruption toolbox is growing exponentially.

Transparency, accountability, vigilance, and preparing for the worst may be the best deterrents to prevent the scourge of corruption from derailing the long-awaited Cuban transition.

Two THE NATURE OF CORRUPTION
AND ITS CONSEQUENCES

A growing body of evidence concludes that corruption has a signifi-cant adverse impact on social and economic development. This finding applies to the corruption usually associated with the pub-lic sector. It also applies to the corruption resulting from the dishonest behavior of individuals or private-sector firms, whether dealing with one another, the public, or government institutions. This emerging consensus reflects the findings of conceptual and empirical analyses of the pathways through which corruption redirects resources away from productive uses and erodes the political and business foundations necessary for sustained economic growth.

The current consensus regarding the deleterious effect of corruption on political and economic development is relatively new. Until recently some analysts posited that corruption had some beneficial effects in dys-functional nations whose resources were largely controlled by dominant elites, had insufficiently developed institutional structures, or possessed in-adequate channels through which particular groups could openly lobby for their interests. A long line of influential political scientists as well as some economists (see Rose-Ackerman 1999, 16–17, for a review), assigned a fa-cilitating function to corruption, as it was presumed that it helped unlock the wheels of slow-moving bureaucracies, thus encouraging economic development.

It also has been posited that in some country settings, deeply ingrained cultural norms legitimize material or social exchanges deemed corrupt in others. What is defined as corrupt has a historical dimension as well. Definitions are mediated by the stage of development attained by a coun-try with respect to contemporary world norms—the generic moderniza-tion concept, enhanced today by the globalization notion. In the modern world, the exchange of goods and services is increasingly regulated by legal rules, commercial practices, and codes of conduct designed to ensure at least minimal standards of transparency and accountability in economic transactions, whether such exchanges occur within the private or public sector or in interactions between the two. But even as these standards are universally disseminated, what is regarded as corrupt continues to be influenced by gradients of interpretation, as every culture makes judgments regarding the severity or tolerance of corruption. To compound the problem, the scope of activities deemed to be corrupt has expanded, as many actions not regarded as such in the past are viewed differently today.

In our discussion of the nature, potential benefits, and assumed cost of corruption, we first examine the groundbreaking analysis of political scientists and other social scientists to gain an appreciation of how the formal study of corruption has been approached from different disciplinary perspectives. Second, we consider contemporary overarching views from the perspectives of political science, economics, and the management disciplines.[1] And third, we review the literature to assess how corruption manifests itself in specific socioeconomic and political sectors. The chapter closes with a summary overview regarding the consequences of corruption.

INSTITUTIONAL AND CULTURAL DETERMINANTS OF CORRUPTION

Nye is representative of analysts who in the 1960s viewed corruption as partly arising from inadequate institutional structures. On the basis of a review of developing countries' experiences and while acknowledging a multiplicity of determinants of corruption, among them distributional and political factors, Nye (1967/2002, 282) assigned a major role in the existence of corruption to the inability of governments to enforce rules. This failure to effectively enforce rules resulted in part from institutional weaknesses, which, in a vicious circle, tended to further undermine the legitimacy of institutions. Given these circumstances, corruption was seen as having a functional role, as it allowed some corrupt officials and their cronies to accumulate capital (that could be used for investment), helped reduce red tape (the "grease" factor argument), provided an impetus to entrepreneurship, and in a perverse fashion, increased the managerial capacity of the state by facilitating transactions (Nye 1967/2002, 284–290).

Leff (1964/2002, 311–315) carried this line of reasoning further. In cases where the economic policy environment is not conducive to growth, he argued, corruption can exert a corrective role. He called attention to the potentially facilitating effects of corruption: bribes, under some circumstances, can overcome government indifference or misguided priorities, act as a defense against poor policies, reduce economic uncertainties, or serve as a tool to promote innovation when facing a rather immobile state resistant to change. Leff (1964/2002, 315) noted that "most of the arguments concerning the negative effects of corruption are based on the assumption that development can best proceed through the policies of an uncorrupted government and bureaucracy . . . this assumes that the government really wants economic development."

This argument, while not germane to most countries in the twenty-first century, seems to still resonate in the few countries that continue to cling to the past and where preserving the political status quo takes precedence over socioeconomic development, as was the case in the Taliban's Afghanistan. It also continues to be the case in North Korea and Cuba, two countries where the main objective of governing elites is holding on to power regardless of how doing so affects the well-being of the population. By tolerating—or, minimally, not prosecuting—petty corruption and other forms of proscribed market activities (see Chapters 4 and 5), Cuba's government diffuses potentially destabilizing social tensions. Huntington (1968/2002, 257) provided the classic formulation for this argument when he observed that "corruption itself may be a substitute for reform and both corruption and reform may be substitutes for revolution."

The role of culture in corruption continues to be the focus of controversy, although most scholars are of the view that culture is a determining or at least conditioning factor. Lipset and Salman Lenz (2000, 116) note, for example, that "quantitative evidence points to a link between corruption and social diversity, ethno-linguistic fractionalization, and the proportion of a country's population adhering to different religious traditions." Few will argue with the notion that in many cultures, mutual obligations in many sorts of transactions, embodied in social networks and kinship relationships, remain paramount. Studies conducted in Africa—also applicable to some degree to Latin America and other regions—highlight the significance of these relationships. They also indicate how difficult it is for members of certain cultures to separate what is corrupt from what is not, as normative expectations guide behavior. In some societies, Scott (1972/2002, 130) indicates that "group loyalties are still centered at the family, village or ethnic group level" rather than at the national level. In contemporary China, for example, what may be viewed as corrupt may be influenced by Confucian traditions based on mutual relationships dependent on loyalty, favor, and friendship (Hao and Johnston 2002, 594). The same is true in many African countries where ethnic ties and bonds of obligation within extended families often straddle the line between what is culturally expected and nepotism. Individuals so disposed regard opportunities to reward family and friends, afforded by what is perceived elsewhere as corruption, instead as instruments for the satisfaction of primary social obligations; they often fail to appreciate the detrimental consequences of those actions for the elusive, and not always recognized, common good. This is consistent with the classical notion of "amoral familism" described by Banfield (1958) in his study of southern Italy, where he found that kinship obligations foment practices inimical to contemporary good governance practices by buttressing corrupt behavior.

A modern variant of normative guidelines that arise from a political culture centered on the ideological premise of state ownership of the means of production was documented in the former Soviet Union. Citizens there relied on the use of personal connections and other illicit practices to obtain scarce goods and services. The typical strategy was to entice (whether through personal, professional, or other contacts) gatekeepers who controlled coveted goods or services to make them available to the petitioner. This represented a Soviet variance of a clientelist tradition seen in many other settings (DiFranceisco and Gitelman 1984/2002, 547).

In more traditional societies with less developed official administrative infrastructures, relentless calls on public officials by relatives and kin help perpetuate corruption. Nepotism is not that infrequent either in countries purportedly having well-developed ethical guidelines and administrative structures, suggesting how powerful and universal is the role of family and social obligations.

On the basis of theoretical contributions by classical social scientists, such as Emile Durkheim and Robert Merton, and analysis of data sets, such as the World Values Survey, Lipset and Salman Lenz (2000) posit that the incidence of corruption in certain cultures is mediated by economic conditions. Such is the case in cultures stressing economic success but failing to provide opportunities. As will be discussed in Chapter 3, this perspective may provide a theoretical foundation to account for the prevalence of corruption in Cuba during the early to mid-1900s. The effect of religion is assumed to operate through the level of tolerance ascribed by different religions to particular behaviors and also as mediated by kinship and family obligations. Strict adherence to personal responsibility codes, as in many Protestant traditions, presumably are less conducive to corrupt practices than religious views that assign to the clergy a forgiving role for human transgressions.

Corruption may also be a means to redress social or political inequities. Marginalized socioeconomic or ethnic communities sometimes resort to corruption as one of the few means available to them to gain some access to wealth and power. While few would justify corrupt acts on cultural terms in societies where contemporary governance concepts are being assimilated and legal sanctions against corruption are available, not many would disagree with Médard's (2002, 381) conclusion that "if nothing or little can be explained by culture, nothing can be understood without it."

Above and beyond formal legal requirements, culture also contributes to the definition of what is corrupt and how worthy of punishment different corrupt acts are. If the population tolerates corrupt acts, most citizens would be opposed to severe punishment. Heidenheimer (1970/2002, 152) elucidates this point through three types of corruption defined in terms of elites' and communities' perceptions:

> "[B]lack corruption" . . . is one which a majority consensus of both elite and mass opinion would condemn and would want to see punished on grounds of principle. "Grey corruption" indicates that some elements, usually elites, may want to see the action punished, others not, and the majority may well be ambiguous. "White corruption" signifies that the majority of both elite and mass opinion probably would not vigorously support an attempt to punish a form of corruption that they regard as tolerable. This implies that they attach less value to the maintenance of the values involved than they do to the costs that might be generated as the result of a change in rule enforcement.

Many low-level corrupt acts in Cuba today, illustrated in Chapters 4 and 5, seem to fit the category of white corruption. They arise from the excessive interference by the state in economic behavior and state ownership of the means of production, coupled with scarcity of consumer goods. Meanwhile the Cuban elite—at least rhetorically—claims to deplore the many instances of grey corruption in which the population routinely engages in part because it results in some individuals getting ahead and threatening the equality ideals of the socialist government. The level of ambiguity responds to the characteristics of the particular cultural milieu as it is also influenced by normative factors associated with changing definitions of what is considered corrupt.

Under modernizing influences—and more recently, the increasing homogenizing effect of the globalized economy—a trend toward convergence has emerged in the definition of what is corrupt and how societies should prevent and approach corruption. This applies not only to countries of the so-called developing world (although some countries, such as Cuba and North Korea, still remain largely marginalized from these influences), but also to the industrialized world, where a major definitional transformation has occurred. Anechiarico and Jacobs (1996/2002, 667) relate how these changes evolved in New York City and elsewhere as the "concept of corruption has expanded over the twentieth century to embrace more, and more varied types of conduct." They go on to note that many states in the United States, and by extension other countries,

> have expanded the concept of bribery to cover gifts and payments to public officials (so-called anti-gratuity statutes) whether or not there was an intent to corrupt or a provable *quid pro quo*. Politicians have been indicted for using their employees to provide personal services or work on their campaigns. Officeholders have been convicted for using campaign funds for personal use. Former public employees have been branded corrupt for engaging in lobbying and other private business after they left office. Low-level employees have been dismissed for petty thefts, and even for doing personal business during work hours. Conflict-of-interest laws and financial disclosure requirements have proliferated. Today, it is considered corrupt just to be in a decision-making role that *could be* affected financially by the decision, regardless of the decision actually rendered. Officials face disciplinary action if their conduct creates the "appearance of impropriety."

The vast majority of political scientists would agree that, at present, the relationship between corruption on the one hand and political stability on the other tends to be direct and unambiguous, as corruption is widely acknowledged to have a corrosive effect on legitimacy by undermining the rule of law. A concern is that with the spread of democratic governance and a concomitant alleged or real increase of corruption as levers of economic and political power become increasingly decentralized, political legitimacy suffers as citizens become ever more distrustful of government. Seligson (2002, 429–431), on the basis of survey research in four Latin American countries, found that corruption eroded the legitimacy of political systems by adversely impacting interpersonal trust, a concomitant of positive civil society relationships. Particularly worrisome is corruption perceived as a threat to the integrity of democratic political processes. Tanzi (2002, 31–32) alludes to the damaging effect of corruption on political party financing (and by extension elections) in democratic systems, where politicians often depend heavily on contributions to cover costs of party organizations and of political campaigns. These problems are common in all electoral systems that, despite many reform attempts across countries, continue to be vulnerable to subterfuge and regulatory loopholes.

These findings give added urgency to the need to address the corruption issue as a policy priority to promote economic development and political stability. The key, Johnston (1997, 69) suggests, is to encourage the emergence and consolidation of sustainable democracies "where officials and private parties can influence each other but also resist exploitation by the other and where wealth and power interests are sufficiently balanced so that neither resource must chase the other."

EFFECTS OF CORRUPTION ON ECONOMIC PERFORMANCE

An extensive literature on the economic consequences of corruption concludes that corruption distorts markets and resource allocation, thereby reducing economic efficiency and growth. The distortions created by corruption, Rose-Ackerman (1999, 9–10) finds, arise when individuals and firms are willing to make illicit payments to public officials to obtain beneficial treatment. Illicit payments thus flow to corrupt officials to reward them for allocating resources or making decisions that favor the briber; as bonuses to corrupt officials for allowing bribers to avoid taxes, customs duties, and other payments to the government; and, in extreme cases, in return for facilitating criminal activity or protecting such activities from being investigated or prosecuted.

Tanzi (2002, 45–46) has identified some of the ways in which corruption distorts markets and resource allocation: (1) reducing the ability of governments to impose necessary regulatory controls and inspections to correct for market failure; (2) distorting the nature of economic incentives; (3) creating an environment in which individuals allocate their talents and energies to rent-seeking behavior and corrupt activities rather than to productive activities; (4) creating an arbitrary tax with high social costs, consisting of the bribe plus the cost of searching for those to whom the bribe should be paid; (5) distorting the role of government as arbiter of contracts and as protector of property rights, allowing individuals to buy their way out of contracts or preventing individuals from exercising property rights; (6) reducing the legitimacy of the market economy and even of democratic governance; and (7) increasing poverty as it reduces the income potential of the most economically disadvantaged, thus having a detrimental impact on income distribution.

Various authors illustrate damaging economic effects of corruption:

- Corruption that requires that entrepreneurs either pay an up-front bribe to start a business or make payments of part of the proceeds of the investment acts as a tax that diminishes the incentives to invest (Wei 1997). This form of corruption lowers investment and retards economic growth. However, because bribes differ from taxes in one crucial way—namely, unlike taxation, corruption is illegal and must be kept secret—corruption is more distortional than taxation, creating opportunities for government officials to change the mix of economic activity toward those that can result in bribes (Shleifer and Vishny 1993, 611–612).

- Corruption tends to hurt innovative activities more than everyday production, with negative implications for long-term growth. Innovators need business, water, fire, health, and other permits in order to start a new firm. The innovator is also likely to need licenses to import machinery, equipment, and raw materials, as well as tax documents and a panoply of other government-issued documents. The innovators' demand for these government-produced goods (permits) is inelastic, and therefore they are targets of corruption. Because innovators frequently do not have the resources to pay bribes, they are often deterred by corruption from carrying out their plans, with a concomitant adverse effect on jobs, output, and economic growth (Murphy, Shleifer, and Vishny 1993).

- To the extent that taking bribes is more lucrative than carrying out productive work, human resources will be misallocated, with some talented and better-educated persons choosing to take jobs where bribes can be obtained rather than engaging in productive work (Mauro 1998). This misallocation of human resources has adverse consequences for the country's long-term growth rate. Murphy, Shleifer, and Vishny (1991, 530) have argued that "a society whose institutions allow talented people to reap the rewards of entrepreneurship and innovation is likely to prosper, but a society whose talent flows to government or private rent seeking is likely to stagnate."

- Corruption in the form of tax evasion reduces government revenue and leads to ever-higher taxes on the limited number of firms that do comply with the rules. Higher tax rates, in turn, push firms to go underground (into the informal sector), reducing the number of taxpaying firms even more. The overall decline in government revenues limits the ability of the state to provide essential services, including the rule of law (Gray and Kaufmann 1998).

- Corruption in government contracting can lead to lower quality of goods and services procured by the state. This may result, for example, in transportation disruptions or flooding of certain areas if low-quality construction services are used in infrastructure projects (e.g., bridges, dams) that subsequently fail. Supply stretching, another corrupt practice that lowers the quality of a product distributed by the state (e.g., adulteration of fertilizer or pesticides purchased by the state and distributed to farmers), can lower production yields or fail to curb destructive pests, with a negative impact on agricultural production (Alam 1990, 91).

- Corruption may distort the composition of government expenditures in favor of those that are apt for bribe seeking that can be kept secret (e.g., large infrastructure projects, military weapons procurement) to the detriment of other forms of expenditures (e.g., salaries of teachers, textbooks) about which it is more difficult to suppress information (Mauro 1998). Tanzi and Davoodi (2002) found that political or "grand" corruption is often tied to capital projects, especially in the presence of weak or underdeveloped controlling or auditing institutions. Corruption distorts the decision-making process connected with public investment projects; it is likely to increase the number of projects undertaken in a country and to change their design by enlarging their size and complexity. The corruption-induced increase in public investment comes at the expense of productivity, and the net result is that public investment ends up having a negative impact on growth.

- Corruption undermines the positive impact of foreign aid on development. As with government expenditures, corruption distorts the selection of projects toward those that are more likely to result in bribes, irrespective of their impact on economic development. For example, corruption explains the decision of the manager of a bottle-making factory in Mozambique who, presented with a fairly simple labeling machine costing $10,000 pressed for a much more sophisti-cated machine costing $100,000. The latter clearly exceeded the needs of his plant. However, the purchase of the more sophisti-cated machine circumvented international donors' guidelines applicable to a more generic machine that would have required

soliciting several bids and choosing the best offer. By bypassing
the process, the opportunity would be created for the supplier of
the unique machine to over-invoice for the machine while sharing
some of the profits with the manager and his ministerial counterparts (Shleifer and Vishny 1998, 105).
- Corruption generally undermines the state's legitimacy and
leads to instability. Instability, in turn, has an adverse impact on
the investment climate and on private investment (Gray and
Kaufmann 1998).

Turning to the quantitative effects of corruption on economic performance, Mauro (1995) in a seminal study used indices of corruption, red
tape, and efficiency of the judicial system for about seventy countries to
identify the channels through which corruption and other institutional
factors affected economic growth and to quantify the magnitude of these
effects. He found statistically significant negative associations between corruption and investment and between corruption and growth. In a subsequent study of ninety-four countries, Mauro (1997) found that a reduction
in corruption of 2.38 points on his 10-point corruption scale would
increase a country's annual investment by 4 percent of GDP and would
increase annual growth of GDP per capita by 0.5 percent. Furthermore,
Mauro (1998) confirmed that corruption altered the composition of government expenditures to favor public investment—more susceptible to
corruption—to the detriment of expenditures on education and perhaps
public health; a country that improved its corruption index from 6 to 8 on
Mauro's 10-point corruption scale typically would increase expenditures
on education by 0.5 to 1.0 percent of GDP, a considerable increase likely
to have a favorable impact on long-term economic growth and development. Findings of other econometric studies reviewed by Tanzi (2002,
48–49) indicate that corruption resulted in a lower level of expenditures
for the operation and maintenance of existing investments—for the same
reasons as it tended to decrease expenditures on public education and
health—thus reducing the productivity of the infrastructure; corruption
also acted as a tax, reducing overall levels of government revenue and limiting the ability of the government to carry out necessary expenditures.

Corruption is also seen as a potentially destabilizing influence to the
increasingly globalized economy, as the absence of and/or the failure to
adhere to clear competitive standards will be detrimental to firms from
countries not willing to pay bribes. Glynn, Kobrin, and Naím (1997, 13)
have noted that "widespread corruption threatens the very basis of an

open, multilateral economy. Multilateralism depends on trust and a belief that others will play by the rules."

In the past few years the international community has taken heed of this warning, as evidenced by several major international anticorruption conventions—sponsored by the Organization for Economic Cooperation and Development (OECD), the Organization of American States (OAS), and the United Nations, among others—defining norms to promote transparency and accountability and minimize the incidence of corruption in transnational business transactions (Abed and Gupta 2002, 7). There is no shortage of suggestions for additional international cooperation initiatives to build support for fighting corruption nationally and globally (see for example Klitgaard 1998).

DETERMINANTS OF CORRUPTION

How a country's public finances are managed is central to the corruption issue and cuts across all sectors of society on which corruption exacts a toll. The weaknesses and vulnerabilities in management of public finances that lead to corruption are well known and generally emanate from the lack of transparency and accountability of governments with dysfunctional legal, political, and control systems. Schaeffer (2005, 3) rightly differentiates poor governance from corruption although noting that the two often have common roots, including civil service incompetence and inefficient institutions. When the ambiance is propitious for widespread corruption, it flourishes in the absence of good governance.

Tanzi (2002) has developed a typology of corruption determinants structured around direct and indirect causes related to the management of public finances. Direct causes of corruption are generally associated with "how the state operates and carries out its functions," while indirect causes relate to how the state is managed and led. Among the direct determinants of corruption identified by Tanzi are: regulations and permits; taxation; spending decisions; provision of goods and services at below-market prices; other discretionary decisions; and the financing of political parties. Indirect causes include: the quality of the bureaucracy; level of public sector wages; the penalty system; institutional controls; transparency of rules, laws, and processes; and leadership example. While Tanzi's taxonomy represents an attempt to bring some order to a very disparate set of causative factors, in fact the distinctions between direct and indirect causes of corruption are not always clear-cut, as there is often considerable overlap. By taking into account how corruption is practiced, Tanzi's framework could be further refined. Hammergren (2000, 4), for example, distinguishes between opportunistic corruption and corruption that is structured so as to become intrinsic to how an organization operates.

How these direct and indirect determinants interact with private interests determines the nature, extent, and magnitude of corruption, as private firms and individuals pay bribes to gain access or retain a service or to obtain a decision favorable to advancing a private interest (Webster 2002, 5). In addition, in some countries where corruption is pervasive, aspiring civil servants may pay bribes to public officials for public-sector jobs that will allow them to extract illicit payments from the public or as means to earn wages higher than those available through private-sector employment (Rose-Ackerman 1997, 38).

Tanzi (2002) approaches the discussion of corruption largely from an economic perspective, thus giving short shrift to cultural perspectives (examined earlier in this chapter) that should be taken into account to generate a richer analytical framework, even though they may be less amenable to policy intervention. Rose-Ackerman (1999, 91–109), in contrast, considers the cultural and political underpinnings of corruption, while taking into account their economic implications. Acknowledging that culture defines what is appropriate, she highlights the potential costs of normative choices when distinguishing private from public roles and what they imply in terms of quid pro quos. Principal-agent relationships mediate the dividing line between what is proper and improper and help define what constitutes, within a given cultural setting, a gift as opposed to a bribe. Her conclusion is that if some traditional, culturally determined behaviors are perceived as corrupt, they "should simply be legalized and reported" (Rose-Ackerman 1999, 110).

Direct Determinants of Corruption

Regulations and authorizations are primary determinants of corruption in administrative systems missing well-defined rules and accountability systems where public officials operate in an environment lacking transparency or where citizens and businesses most frequently come in contact with and depend on decisions made by officials with discretionary authority. Discretionary decision-making power creates the potential for public officials to extract bribes or other illicit payments in exchange for favorable decisions or in processing documents, permits, and licenses to which citizens and businesses are entitled.

State revenue collection, whether through the direct or indirect payment of taxes and customs fees, is often a source of corruption, particularly when rules are unclear or the collection process brings tax collectors in close contact with taxpayers. Among the circumstances that give rise to corruption in taxation, Tanzi (2002, 28) has identified the following: laws that are unclear and difficult to interpret; tax administrators who are poorly paid; inadequate penalties for abuse; lack of transparency; excessive discretionary authority over determination of tax liabilities, audit decisions, and other administrative procedures; and poor controls and supervisory processes.

Poorly structured and managed spending decisions often are behind instances of administrative corruption (Tanzi 2002, 29–30). Most common are those in which the payment of bribes or other illicit favors are responsible for decisions to fund projects not meeting optimal economic or efficiency criteria at the expense of other, more worthy initiatives. Other corrupt acts are connected with government procurement, as when bidder selection is influenced by corrupt officials. When this happens, the cost to government for goods and services is inevitably higher than the market price would have been, since the briber must at least recover the amount of the bribe. Extra-budgetary accounts, generally subject to more lax financial management controls and a wider degree of discretionary authority, are a frequent target of corrupt officials.

Very vulnerable to corruption are those programs in which government seeks to provide goods or services—be they social services (including public housing, utilities, or even pensions), foreign exchange, credit, or rationed items—to the population at below-market prices (Tanzi 2002, 30). As the availability of resources to finance these programs is limited, public officials are usually granted allocation authority; potential recipients of the subsidized goods or services are often willing and/or vulnerable to pay bribes to gain faster or assured access to the benefits to which they are entitled or to obtain benefits to which they are not.

Many other discretionary decisions are susceptible to corruption. Since the nature of these decisions and who benefits from them often have significant economic, financial, and business ramifications, unscrupulous officials are in a privileged position to tilt decisions to benefit bribe payers. Among many such discretionary decisions, Tanzi (2002, 30–31) identifies the following: incentives related to income, value-added, and foreign-trade taxes; discretionary zoning law authority over privately held land; the power to decide and allocate the use of government-owned land; the ability to confer monopoly power over foreign investment; discretion over the sale or use of government resources (e.g., concessions to extract minerals or timber from state lands) and the conditions of sale or use; and discretionary decision-making authority over import, export, or domestic economic activities.

Indirect Determinants of Corruption

The quality of the bureaucracy, often combined with the level of wages paid to public officials, has been identified as a major determinant of corruption (Tanzi 2002, 32–35). The factors that influence the quality of the bureaucracy include the prestige accorded to public service in a given society, how public servants are recruited and rewarded (in terms of career advancement and salary), and the extent to which public service is based on political connections, patronage, and nepotism, as opposed to merit and performance.

The role of remuneration received by public servants in giving rise to corruption, while generally assumed to be significant, is rather elusive, as the level of corruption is mediated by many other factors, such as the professionalism of the public service, national public service traditions, and the availability of nonmonetary incentives. Still, empirical studies suggest that there is an inverse relationship between public-service wages and corruption (Van Rijckeghem and Weder 2002), although the evidence is not consistent across countries. In this regard, an effective intervention has been to substantially increase remuneration of government employees particularly prone to corruption, such as tax collectors, customs agents, and police. Evidence from Argentina, however, contradicts this purported relationship, as a study of hospitals in that country did not find convincing evidence to support the hypothesis that higher wages for procurement officers were associated with lower levels of corruption; the study suggested instead that a more robust predictor of corruption was the degree of impunity (Schargrodsky, Mera, and Weinschelbaum 2001).

Lack of transparency is perhaps the leading cause of corruption, as it permits corrupt officials to conceal their actions and the parties paying bribes to benefit from their transaction (Tanzi 2002, 37). Opacity is commonly manifested in rules and regulations that are vague and difficult to interpret, lack of public information, and complicated and untimely procedures to obtain information.

As in many other areas of economic, social, and political life, the quality of leadership is crucial in determining the extent of corruption. Tanzi (2002, 38) points out that "when the top political leaders do not provide the right example, either because they engage in acts of corruption or, as is most often the case, because they condone such acts on the part of relatives, friends or political associates, it cannot be expected that the employees in the public administration will behave differently."

How corruption is punished when detected and how effectively corrupt acts can be minimized through robust control mechanisms are crucial determinants of the incidence of corruption (Tanzi 2002, 35–37). Immunity from prosecution for public officials and lenient punishment of offenders tend to be associated with higher levels of corruption. Inadequate control mechanisms or inappropriate self-policing procedures (e.g., lack of whistle-blower protections) foster corruption, as does politicized, nonprofessional decision making. In the view of many observers, eliminating immunity for public officials—whether political appointees or career civil servants—and their accomplices outside government may be one of the most effective interventions in curbing corruption. Political will is crucial, as is willingness by political leaders and watchdog agencies to exercise it with the support of civil society actors (Pope 2000, 41–46). Rose-Ackerman (1999, 199) suggests that "[anticorruption] reforms will not occur unless powerful groups and institutions inside and outside government support it."

DETERMINANTS OF CORRUPTION IN SPECIFIC SECTORS

Beyond the general treatment of the causes of corruption, attention is increasingly being directed to understanding the determinants of corruption in specific socioeconomic and political sectors by focusing on their peculiarities and how interactions among stakeholders impede or encourage illegal transactions. The literature often distinguishes how sector corruption manifests itself according to the level of socioeconomic and political development. A good starting point for the analysis is a broad typology used in the context of social delivery services but applicable to other sectors as well. According to this typology, corruption results when private suppliers are willing to pay bribes to gain government contracts; government officials, often in connivance with private individuals, misappropriate public resources for personal use; and government employees extort payments from citizens to provide them with services they are entitled to receive. The rest of this section examines the peculiarities of corruption within different socioeconomic and political sectors, connecting the findings of the literature to the Cuban situation as appropriate.

Corruption and Agriculture

Corruption in the agricultural sector in many countries is often related to issues associated with land title and use; credit availability; access to agricultural supplies; water allocation; product standards and certification; marketing; and domestic and international programs designed to promote agricultural development (Fink 2005, 146–148).

Land titling is vulnerable to corruption because of multiple or uncertain (informal) claims, poor record keeping, and the bureaucratic nature of registration processes. Transition economies, burdened with the legacy of socialist governments—that largely did away with private property rights, arbitrarily expropriated land, and assigned ownership rights to particular individuals or groups—have been particularly vulnerable to corruption. The settlement of contesting property disputes in settings with uncertain and weak rule-of-law regimes has often been done through the payment of bribes or the illegal assignation of title to well-positioned and corrupt government officials.

Problems of this nature are sure to arise in a Cuba in transition, as property rights have been muddled by the land expropriations of the 1960s and shifts in land tenure policies that are still occurring well into the 2000s. Further muddling the process is the large-scale emigration of former landowners and their descendants; the forceful displacement of peasant populations (for example from the Escambray region during the 1960s to combat insurgents); the possible willful destruction of pre-revolutionary landownership registries; and the passing away—after nearly a half-century of socialist rule—of generations of landowners with clear recollection of lawful land boundaries.

Access to credit, supplies, and water is certain also to generate many corruption opportunities in Cuba, at least during the early stages of the transition. Rational access to these production inputs will have to await the emergence of markets for intermediate inputs and of distribution mechanisms, as for several decades they were allocated according to state planning objectives, prioritizing their distribution to state farms and cooperatives, to the detriment of privately owned small farms. Absent proper regulation and oversight, many government bureaucrats will likely attempt to take advantage of their control over access to resources—including those originating from international assistance—and allocate them to themselves or to those likely to pay a bribe. Access to irrigated farmland will be particularly susceptible to corruption, given its high production potential.

The transition to market-driven agriculture will give rise to many other corruption opportunities, particularly if attempts are made to maintain production quotas and control prices, even if temporarily. Many of socialist Cuba's agricultural black markets arose from such attempts to interfere with market allocation, as did sugar agribusiness corruption before socialism that arose from competition among mill owners to acquire production quotas.

Corruption and the Environment

Corruption in the utilization of natural resources results as much from the forces driving malfeasance in other sectors (such as weak procurement procedures, inadequate institutional development and weak regulatory frameworks, and a poorly trained and compensated civil service) as from the intrinsic value of natural resources and how they are exploited. The sector is particularly prone to corruption, as the utilization of natural resources is often managed through complex regulations; natural resources generally must be inventoried if taxes are to be levied (opening the door for illegal transactions); and the risk of punishment for transgressors is low, as offenses often are committed in remote locations away from public scrutiny (United Nations Development Programme et al. 2003, 36).

Corruption in this sector is particularly perverse, as it has been found that the exploitation of natural resources under the influence of corrupt practices often retards rather than accelerates economic growth due to the pernicious effects of rents (Leite and Weidmann 2002). Moreover, corruption is a major factor in "undermining environmental equity and destroying ecosystems" (UNDP et al. 2003, 36). What distinguishes the environmental sector from others, according to Winbourne (2005, 99), "is that corruption here is triggered by large amounts of formal and informal revenues that can be gained from many natural products." The key issue, suggests Winbourne, is the intrinsic "conflict between private interests concerning the commercial value of natural resources (mineral, water, land, forest, wildlife, for example) and reductions in production costs by using environmentally unfriendly technologies, on one side, and, public interests in a healthy habitat, on the other side."

Given this permanent tension, corruption related to natural resources can appear at any time, under a number of guises, and at different levels of decision making. Winbourne (2005, 102–105) identifies three basic levels of corruption in the environmental sector and areas of vulnerability associated with each (Table 2.1).

Grand corruption occurs when decision making related to the development of environmental and natural resources policy is compromised by ulterior motives designed to favor some particular interests. It can lead to

TABLE 2.1. LEVELS OF CORRUPTION AND VULNERABILITIES
IN THE ENVIRONMENTAL SECTOR

Level of Corruption	Areas Vulnerable to Corruption
Grand corruption	• Environmental and natural resources policy and regulations development
Mid-level corruption	• Distribution and designation of environmental/ natural resources and territories for particular utilization (including public procurement)
	• Permitting and certifications such as in issuing permits and certificates for using territories and natural resources and operating industrial sites, including permits for emissions, discharges, and solid wastes
	• Environmental assessments, including Environmental Impact Assessments (EIAs)
Petty corruption	• Enforcement, including inspections by environmental protection agencies and other related agencies to assess whether established environmental standards are being met and policing violations such as poaching, illegal logging, resource trafficking, excessive emissions, and so forth

Source: Winbourne 2005, 103

state capture and generally results from a lack of transparency and accountability in decision making, coupled with broad and unchecked authority granted to public officials, undue influence exerted by powerful foreign interests, and poorly designed and implemented laws regulating financial disclosure and lobbying.

Mid-level corruption involves the designation and assignment of environmental resources for particular uses; how they are regulated through permits and certifications; and how they are influenced by environmental assessments. Petty corruption is connected with the wanton violation of inspections and enforcement of regulations and is usually associated with opportunities available to poorly paid public officials to extract rents to increase their family income. According to Winbourne (2005, 105),

> Petty corruption in the environmental sector occurs mostly during
> environmental inspections and the policing of illegal acts such as

poaching, illegal logging, discharges, emissions, and the like. In this kind of corruption, insignificant amounts of money and low-level officials are usually involved, unless it is part of a vertically organized scheme that can reach into higher levels of government. The most common forms of corruption at this level are bribery, influence peddling, and nepotism. The major reasons for support mechanisms include inspection regulations that are open to overly broad interpretation, insufficient inspection procedures, lack of accountability, low salaries for inspectors, and unattainable environmental standards that are established without consideration of the resources and technologies needed for businesses to meet these standards.

The potential for increased environmental corruption in Cuba is significant. The economic payoff from the country's most dynamic sector, tourism, is heavily dependent on the usufruct of natural resources such as sandy beaches, coastlines, rivers, forests, and so on. Access to these resources is essential to a tourism enterprise and may be influenced by the payment of bribes to government officials. The same would apply to the exploitation of mineral resources (in the case of Cuba, mostly nickel and copper deposits) and oil, where access to licenses and the ability to bend rules and regulations could be subject to illicit payments.

Corruption and Public Education

While acknowledging that large-scale corruption in the public education sector is relatively frequent and costly, Chapman (2005, 66) argues that it is not as detrimental as small-scale corruption. First, as a high-visibility and diffuse government activity, education is prone to patronage and to appeals to local sentiments; second, educational decisions are controlled by gatekeepers with decision-making ability at various levels; and third, educational expenditures are often small and made in many different sites. In Azfar's (2005, 183–187) typology, corruption in the education sector (and the health sector) arises from interactions among providers and clients, providers and suppliers, and payers and suppliers, as well as from administrative processes within the service delivery organization. For Chapman (2005, 66), an insidious and detrimental consequence of petty corruption in the education sector is that "entire generations of youth are mis-educated— by example—to believe that personal success comes not through merit and hard work, but through favoritism, bribery and fraud."

TABLE 2.2. COMMON FORMS OF CORRUPTION IN THE EDUCATION
SECTOR, BY LEVEL

Level of Activity	Type of Behavior
Central Ministry	Kickbacks on construction and supply contracts
	Favoritism in hiring, appointment, and promotion decisions
	Diversion of funds from government accounts
	Diversion of funds from international assistance funds
	Ghost teachers and employees
	Requiring payment for services that should be provided free
	Withholding needed approvals and signatures to extort bribes (e.g., gifts, favors, outright payments)
	Directing construction and services to locations that offer opportunities for personal gain by oneself, family, or friends
	Requiring the use of materials as a way of creating a market for items on which oneself, family, or friends hold an import or production monopoly
Region/district	Overlooking school violations on inspector visits in return for bribes or favors
	Diversion of school supplies to private markets
	Sales of recommendations for higher education entrance
	Favoritism in personnel appointments (e.g., headmasters, teachers)
School	Ghost teachers
	Diversion of school fees
	Inflation of school enrollment data (in countries in which central ministry funds are allocated to schools on the basis of enrollment)
	Imposition of unauthorized fees
	Diversion of central Ministry of Education funds allocated to schools
	Diversion of monies in revolving textbook fund
	Diversion of community contributions
Classroom/teacher	Siphoning of school supplies and textbooks to local market
	Selling test scores and course grades
	Selling change of grade
	Selling grade-to-grade promotion
	Selling admissions (especially to higher education)
	Creating the necessity for private tutoring

TABLE 2.2. (*continued*)

Level of Activity	Type of Behavior
International agencies	Teachers' persistent absenteeism to accommodate other income-producing work Payment of bribes Payment of excessive or unnecessary fees to obtain services Skimming from project funds Allocating (or acquiescing in the allocation of) project-related opportunities on the basis of candidates' connections rather than merit

Source: Chapman 2005, 70

How corruption manifests in the education sector makes these distinctions of more than academic interest (see Table 2.2 for an illustrative list of forms of corruption in the sector). Chapman (2005, 66–68) identifies outright acts of bribery or fraud perpetrated by educational officials at all levels in exchange for decisions favoring one interest or another.

Corruption is also associated with poorly or irregularly paid educational officials, who are often seen as having few other choices than bribes to supplement their low salaries. In some instances, what may be perceived as corrupt by some observers is not regarded as such in the cultural context in which it occurs, as educators are often forced into "cutting corners, ignoring rules, and by-passing procedures in order to move activities forward in ways important to the success of a project or ministry initiative" (Chapman 2005, 67). In other instances, cultural practices condoning gift giving are distorted and used to extort petty bribes. Finally, many acts in the educational sector that appear to be corrupt are actually the result of sheer incompetence resulting from poor management or inadequate infrastructure. Absenteeism and sinecures (ghost workers) are serious concerns in many national educational systems, as is the proclivity of officials to redirect educational resources to their own pockets or toward the support of the agendas of particular political factions. As we discuss in Chapter 3, Cuba's history is replete with alleged incidents of abuse of sinecures in the public education system and the appropriation of the sector's resources by public officials or political party members.

Chapman (2005, 68) concludes that perceptions of corruption in education often determine what forms are tolerated, as often what is perceived as corruption is a result of resource scarcity.

The essential point is that thoughtful, reasonable people can disagree over what constitutes corruption. Even when observers agree
that certain actions constitute corruption, they may differ in their
tolerance of the offense (e.g., when the sale of grades is tolerated because teachers are underpaid). Moreover, those forms most
widely condemned (e.g., contract kickbacks) tend to be the least
visible; those that tend to be the most visible (e.g., forced private
tutoring) tend to be the most widely tolerated.

Corruption and Public Health

As with public education, the public health sector is prone to corruption
because of the very diffuse nature of the demand and the multiple public
suppliers involved. Corruption in the public health sector is responsible
for an enormous loss of public resources and results in the denial of basic
health services to needy citizens. Cross-country econometric studies suggest that countries with a high prevalence of corruption are likely to have
higher infant and child mortality rates and a higher percentage of low birth
weights (Gupta, Davoodi, and Tiongson 2002).

Vian (2005, 44) has noted that the public health sector is particularly
vulnerable to corruption, as it provides a wide array of services in multiple
locations, expenditures are quite significant, and demand is broad and often
immediate. Furthermore, "there are many kinds of processes and expenditures occurring in the health sector, from expensive construction and high
tech procurement, with attendant risks of bribery, collusion and ex-post
corruption, to frontline services being offered within a provider-patient
relationship marked by imbalances in information and inelastic demand
for services." Table 2.3, developed by Vian, summarizes the areas or processes in the health services sector that are particularly susceptible to corruption, associated types of corruption and problems, and their indicators
and results. Most damaging and costly seem to be those corrupt practices
related to the procurement and distribution of medical supplies, including
diversion of resources to private hands, and the tendency for poorly paid
health personnel to engage in unregulated and often illegal provision of
health services in exchange for informal payments; to these, Azfar (2005)
would add ghost workers (see also Di Tella and Savedoff 2001).

With public health sectors under economic pressure everywhere, Vian
observes as well, corruption can exacerbate inequalities in delivery of services by creating opportunities for health personnel and patients to con-
nive to provide services or scarce medications to those willing to make

TABLE 2.3. TYPES OF CORRUPTION IN THE HEALTH SECTOR

Area or Process	Types of Corruption and Problems	Indicators or Results
Construction and rehabilitation of health facilities	Bribes, kickbacks, and political considerations influencing the contracting process Contractors failing to perform and not being held accountable	High-cost, low-quality facilities and construction work Location of facilities that does not correspond to need, resulting in inequities in access Biased distribution of infrastructure favoring urban and elite-focused services and high technology
Purchase of equipment and supplies, including drugs	Bribes, kickbacks, and political considerations influencing bid specifications and winners Collusion or bid rigging during procurement Lack of incentives to choose low-cost and high-quality suppliers Unethical drug promotion Suppliers failing to deliver and not being held accountable	High-cost, inappropriate, or duplicative drugs and equipment Inappropriate equipment located without consideration of true need Substandard equipment and drugs Inequities due to inadequate funds left to provide for all needs
Distribution and use of drugs and supplies in service delivery	Theft (for personal use) or diversion (for private-sector resale) of drugs or supplies at storage and distribution points Sale of drugs or supplies that were supposed to be free	Lower utilization Patients not getting proper treatment Patients making informal payments to obtain drugs Interruption of treatment or incomplete treatment, leading to development of antimicrobial resistance

(continued)

TABLE 2.3. (*continued*)

Area or Process	Types of Corruption and Problems	Indicators or Results
Regulation of quality in products, services, facilities, and professionals	Bribes to speed process or gain approval for drug registration, drug quality inspection, or certification of good manufacturing practices Bribes or political considerations influencing inspection results or suppressing findings Biased application of sanitary regulations for restaurants, food and production, cosmetics Biased application of accreditation, certification, or licensing procedures and standards	Subtherapeutic or fake drugs being allowed on market Marginal suppliers being allowed to continue participating in bids, getting government work Increased incidence of food poisoning Spread of infectious and communicable diseases Poor-quality facilities continuing to function Incompetent or fake professionals continuing to practice
Education of health professionals	Bribes to gain place in medical school or other pre-service training Bribes to obtain passing grades Political influence, nepotism in selection of candidates for training opportunities	Incompetent professionals practicing medicine or working in health professions Loss of faith and freedom due to unfair system
Medical research	Pseudo-trials funded by drug companies that are really for marketing Misunderstanding of informed consent and other issues of adequate standards in developing countries	Violation of individual rights Biases and inequities in research

TABLE 2.3. (*continued*)

Area or Process	Types of Corruption and Problems	Indicators or Results
Provision of services by frontline health workers	Use of public facilities and equipment to see private patients Unnecessary referrals to private practice or privately owned ancillary services Absenteeism Informal payments required from patients for services Theft of user fee revenue, other diversion of budget allocations	Government losing value of investments without adequate compensation Employees being unavailable to serve patients Reduced use of services by patients who cannot pay Impoverishment as citizens use income and sell assets to pay for health care Reduced quality of care from loss of revenue Loss of citizen faith in government

Source: Vian 2005, 45–46

illegal payments. This is an apt description of what began to occur in Cuba in the early 1990s as, in the absence of foreign subsidies, the health care system deteriorated and patients who needed scarce medications were left to their own devices.

The situation in Russia during and after the transition away from socialism closely parallels what has been occurring in Cuba during the so-called Special Period that began in the early 1990s. The Special Period is an economic state of emergency triggered by the dissolution of the Soviet Union and political and economic changes in Eastern Europe that reduced trade and economic assistance from these nations and has had severe repercussions on the Cuban economy. Prior to the transition, the Russian state (then part of the Union of Soviet Socialist Republics) had expanded the public health care system to an extent not sustainable in a market economy. The number of physicians was excessive, and they were poorly compensated; pharmaceutical products were subsidized and tightly controlled. With the collapse of the socialist system and the emergence of a market economy, health-sector subsidies were dramatically cut at the same time that salaries of health personnel lost much of their purchasing power as a result of general inflation. Despite this situation, writes Vian (2005, 55),

The [Russian] government refused to recognize that it could not
support the health establishment it inherited; it would neither
downsize, redefine the package of free services, nor institute formal
fees that might be managed in such a way to reduce the impact on
the sickest and poorest. Patients were forced to pay market prices
for drugs . . . and . . . under-the-table payments for medical services
have soared as health providers try to assure themselves a living
wage, and patients try to obtain the care they need.

Corruption and the Energy Sector

Certain peculiarities of the energy sector make it vulnerable to corruption, according to Ruth (2005): the opportunities to generate considerable
rents from extraction, transformation, and use activities; the time-sensitive
nature of some activities (e.g., extraction of natural gas associated with oil
production or distribution of electricity); the considerable capital investments required; and the extent to which the sector (whether state-owned
or privatized) is regulated by the state. Ruth (2005, 116) notes,

> Because of the growing need for energy and limited sources of sup-
> ply, governments have both natural monopolies in the energy sector
> and high interests to protect their energy supply from disruption.
> The supply chain from energy extraction to transformation and use
> typically involves complex infrastructure systems, many institutions
> and jurisdictions, and potentially a large number of end users. Within
> this energy scenario, ample opportunities exist for high profits and
> resource rents, and for individuals to engage in corrupt practices to
> gain access to, or use, the power associated with access to energy.

Ruth (2005) further notes that corruption may occur as energy producers
are compelled to make "facilitation payments" to ensure prompt delivery of
goods and services essential for extracting energy resources or as resources
are diverted to private hands due to difficulties in properly tracking the large
amounts of fuels that have to be transported or distributed. Distribution of
energy products to consumers (e.g., gasoline, cooking gas, electricity) gives
rise to yet another set of opportunities for corruption when regulatory and
control systems are ineffective. These corrupt practices might manifest as
illegal sales, faked ration coupons, falsified meter readings, or condoning of
illegal electricity hookups. In countries where the energy sector is subsidized, corruption may be associated with the discretion enjoyed by officials

to allocate the subsidies. Opportunities for grand corruption are plentiful, for example when officials take advantage of their decision-making authority in the acquisition and importation of capital goods or in granting licenses or when government officials use inside information for their own benefit or to the benefit of those who pay them.

Corruption and the Justice System

The justice system, broadly defined, encompasses courts, judges, prosecutors and public defenders, public law enforcement authorities (including police), the private bar, court personnel, and enforcement institutions such as prisons. Corruption in the justice system occurs whenever authority is misused for personal gain, resulting "in the improper delivery of judicial services and legal protection for citizens" (Pepys 2005, 13).

Corruption in the justice system, a fundamental anticorruption pillar, should not be underestimated, as it can severely undermine the effectiveness of all other anticorruption initiatives (Pope 2000). The roots of corruption in the justice system are varied but typically are connected with the ability of judges and other officials of the judicial system to use discretionary power to bend the law or regulatory framework to benefit one or another party in disputes in exchange for bribes or other favors (Hammergren 2000, 3). In many countries, major contributing factors are low wages and poor working conditions, coupled with inadequate procedures, including lack of training. In poorly managed court systems where backlogs tie up cases for months if not years, delays are often broken through the payment of bribes. Judicial decisions are sometimes influenced by bribes, and other times they are forced upon judges by political parties or by powerful interests who are able to operate with impunity.

Pepys (2005, 16–18) observes that corruption in the justice system could occur anywhere along a procedural continuum that extends from filing a complaint or initiating an investigation to reaching a judgment or enforcing a sentence. Fear of retribution often is an instrument used to pervert the intent of the law, as is the paying of bribes to influence whether a decision is enforced and how. In some cultures more than others, familial obligations and relationships also contribute to corruption, as do nontransparent administrative procedures that could be utilized to determine outcomes. Pepys (2005, 18) describes how the latter operates:

> Another insidious form of corruption comes from within the justice system itself. Chief police officers, prosecutors, or judges can

exert significant administrative authority over their subordinates. By the simple act of assigning an investigation to a certain police officer, or a case to a certain prosecutor or judge, the outcome of the investigation or case can be determined. In some courts, the senior judge reviews the decisions of the other judges to assure the "correctness" of their opinions. Although the purpose of the review may be to seek accuracy of the facts and law, such internal pressure can have the effect of ensuring that judges comply with the senior judge's position in order to maintain good relations and secure their favor.

Corruption and Military Spending

Military spending has very frequently been associated with corruption. Military procurements tend to be quite sizable, specifications are very technical, and few suppliers are able to deliver the desired products or services. Allegations abound of military purchases made contingent on the payment of bribes, particularly—but not exclusively—by military regimes lacking proper accountability and transparency safeguards.

Corruption in military expenditures may have increased since the end of the Cold War, as reduced purchases and idle hardware production capacity have prompted international arms suppliers to step up questionable marketing strategies to sustain sales and production. The secrecy that often accompanies military affairs in general and arms sales in particular contributes to this state of affairs.

Econometric studies also suggest that corruption tilts budget allocations toward military spending and away from more productive social sectors (e.g., education, public health) as opportunities for illicit enrichment tend to be more plentiful in military spending than in other public service sectors (Gupta, de Mello, and Sharan 2002).

Corruption and the Political System

Corruption in the political system takes many forms and ranges from illegal actions in the process whereby candidates for office are selected (e.g., campaign financing, vote buying) to how politicians use their power once in office. Ruling parties in particular tend to enjoy a great deal of discretionary authority since they shape political and economic agendas and "also monitor the bureaucracy, control the distribution and management of public resources, and supervise the activities of public corporations"

(Blechinger 2005, 33). The expectation to profit, or to continue to profit, from the fruits of power has also been a powerful determinant of the desire of many political leaders to extend their terms in office, often by non-democratic means (Blechinger 2005, 28). Table 2.4 summarizes a typology of corruption in the political process, developed by Transparency International, that identifies vulnerable actors and likely outcomes.

A frequent avenue for corruption to become embedded in electoral politics is political party financing. The Latin American experience indicates that regulations designed to promote transparency and prevent undue influence of private parties in political processes are often perverted by the general ineffectiveness with which they are implemented. Procedures to report political donations are often complex and difficult to enforce; government subsidies to political parties, while generally more open to public scrutiny, are subject to manipulation; rules to monitor campaign spending can be bypassed with relative ease; and poorly audited financial records are not conducive to transparency (Casas 2005, 26–30). The key to controlling corruption in political party financing is a complex nexus of oversight and regulatory institutions, together with ethical commitments by politicians cognizant that they are being watched by a civil society intolerant of dishonesty and manipulation (Ferreira 2005).

Illegal activities conducted by or on behalf of political parties have often been at the vortex of corruption in many societies, pre-revolutionary Cuba serving as a fitting example. In the multiparty system that existed in Cuba before 1959, political parties competed for popular support in order to achieve power. If they succeeded, they often gave free hand to their partisans appointed to positions of power to extract rents, confer financial and business favors on selected constituencies, or even commit outright fraud. Specific abuses of this nature—in Cuba and elsewhere—include taking bribes, demanding extortion payments, appointing supporters to public positions from which they can benefit personally, making decisions that advance the economic and financial interests of particular groups associated with the party, and channeling government resources to officials and individuals affiliated with the party.

In today's Cuba, where authority is vested in a single, all-powerful, official party and the state controls most aspects of economic life, the risk of grand corruption and state capture is highest because of the absence of countervailing political and social forces. As discussed in this book, dismantling such a system poses particularly difficult challenges, as deep transformations must be accomplished in an environment lacking transparency and unambiguous rules. Preventing in Cuba the experiences of the former

TABLE 2.4. TYPES OF CORRUPTIVE POLITICAL PRACTICES AND
THEIR OUTCOMES

Practice	Vulnerable Actor/Group	Outcome
Vote buying	Voters, politicians, and candidates	Bribing voters, offering incentives (gifts, food employment), and buying votes in legislative issues
Funding from illicit sources	Candidates and political parties	Accepting money from drug traffickers or foreign sources
Political patronage	Candidates, political parties, government officials, civil servants, party members, the public at large	Engaging in bribery, kickbacks, political favors, and outright theft involving party loyalists
Nepotism	Candidates, political parties, government officials, and civil servants	Exercising favoritism involving candidates nominating relatives for public administration positions in exchange for political support
Selling of appointments and access to information	Public servants and candidates	Gaining access to jobs, seats, or posts in government through contributions
Abuse/misuse of public resources	Public sector, government	Using public resources for political gains and capturing state resources to fund campaigns, companies, organizations, and individuals
Personal enrichment	Candidates and politicians	Taking contributions intended for elections; securing better positions to participate in political process and pick favorites to win
Demand for contributions from public servants	Public servants and civil service	Imposing fees for office holders and forcing public servants to become party members

TABLE 2.4. (*continued*)

Practice	Vulnerable Actor/Group	Outcome
Violation of political party finance regulations	Political parties and candidates	Accepting donations from sources that are prohibited; spending more than the legal ceiling allows; inaccurate accounting and reporting and lack of transparency in funding
Contributions for contracts and policies	Private sector	Making payoffs in exchange for political support in the form of licenses, contracts, and legislation

Source: Based in part on Transparency International 2004b, adapted by Casals and Associates 2004b

Soviet Union and other ex-socialist states that saw unprecedented levels of corruption upon the dismantling of the totalitarian system, often with the connivance of officials from the ancient regime, will require an explicit anticorruption emphasis in the Cuban transition strategy.

Corruption in Public Construction

Public construction projects are beyond a doubt one of the most vulnerable areas to corruption regardless of sector. Large infrastructure projects in particular are often targeted. We have already noted how resource allocations are frequently tilted toward construction projects and away from other uses. The usually large size of construction projects and the asymmetry underlying the understanding by public-sector regulators and the public on the one hand and builders on the other of what a large construction project entails—from planning and design to actual delivery—opens many windows for corrupt transactions. Other contributing factors are difficulties in comparing bidding costs, as construction projects are many times specific to a particular setting and, being government-regulated, open to bribery. Construction projects, in addition, usually entail complex contractual links, each providing opportunities for corrupt transactions. Another feature of construction that makes it prone to corruption is that projects proceed in stages; later stages may conveniently conceal (e.g., concrete over steel) shoddy construction practices, or lower-quality materials may be used to save resources for illegal payments. Further, the industry is highly secretive due to intense commercial competition and because lenders, including national banks and international financial institutions, commonly fail to exercise due diligence in their evaluation and selection of contractors (Stansbury 2005). These problems are often exacerbated in post-conflict reconstruction situations when basic control mechanisms may be set aside due to humanitarian pressures (see, for a review, Transparency International 2005).

Corruption in Other Sectors

Other sectors particularly prone to corruption include immigration and labor law enforcement. Corruption in the former is driven by the imbalance between the number of potential immigrants and the setting of quotas by destination countries to limit legal admissions. To bypass these limits, migrants seek unauthorized entry by paying off immigration control officials in transit or destination countries or purchasing passports and visas from corrupt consular officials. While the intent of labor laws is often circumvented by employers willing to bribe inspectors to look the other way, just as often corrupt inspectors extract bribes from establishments by threatening to drum up labor violations.

Law enforcement is equally vulnerable to corruption. The most visible and notorious example is the bribe extracted by police officers for alleged traffic violations. This practice is ubiquitous in many developing countries, where it is common to see police checkpoints solely established for this purpose.

CONCLUSION

In summary, as stated by Transparency International (in Pope 2000, 6–7), corruption has multiple adverse impacts on political, economic, and social development. Among many other reasons, corruption is detrimental because it:

- obstructs how governments seek to allocate resources by inducing inefficiency and waste;
- discourages the operation of the market by interfering with the ability of businesses to operate by introducing unpredictability and barriers to entry and discouraging investment;

- increases administrative costs to taxpayers;
- diminishes the resources available for public purposes, when it involves kickbacks;
- erodes public morality and administrative probity;
- undermines respect for government authority and thus legitimacy;
- encourages citizens to be corrupt when public servants are corrupt;
- encourages corrupt politicians and officials to avoid unpopular decisions that run counter to their self-interest;
- results in productivity losses as more attention is devoted to how to circumvent the system rather than to advancing through hard work;
- often leads to costly, unproductive, and unnecessary litigation; and
- tilts the balance in favor of money rather than the satisfaction of human needs.

The cost of corruption to the welfare of those in greatest need is especially insidious. In a comprehensive review of the literature, Chetwynd, Chetwynd, and Spector (2003, 15) conclude that corruption "does exacerbate and promote poverty," although how it does this was found to be complex and mediated by economic and governance factors. Corruption reduction programs, they suggest, could advance poverty alleviation programs to the extent that they would contribute to increased economic growth, encourage more equitable income distributions, lead to more effective governance institutions, provide better government services, and increase citizen confidence in government. These recommendations to reduce poverty are consistent with a sustained attack on many of the causes of corruption discussed in this chapter.

Three ROOTS OF CORRUPTION IN CUBA

The roots of administrative corruption in Cuba can be traced back to political, institutional, administrative and rule-of-law practices during four centuries of Spanish colonial rule. These institutionally and culturally determined practices were reinforced by political and economic developments on the island during the Republic (1902–1958). They were later greatly transformed by the 1959 Revolution but persisted, taking new forms under different ideological and institutional premises, only to reemerge in pre-revolutionary incarnations following the 1989 socialist bloc collapse. As a result, traditional forms of corruption coexist in contemporary Cuba with equally pernicious forms of corruption that are typical of countries with centrally planned economies or transitioning from command to market economies, creating a complex national landscape of corruption. The juxtaposition of these three corruption trends (traditional, socialist, and transitional) is ominous and portends a very challenging transition scenario for Cuba. Regardless of the circumstances under which the long-awaited Cuban transition materializes, it will likely be accompanied at every step of the way by the specter of corruption.

This chapter provides a historical overview of the nature and extent of corruption in the country before 1959, pinpointing connections that link corrupt practices of the past with contemporary ones discussed in Chapters 4 and 5. This historical perspective also draws attention to the likelihood that corrupt practices of long ago will reappear once the transition gets under way—barring a miraculous economic recovery sweeping enough to offset the historical propensity of many Cubans to bend rules in the pursuit of self-interest or the average Cuban's proclivity to seek a minimum of economic security under the umbrella of the state. Awareness of these historical continuities is essential to understand the current and prospective nature of corruption in Cuba and the policy levers that might be available to minimize it. As we consider them, we are inevitably drawn not only to rule-of-law issues, but also to the political and economic realms and to how transitional and post-transition Cuba should address concerns related to governance, growth, equity, and the provision of social services.

To set this discussion into its proper context, it is essential to balance the tendency of some Cuba analysts to overstate the significance of country-specific circumstances while neglecting to assign proper weight to more universal determinants of corruption. While specific features of Cuban history can enrich our understanding of the texture and causes of corruption in the country, they should not divert attention away from major determinants of corruption that transcend national borders and that are in large measure responsible for its common occurrence. A considerable body of evidence speaks to the universality of corruption across cultures and historical periods. This same comparative literature describes why some societies have succeeded in curtailing corruption and the types of interventions that have been effective in controlling or at least minimizing it.

From this perspective, therefore, it is indeed useful to understand how corruption manifests itself in any given national context, both from historical and institutional perspectives. It is hardly insightful at the more general level to say that greed or economic necessity drives corruption or that corruption results when unethical individuals conclude that the potential gain from bending the rules exceeds the potential cost of being caught and punished. But it is useful to grasp an understanding of why corruption is often condoned, even encouraged, by the political, economic, and social order. Thus, we briefly examine corruption practices in Cuba since colonial days but focus particularly on the period between 1902, when the country achieved its formal independence, to 1959, when the revolution led by Fidel Castro came to power.

Before we do so, however, it is worth pointing out that in Cuba, as in any other country, it is difficult to separate myth from reality when addressing the corruption issue. By their very nature, acts of corruption are carried out in the dark and in connivance between the parties involved. Thus, cases in which incontrovertible evidence comes to light that a corrupt act has occurred are the exception rather than the rule. Instances of petty corruption, as when an official demands a small bribe for a routine government service, are more blatant and thus less likely to be made in the dark than when a businessman pays a large bribe behind closed doors to a politician. In the more egregious cases, the rare instances when evidence is available are likely to result from judicial interventions or because it has been provided by one of the involved parties. This means that most corruption information must be regarded as "allegations" rather than fact. This being said, it is not far-fetched to assume that many corruption allegations have a basis in fact, although it is generally difficult to establish their truthfulness beyond the shadow of a doubt absent legal proceedings. In some cases, actions taken by politicians and bureaucrats are so blatant, or so lacking in transparency, that despite the absence of definite evidence of malfeasance, it is reasonable to assume that they were motivated by some ulterior, generally dishonest, objective. These caveats must be kept in mind in the historical review that follows and more generally in our discussion of corruption in contemporary Cuba in subsequent chapters.

COLONIAL CUBA

It is not an exaggeration to state that the seeds of corruption arrived in Cuba with Columbus' fleet during his voyage of discovery in 1492. The enormous personal risks endured by the seafarers, while partially motivated by the challenges of the unknown, were also driven by expectations of acquiring great personal wealth. That many *conquistadores* did just that by pillaging the riches of the Americas need not be recounted here. Although Cuba's mineral wealth was limited and most early settlers soon departed for more promising pastures in continental gold-rich destinations like Mexico and Peru, colonial administrators early on instituted mechanisms to extract for the Spanish crown as much wealth from the island as possible.

Marrero (1974, 233–235) writes that even before Diego Velázquez, Cuba's first governor general, had completed the island's occupation, he appointed officials to oversee the management of colonial resources and prevent undue personal gain, since fraudulent practices were feared. As early as 1559, the custom of selling public positions to the highest bidder—in particular potentially profitable posts in justice administration and tax collection—was in evidence in Cuba (ibid., 247–248). These practices, common in medieval Europe and in the American Spanish empire, were justified, as it was difficult for central governments to monitor local officials due to widespread dishonesty, considerable geographical distances, and primitive administrative techniques. Through this practice, governments avoided the risks inherent in the transfer of monies; moreover, since officials had a personal stake in results, they more competently performed their duties (Swart 2002, 96). With the passing of time and as states consolidated their authority and administrative procedures improved, the practice of selling offices gradually withered away. Nevertheless, the consequences of this practice continue to permeate, even to this day, the culture of public administration in countries that never managed to completely erase the legacy of profiting from public office. Equally profitable became the sale by public officials of amnesties for common crimes, a practice extended to other types of infractions (Marrero 1975, 213).

By the seventeenth century, frauds of all sorts were common in colonial Cuba; rare was the high-ranking public official or businessman who was not involved. Repeatedly, audits revealed malfeasance on the part of captain generals, governors, and navy and army officers (Marrero 1975, 147, 229–234). Yet, in Cuba, as in the rest of Spanish colonial America, such audits rarely led to prosecutions, unless suspected parties were in the sights of powerful political enemies (Montaner 2001, 46). This state of affairs has been blamed primarily on two factors. First, few Spanish officials went to Cuba with any other intent than enjoying the privileges of office and/or becoming rich, whether licitly or illicitly (Masó 1998, 299). And second, in exchange for absolute loyalty, the crown looked the other way as long as its imperial interests and share of colonial wealth were assured (Montaner 2002, 26). But even within this laxity, some order had to be imposed. In 1637 a *tribunal de cuentas* (court of accounts) was established in Havana and entrusted with the oversight of the fiscal affairs of Santiago de Cuba and Florida (a Spanish colony at the time), as well as with the financial oversight of the Spanish fleets and the city's customs house (Masó 1998, 56).

Madrid contributed substantially to the prevailing culture of disrespect for the law by imposing mercantilist policies that only allowed trade between Cuba and the port of Seville. The opportunities for illicit and profitable contraband with British, French, and Dutch traders were plentiful and embraced with relish by Cuba's inhabitants, often in connivance with the local authorities (Marrero 1975, 105–153). By the eighteenth century, few Cubans paid much attention to fiscal or commercial regulations. Official *contaduría* (accounting) documents unearthed by Marrero (1978, 171) in the Archives of the Indies illustrated the futility of trying to eliminate contraband, concluding that "no measures were sufficient to extinguish" it.[1]

Superimposed on this complex governance scenario was the institution of slavery, whose role in the emergence of a national culture of corruption should not be underestimated. Slavery, by its nature, entails the exploitation of human labor and disregard for the rights of others. The cruelty of slavery engenders a desire on the part of the enslaved to even the score with the perpetrators by one means or another. Thus, while slave owners saw nothing wrong in extracting profit from the labor of others, slaves found no fault in taking from those in authority, so long as they were not caught and punished. Even after slavery was abolished, powerful former slave owners relied on numerous subterfuges to maintain control over the ex-slaves and continue to profit from their labor, violating both the spirit and the substance of laws designed to set the slaves free (Scott 1985). This insidious relationship, perpetuated by a sense of racial superiority, was also to shape later relations of dependency, whether on a former master or on an influential politician.

Early in the nineteenth century, contraband continued unabated. The authorities reached the conclusion that to reduce its level it was necessary to offer public servants employment tenure and higher salaries (Masó 1998, 214). The continuation of the illegal slave trade for years after 1820, when Spain formally agreed to its abolition (Thomas 1971, 200), is a testimony to the willingness and ability of some Cubans—often in connivance with Spanish colonial authorities—to continue to engage in contraband despite the British navy's surveillance of the island's sea lanes (Masó 1998, 454; Thomas 1971, 156–167, and 1997, 638–648). The introduction of indentured laborers from China and Mexico after the end of slavery to provide cheap labor to the sugar industry only deepened the one-sided relation of dependency between the workers and their overseers, further contributing to the culture of corruption.

Meanwhile, the prevalence of fraud had not been reduced to any significant extent. By the close of the nineteenth century, fraud was reportedly as common as ever, despite measures to limit its occurrence instituted by several captain generals. During the administration of Captain General Manuel Salamanca (who only served for one year, 1889), three hundred public officials were prosecuted for fraud (Masó 1998, 299). Administrators of La Habana's Customs House were said to become wealthy within six months of assuming office.

Spain's loss of its continental empire, including its former Meso- and South American colonies, did not bode well for anticorruption efforts in Cuba. Spain's resolve to maintain its colonial hold on the island led to the weakening of administrative controls, particularly when Cubans resorted to armed conflict to achieve independence. Quiroz (2003, 18) concludes, "Increased colonial corruption was a consequence of the systematic weakening and, at times, violent destruction of the local institutional bases of Cuban autonomy through discrimination, racial checks, war, expropriation, and exile." Most colonial administrations felt that Spain's continued dominance of Cuba could be achieved by condoning the corrupt practices of officials willing to do whatever was necessary—regardless of the consequences for the local population—to ensure the island's allegiance to Spain. As a result, by the last decades of the century, as Cuba was being devastated by war, it was also overwhelmed by corruption. Quiroz estimates, on the basis of colonial administrative records, that during the last few decades of the nineteenth century between 20 and 50 percent of public revenues were being siphoned away by corrupt officials.

So prevalent was corruption that it has even been identified, together with administrative inefficiency and the brutality of forced resettlement measures, as contributing to the deaths of tens of thousands if not hundreds of thousands of Cubans during the country's War of Independence (1895–1898), at a time when Cuba's population was less than 2 million. Such unprecedented loss of life occurred as rural inhabitants were forced to leave their homes and farms to resettle in cities (the so-called *reconcentración*) on orders of Spain's Captain General Valeriano Weyler to deny popular support to rebel forces in the field. Poorly fed and housed, many *reconcentrados* fell victim to communicable diseases and starvation (Echerri 2004). Resources assigned by the Spanish government to ease the plight of forcibly resettled Cubans were presumably diverted by corrupt officials.

In summary, fraud, corruption, and laxity in applying the rule of law were generalized during the four centuries of Spanish colonial rule. Tenure in public office was commonly seen as a license for enrichment. Posts through which individuals appropriated public revenues for their own use—or via illegal but tolerated practices, such as complicity in contraband—were routinely sold to the highest bidder. Further, "civil servants and judges were paid so little, or had themselves paid so much for their jobs, that corruption was the only effective method for recompense" (Thomas 1971, 738). A contraband tradition deeply rooted in an island nation at the crossroads of colonial trade had provided a livelihood to countless individuals over successive generations, and consequently rules and regulations meant little. Tax avoidance was the norm. In this environment of maximization of economic benefits regardless of the legitimacy of the means, nepotism also flourished. By the end of the nineteenth century, Spanish fears of losing Cuba aggravated the corruption as Madrid became ever more tolerant of corrupt officials as long as they defended the colonial status quo.

Montaner (2002, 27–28) notes that the situation in Cuba was not different from that prevailing in the rest of colonial Latin America, where the public treasury was often regarded as the main route to employment or wealth and where integrity among public officials was the exception. By the dawn of the twentieth century, a Cuba decimated and impoverished by thirty years of war and about to achieve independence under American tutelage and where corruption has flourished as never before was ill prepared for self-governance despite the enormous sacrifices of two generations. The colonial legacy of deeply ingrained malfeasance internalized over several centuries of Spanish rule and laxity in upholding the rule of law would undermine the foundations of the new republic.

THE AMERICAN OCCUPATION

Between 1898 and 1902, the country's devastation and the presence of American occupation forces appeared to have arrested corruption. A contributing factor may have been the nature of the short-term U.S. military administration. Another was the Foraker Amendment approved by the U.S. Congress in 1899, which prohibited the U.S. military government from granting commercial concessions. The concern was that contracts or commercial concessions awarded under such circumstances could have led to potentially questionable deals, although the amendment only began to be applied in 1900, too late to arrest the first wave of speculators who swarmed to Cuba seeking profitable ventures soon after the war ended when land and other assets could be acquired cheaply (Thomas 1971, 438–439, 464–465).

Cuba-U.S. trade and investment relations increased quite substantially after 1903, when a reciprocal commercial treaty was signed whereby Cuban commodities, mainly sugar, received a 20 percent tariff preference in the U.S. market, while U.S. products were granted tariff preferences ranging from 25 to 40 percent in the Cuban market (Thomas 1971, 469). Large-scale foreign investment, principally from the United States, the continued presence of Spanish interests in some economic sectors, and the volatility of the international sugar market (discussed below) had dire economic and political consequences during the early Republic, creating conditions under which corruption would flourish (Domínguez 1978; Pérez 1995; Thomas 1971).

THE EARLY REPUBLIC

Following nearly four years of U.S. occupation, Cuba's first president, Don Tomás Estrada Palma, assumed office on May 20, 1902. His term, which lasted until 1906, was to be the only presidential period during the Republic characterized by honest stewardship of the nation's resources. Estrada Palma's integrity was manifest in his personal behavior and in actions he took to prevent corruption and other questionable practices. He collided with members of the National Congress, eager for preferential treatment in the award of government construction contracts, and harshly criticized congressional perks (Márquez Sterling 1969, 328). Estrada Palma vetoed attempts to legislate sweeping parliamentary immunity and reinstate the national lottery—first established in 1812 under Spanish colonial rule (Thomas 1971, 150) but banned under the American occupation— although on the former he was overruled by the legislature (Chapman 1927/1969, 513). The National Congress was also tainted for its approval of lavish salaries for public officials and for the way it handled compensation for veterans of the War of Independence, including payments to fictitious elements (Thomas 1971, 471).

However, the Estrada Palma administration was marred by electoral irregularities during the 1904 midterm elections (Márquez Sterling 1969, 328) and again as Estrada Palma sought reelection in 1906 (Masó 1998, 471–477). Estrada Palma also was criticized for the wholesale dismissal of government employees not affiliated with his own political party, a spoils system that would haunt Cuba for decades to come (Thomas 1971, 473). Despite these irregularities, the Estrada Palma administration, in the judgment of historians, provided a standard of administrative integrity unmatched by subsequent Cuban republican governments (Masó 1998, 475).

By the time of the second American intervention (1906–1909)—provoked by Estrada Palma's resignation from the presidency following election-related disturbances and justified by the Platt Amendment's clause that gave the United States the right of intervention "for the maintenance of a stable government"—some administrative malpractices began to reemerge just as a changing economic environment was opening the door to novel corrupt practices. The role that Charles E. Magoon, the U.S. administrator from 1906 to 1909, may have played in the blossoming of corruption in republican Cuba is subject to debate. Some historians have contended that he condoned corrupt practices, while others have argued that corruption was present during his administration despite his best intentions. There are also disagreements regarding his personal integrity; many Cubans of his day alleged that Magoon was corrupt, a charge dismissed by Chapman (1927/1969, 232–233) and Thomas (1971, 484), the latter emphatically concluding that "Magoon was not, in fact, corrupt."

What does not appear in doubt is that in his zeal to forge social peace among contending political factions following the 1906 disturbances,

Magoon caved in to patronage demands, relaxing administrative discipline and legitimizing the granting of sinecures (popularly referred to as *botellas*), rewarding political cronies with government jobs in exchange for only nominal work (Jenks 1928, 97; Masó 1998, 343). As several historians have noted, however, it would be absurd to blame Magoon for the introduction in Cuba of sinecures and other actions lacking in transparency, as such practices dated back to the days of the captains general (Chapman 1927/1969, 254; Masó 1998, 478). Márquez Sterling (1969, 343), however, criticizes Magoon for legitimizing patronage and other questionable procedures that would eventually become deeply entrenched in the Cuban polity. Magoon likewise is held responsible by other historians for undermining the autonomy of court judgments, and thus judicial independence, by granting an excessive number of pardons, actions that have been justified by some historians on the grounds that he was "overmagnanimous" (Thomas 1971, 485) rather than for monetary gains. The Magoon administration, moreover, failed to eradicate public-service corruption, evidenced by the prosecution in 1908 of high-level officials on charges of embezzlement (Thomas 1971, 492).

It has also been alleged that Magoon favored some of his collaborators and American firms through the award of profitable concessions (e.g., for Havana's electric cars) and poorly supervised the execution of public works contracts (Thomas 1971, 493; Masó 1998, 479). As Magoon's tenure was coming to a close, Cuba became "a virtual paradise for contractors with and without experience" (Jenks 1928, 102). These contracts were said to have drained the nation's resources, although Magoon's legacy of building roads and other infrastructure has been characterized as commendable.

On the positive side, the Magoon administration is credited with a legacy of modern legislation consistent with the country's 1901 Constitution that replaced many laws dating to the Spanish colonial era. Among them were those intended to strengthen public management and accountability, such as the state accounting and municipal accounting laws, as well as a civil service law designed to create a professional corps of government officials and provide tenure to public servants (Masó 1998, 478–479; Thomas 1971, 484). These laws, however, proved ineffective in practice.

By the end of the second U.S. intervention in 1909, conventional corrupt practices, ingrained in the national ethos after several centuries of colonial rule that had been temporarily suppressed during the first U.S. intervention and the Estrada Palma administration, began to resurface. At the same time and under American hegemony, more modern forms of malfeasance, dependent on the sale of influence and large-scale foreign investment, assumed center stage as Cuba entered an unprecedented period of economic prosperity fueled by the growth of the sugar industry.

The Administrations of Presidents Gómez, Menocal, and Zayas

The presidential tenure of José Miguel Gómez (1909–1913) opened the door for pervasive corruption. As practically every other president who followed, President Gómez assumed office denouncing the alleged excesses of his predecessor (Magoon, in this case) and promising to clean up public administration and put an end to unethical deals. Once he assumed power, Gómez rescinded many of the public works contracts let under Magoon, claiming they had been awarded through favoritism and suspect procedures (Jenks 1928, 101–102).

Shortly after Gómez took office, his administration was shaken by a scandal associated with a contract to dredge the Havana harbor for which bribes allegedly were paid to Cuban officials and legislators, some of whom were stockholders of the Houston, Texas-based company subcontracted to do the dredging (Masó 1998, 484; Schwartz 1997, 20–21). These officials included persons with close ties to the speaker of the house and the minister of public works. The matter was particularly egregious since the potentially very profitable contract, awarded to the Cuban Ports Company, foresaw a thirty-year concession to collect shipping levies based on the tonnage of merchandise handled by the port (Jenks 1928, 121–123).

The Gómez administration was also involved in the notorious "Arsenal" land deal whereby British-owned United Railway agreed to relocate its main train station to the outskirts of Havana to permit the construction of new public buildings in its former central location. Public support for the scheme fizzled as it was alleged that the magnitude of the transaction had been understated and fraud was suspected (Thomas 1971, 506). It was also claimed at the time that some of Cuba's most influential newspapers were handsomely paid to endorse the Arsenal deal (Chapman, 1927/1969, 338), as "all newspapers were recipients of government subsidies and so could never be regarded as arguing their own point of view" (Thomas 1971, 505). Many similar deals were reportedly consummated by the Gómez administration. Outright theft was reputed to have been common as well; it was estimated that during the Gómez presidency "customs lost between 15% and 25% of its revenues through corruption" (Thomas 1971, 506).

Gómez legalized the national lottery,[2] banned in 1898 by the American occupation and whose re-establishment had been vetoed by President

Estrada Palma. The lottery, under successive administrations, became one of the primary sources of sinecures, utilized by presidents at will "as a private source of income, to be used either personally or in holding the support of political friends" (Foreign Policy Association 1935, 364). Gómez also engaged in political patronage, providing jobs to family, friends, and political cronies, further increasing the size of the public sector and raising the armed forces ceiling for active members (Chapman 1927/1969, 277, 390; Thomas 1971, 511).

Most high-level corruption during the Gómez administration apparently did not involve the outright theft of government resources, but rather under-the-table payments of bribes or hefty fees to associates of high-level government officials and legislators in exchange for political influence (Masó 1998, 485). This political influence was used to craft laws to favor particular interests, akin to what we would label today as state capture. Other forms of political and administrative corruption that blossomed in the Gómez administration included the issuance of executive and legislative amnesties for criminal offenses, often tailor-made for particular beneficiaries, and less-than-transparent procurement procedures in awarding government contracts for the purchase of goods and services.

The rather significant infrastructure development program sponsored by the Gómez administration—like the one implemented just a few years earlier by Magoon during the second U.S. intervention—provided bountiful opportunities for corrupt practices generally associated with a growing economy. During this period, Cuba expanded its transportation, sanitary, agricultural, industrial, and urban infrastructure to accommodate significant flows of foreign direct investment (FDI). These investments included the construction of new roads and bridges, urban aqueducts and sewerage systems, the national presidential palace, and railroad lines and ancillary facilities; paving of city streets; modernization of the telephone system; and the purchase of navy vessels and other military equipment and supplies (Chapman 1927/1969, 289–290; Masó 1998, 349; Thomas 1971, 504–505). Gómez personally "gained a great fortune out of the presidency" (Chapman 1927/1969, 286; see also Arencibia Cardoso 2002, 53).

By the close of Gómez' term of office, "revulsion about administrative corruption was already pervasive," with political opponents including veterans of the War of Independence demanding probity in the management of the state (Ibarra 1998, 66). A famous phrase coined by the people to describe Gómez, whose nickname was "El Tiburón" (the shark), made a fitting epilogue to his contribution to Cuba's history of corruption: *El tiburón se baña, pero salpica* (The shark bathes, but he also splashes). Thus while Gómez stole public resources, he shared the spoils with others (Masó 1998, 481).

As did President Gómez before him, Mario García Menocal assumed office claiming to be committed to administrative probity. In fact, Menocal's electoral slogan was "Honesty, peace, and work" (Masó 1998, 491). During the early years of his two-term administration (1913–1921), Menocal considered but was eventually dissuaded from prosecuting President Gómez for wrongdoing. In part due to U.S. pressures—based on concerns about the way the Gómez administration handled the Cuban Ports Company concession (presumably in violation of Article II of the Permanent Treaty) and U.S. bondholders' exposure to financial damage—Menocal derogated the concession and compensated investors, at a substantial loss to the Cuban treasury (Jenks 1928, 122–125; Masó 1998, 489). Why Menocal decided to revoke the concession has never been made entirely clear. U.S. pressure was one factor, but Chapman suggests that there were others as well: that some Menocal associates had been left out of the deal; that the Cuban Ports Company refused to contribute to Menocal's political coffers; or that Puerto Padre, a port of significance to the Cuban American Sugar Company, in which Menocal held a substantial ownership share, was not designated as one of the dredge sites. Chapman (1927/1969, 339) concludes, however, that the most likely reason was "the political capital he [Menocal] was able to make out of the affair."

Corruption intensified during President Menocal's administration. Partly mediated by Cuba's sugar boom during and after World War I, forms of corruption multiplied. While the abuse of political office for personal gain in granting concessions and earning illicit commissions continued, outright fraud became more common, as when contractors collected fees for undelivered projects or "payments [were] made for imaginary roads and fictitious bridges over non-existent rivers" (Chapman 1927/1969, 395). State-owned lands passed into private hands under obscure circumstances. In these dubious operations, legislators and public officials often colluded with contractors and landowners. Foreign loans also became an expedient source of riches for corrupt officials, as they allegedly involved occasional under-the-table payments by international bankers (Thomas 1971, 526). Finally, emergency measures imposed during World War I opened new venues for corruption, such as manipulations of price controls and the sale of export and import permits. When international sugar prices collapsed, creating havoc in the banking sector, well-connected individuals acquired bank assets at very favorable prices (Masó 1998, 494).

Some of the profits captured by national investors associated with the Cuban Ports Company were reinvested in land development deals and eventually in tourist development schemes that opened still other avenues for corruption. These tourism projects, often made possible by enabling legislation custom-made to favor special interests, were conceived in connivance with corrupt politicians who stood to benefit financially from direct or indirect participation in the projects (Schwartz 1997, 31–33). For example, Menocal signed bills granting licenses to operate gambling establishments, including legalized betting on horse racing and jai alai; the latter license was said to have been awarded to his relatives (Chapman 1927/1969, 391; Thomas 1971, 533–534).

Menocal's administration expanded the roster of public employees, including the military, and granted *botellas* to political supporters and opponents alike to parcel out the spoils of prosperity and encourage social peace (Chapman 1927/1969, 390, 396, 417). Electoral fraud accompanied administrative corruption, with reports of ballot-box tampering, intimidation, and the purchase of votes (Márquez Sterling 1969, 357). It was alleged that Menocal personally benefited handsomely from corruption: his personal wealth is said to have increased from about $1 million when he became president to some $40 million—or about $5 million for each year he served as president—by the time he completed his term of office (Chapman 1927/1969, 395; Thomas 1971, 525).

However, it was the tenure of Alfredo Zayas (1921–1925) that set a new standard for corruption in republican Cuba. Described as the "maximum expression of administrative corruption" (Masó 1998, 504) the Zayas presidency attained such notoriety by allowing corruption to spread to all areas of public life, even into proscribed activities like prostitution. Particularly objectionable was the nepotism that characterized his administration—Zayas relied on his relatives and friends to illegally amass wealth—as well as the graft associated with land deals and the importation of seasonal Caribbean laborers for the sugar harvests (Chapman 1927/1969, 428–434, 481). The National Congress was Zayas' willing partner in the consummation of many corrupt deals, as when it approved, in the wee hours of the night without debate and absent the required legislative quorum, twenty-nine bills for presidential signature (ibid., 495). When queried as to why he had signed a $2.7 million dredging contract approved by the Senate in secret session, Zayas was insolent enough to reply that "he had 300,000 good reasons for signing it" (Thomas 1971, 572). In today's lexicon, petty and grand corruption coexisted like never before during the Zayas administration.

*Political and Economic Determinants
of Corruption in the Early Republic*

By the end of the Zayas administration, nearly a quarter-century after the establishment of the Republic, corruption already was deeply embedded in the national fabric. A rapidly growing economy dominated by foreign investment, mostly from the United States, made possible the development of the national infrastructure—built primarily to serve the needs of the sugar industry and the country's major urban areas, Havana in particular. At the same time, the native-born population in rural areas faced sharply different conditions. While foreigners tended to occupy the more desirable urban jobs, Cuban citizens were relegated to unskilled jobs, many associated with the seasonal sugar industry. The upper economic reaches were closed to Cuban citizens by virtue, on the one hand, of the continued economic dominance of former colonial Spanish commercial interests— protected under the Treaty of Paris that ended the Spanish-American War of 1898 as a means to promote social harmony in Cuba—and, on the other, by the overwhelming presence of foreign capital in the country's most dynamic agricultural and modern urban sectors. Excluded from the centers of economic power, Cubans turned to the state for financial security and upward mobility:

> Public administration in general and politics in particular acquired a special economic significance. It was to government that Cubans looked for economic security. State revenues became the principal source of economic solvency as Cubans came to define their material well being in political terms. Public office, patronage appointments, and civil service became ends; politics and electoral competition became ends. . . . This development underscored the emerging social reality of the early Republic: the origins of a new elite organized around the control of the state and dependent upon control of public administration as the principal source of wealth and a means to property. (Pérez 1995, 214–215)

This situation was not then and is not today unique to Cuba. In many countries, as noted by Huntington (1968/2002), it has been more profitable to be affiliated with public administration or to be a politician than to be a businessman or farmer. Wealth acquisition follows from the failure to establish a clear distinction between public roles and private interests.

Contributing to this state of affairs in Cuba was the function played by the state as employer of last resort at a time when private-sector jobs were scarce (other than in the agricultural sector, shunned by most native white workers) and many non-Cuban immigrant employers (mostly Spanish-born) preferred to hire fellow immigrants. The nation's educational system and a shunning of technical careers by the Cuban middle class made matters worse, as relatively few professionals had the proper background to work in the emerging modern sectors of the economy. The national university was fraught with corruption, "with many 'professors' being paid without teaching, being merely political henchmen or relations of the president" (Thomas 1971, 564). Thus, educated Cubans had little choice but to drift into public-sector employment, further feeding the existing tradition of nepotism. The bureaucracy and the military expanded to accommodate the inflow of persons seeking employment, thereby enhancing the redistributive role of the state (Foreign Policy Association 1935, 6–8).

Political patronage completed the picture of corruption and electoral fraud. Influenced by the demonstration effect of corruption at the highest levels of government, few Cuban officials had the motivation to act honorably and forego opportunities for increasing income or acquiring wealth. Large-scale firings of government officials with every change of administration meant that politicians had to satisfy their promises to supporters during the limited time they could enjoy the fruits of power (Ibarra 1998, 66; Pérez 1995, 220). The lack of job security encouraged public employees to act quickly to put a little something aside for a rainy day. In such an environment, petty corruption was widespread.

The rule of law was weakened by political corruption and an ineffective justice system. With a predatory political system, elected officials approached the national treasury as if it were their own. The political will to confront corruption was lacking, and in fact politicians actually led the pillage of the state. "Congressional and Executive impunity," in the words of the Foreign Policy Association (1935, 6), "further contributed to the reckless abandon with which Cuban politicians approached the national treasury. Article 53 of the 1901 Constitution, in the absence of effective control institutions, provides blanket immunity declaring that a member of the national Congress could not be prosecuted for any offense except with Congressional consent."

As if this were not enough, hundreds of Cuban politicians had been indicted for various criminal offenses, and some were even convicted, but few served any sentences. Blanket amnesty bills frequently served both to cleanse convictions for past crimes and to remove the threat of conviction for questionable acts committed while in public office. Estrada Palma issued six comprehensive amnesty bills during his tenure, while the administrations of Gómez, Menocal, and Zayas on average issued thirty each. Presidential pardons, more often than not obtained under questionable circumstances, were even more frequent, ranging from hundreds during the presidencies of Estrada Palma and Zayas to thousands under Gómez and Menocal (Pérez 1995, 217–218).

Rounding the corruption circle was the absence or general ineffectiveness of control institutions. Although customs duties represented more than half of the state's revenues, they were inadequately tracked and thus subject to misappropriation. The public procurement apparatus was totally perverted, as most government contracts were awarded at inflated cost and contingent upon the payment of commissions or subject to other collusive arrangements with dishonest public officials. Lax accounting resulted in poor financial controls. Furthermore, government accounts were audited poorly if at all, which prevented the systematic detection of fraud and other irregularities. The accountability unit within the Ministry of Finance could not conduct independent audits because it was subordinate to the finance minister (Foreign Policy Association 1935, 7–8, 373–374).

In summary, by 1925 corruption was an integral part of republican Cuba's daily economic and political life. Low-level officials, often appointed as political patronage, depended on petty corruption to supplement meager salaries or accumulate savings, given their lack of job security in a highly politicized civil service. And just as petty corruption was rampant, so was grand corruption. To survive and prosper, businesses had to "take care" of public officials. The most ambitious and entrepreneurial, ironically, looked to political corruption, as it "was, in fact, an effective method of capital accumulation in a capital scarce economic environment" (Pérez 1995, 216).

NEW AND OLD CORRUPTION MODALITIES

Gerardo Machado assumed the presidency (1925–1933) promising to confront corruption in the public sector. At least initially, he managed to keep his promise, and even though the controls he instituted weakened as the economy struggled and he began to assume dictatorial powers, low-level administrative corruption appears to have been reduced to levels below those prevailing in prior administrations. Machado endeavored to improve the performance of the public sector and, while doing so, reduced both the number of phantom workers on the government's payroll and opportunities for under-the-table petty transactions. As part of his moralizing campaign, Machado confronted illegal gambling and prostitution and even promised—though he did not keep the promise—to do away with the national lottery (Thomas 1971, 572–573). His success in tackling corrupt practices rested on his control of the bureaucracy, including public procurement, and by the fear his authority inspired in politicians and public officials.

While most forms of low-level and petty corruption declined during the Machado administration, the same cannot be said about grand corruption (Masó 1998, 521, 526). Machado's reining in of some types of low-level corruption was based on centralizing state management, which eventually resulted in concentrating opportunities for corruption into fewer hands. Schwartz describes an example:

> All government purchases—from food for public institutions to
> electrical goods for government offices, from boots for the army
> to medicines for hospitals—passed from lower-level in the offices
> in the various ministries up through the bureaucracy by means
> of recommendations to a Superior Procurement Court (Tribunal
> Superior de Subastas), a board set up to select winning contract
> bidders. . . . Thus, in the guise of a reformist watchdog function,
> Machado centralized both government purchasing procedures and
> the potential collection of bribes. (Schwartz 1997, 61–62)

Bardhan (2002, 326) finds that this form of corruption has "less adverse consequences for efficiency than decentralized bribe-taking, because in the former case the bribee will internalize some of the distortionary effects of corruption" as the potential number of points at which different officials could extract rents is reduced. This may help explain the general praise heaped by contemporaries and historians on the accomplishments of the Machado administration in developing the country's infrastructure despite the centralization of corruption.

Under Machado, a more activist state—more directly involved in financing and promoting development projects—opened greater corruption options. Corruption on a grand scale was most evident on an extensive public works program, funded through special taxes and foreign loans, whose most visible legacies are Cuba's Central Highway and National Capitol. Many of these projects carried highly inflated costs, providing ample margins for well-placed functionaries to siphon off money (Foreign

Policy Association 1935, 369, 372–373). There were even allegations that the U.S. company contracted to build the Central Highway, Warren Brothers, was working in connivance with Machado and his associates (Márquez Sterling 1969, 425; Masó 1998, 526; Thomas 1971, 581–582). Information provided to the U.S. Congress suggested that Chase Bank of New York in particular, along with other banks, wittingly or unwittingly collaborated with the Cuban government to secure public works loans whose proceeds allegedly went in part to line private pockets. Other allegations lodged against Chase Bank included making personal loans— that were not repaid—to the president, to some of his associates, and to companies they managed (Foreign Policy Association 1935, 390–391).

Another means to riches skillfully manipulated by the Machado administration and its political cronies was the use of insider information to profit from private-sector deals. This was nothing new—the practice was common during prior administrations—but it rose to new heights during the Machado administration. Trading on insider information was fueled by the expansion of the urban infrastructure of Havana and other secondary cities, often in conjunction with economic diversification plans conceived around real estate developments and infrastructure for the tourism industry. The Miramar neighborhood, to this day one of Cuba's most desirable, was built west of Havana after the government constructed an iron bridge spanning the Almendares River that made such land accessible and provided paved streets and public utilities to support the area's development. Tourist concessions were also part of the scheme, as tourist attractions and the plushest real estate developments were generally placed in close proximity to each other to enhance the appeal of Cuba to the moneyed international tourist elite (Schwartz 1997, 37).

While public-private cooperation in economic development projects is common in market-driven economies and legitimate when conducted in a transparent fashion, it is a questionable source of private gain when transactions are conducted in the absence of public scrutiny and with the intent to enrich a few well-placed businesspeople and colluding political associates. Schwartz describes how a simple, familiar process becomes underhanded when insiders are privy to information:

> A city council plans a new park, for example, or chooses a transportation corridor. An astute individual, most likely a political insider, goes to the area under consideration and buys property. When the city officials publish their plans and precipitate an increase in land values, the investor enjoys a profit. If speculators buy land first and

then manipulate the legislative process to push a project, is that business or corruption? Shady dealings or visionary leadership? (Schwartz 1997, 17–18)

The collapse of the sugar industry in the mid-1920s enhanced the discretion of public officials over the economy and created opportunities for corruption. After expanding rapidly in the first quarter of the century, the Cuban sugar industry confronted a world market glut and plummeting world prices for sugar. In an effort to prop up international prices, Cuba took the painful step of unilaterally reducing sugar production. The Verdeja Act, passed in May 1926, granted the government the authority to determine the length of the *zafras* (sugarcane harvests) and to limit output. This was the beginning of a deliberate policy of production limits that affected Cuban sugar output—with some exceptions—for the next three decades and created opportunities for corruption in the allocation of production quotas.

In 1927 the Tarafa Act created a permanent commission charged with determining annually the level of sugar production for export, presumably levels that would not disrupt the international market. For example, the 1927 crop was limited to 4.5 million tons (compared to about 5.1 million tons in 1926), with each sugar mill directed to produce 92.25 percent of what it had produced in 1925 except for "special circumstances." When they were announced in February 1927, the quotas set by the Machado government varied greatly across mills and from the prescribed norm; for example, the mills belonging to the American Refining Company received a quota equivalent to 98.2 percent of the preceding year's production, while Cuban Cane's western plantations were allocated only 69.5 percent and its eastern plantations 84 percent (McAvoy 2003, 188–189). Referring to this incident, sugar magnate Manuel Rionda wrote at the time:

> It was rumored that the reason why some companies received such good treatment was due to their having paid somebody $1 to $1.50 a bag. . . . I said that I did not believe that there was anything of that kind and that I did not know of anybody having paid anything. . . . It is unfortunate, however, that Cunagua and Jaronú [two sugar mills] had such a good treatment accorded to them, while others received a bad deal. I am sorry for [Machado's] reputation. In the course of discussion I said that if they had employed Mr. Vázquez Bello [formerly Machado's campaign manager and at the time Secretary of the Interior] before, they probably would have had better treatment. (Cited in McAvoy 2003, 192–193)

Machado's decision to seek an extended presidential term as well as reelection angered his opponents, in part because it "antagonized those members of the political class who felt that the reelection violated the redistributive nature of Cuban elite politics" (Whitney 2001, 56). Most Cuban political parties would have been content to alternate in office, since that gave them a periodic chance to reward supporters by gaining access to sources of wealth. Facing an emboldened political opposition, Machado was forced increasingly to depend on corruption and violence to remain in power. Machado's ouster in 1933, following several years of civil upheaval and promoted by U.S. president Franklin D. Roosevelt, was undoubtedly precipitated in part by public discontent with his desire to perpetuate his grip on power and by popular disgust with corruption in his administration. The explanation would not be complete, however, were we not to take into account the devastating effects of the Great Depression on Cuba's economy and the resulting inability of his government to continue pursuing the customary redistributive policies upon which so many Cubans had come to depend. For years to come, and in different forms, the redistributive state would continue to define Cuba's history, even into the twenty-first century.

THE REVOLUTIONARY INTERREGNUM AND BATISTA

The end of Machado's government in 1933 and his replacement by a five-person junta (the Pentarquía) was supposed to bring to a close Cuba's long corruption history. Idealistic young revolutionaries issued manifestos after Machado's overthrow calling for limits to amnesty for convicted corrupt officials, the establishment of special tribunals to which public servants had to disclose their assets upon assuming office, and the abolition of the national lottery. The goal was to do away with banality and corruption in public life (Márquez Sterling 1969, 408). Corruption declined during the next few years because of revolutionary effervescence and political instability, but perhaps mostly because of the substantial fall in the revenues reaching the public treasury (Gellman 1973, 209). The Cuban economy, already weakened by the collapse of international sugar trade, suffered yet another blow as the Great Depression turned the United States inward, depriving Cuba of tourism revenues.

The one-hundred-day civilian Pentarquía government led by Ramón Grau San Martín, who would become Cuba's president from 1944 to 1948, proscribed the political parties of the Machado era as well as the Superior Electoral Tribunal; did away with the amnesty laws approved under the Machado regime; and established special tribunals to prosecute cases of political repression and charges of graft and fraud (Márquez Sterling 1969, 446).

Interestingly, one of the main accomplishments of the interim administration for which he received much praise was the so-called 50 Percent Law, whereby half of all employees in industrial, commercial, and agricultural enterprises had to be native-born Cubans (Foreign Policy Association 1935, 212–213). That such a protectionist law was overwhelmingly approved reveals the national concern about unemployment. This was but one of many attempts by domestic labor and business sectors to protect their interests in a Cuba where the state played a significant role in the distribution of the nation's wealth. In addition to the economic distortions they produced, these interventionist policies were to, in due course, dramatically influence the course of rent seeking and corruption in the country.

The mid- to late 1930s were a time of political instability in which several caretaker governments presumably ruled Cuba. However, real power rested in Fulgencio Batista's hands. Once Batista became Cuba's strongman, old corrupt habits soon returned. Shortly after assuming de facto control of the government in 1934 from his position as head of the army, Batista encouraged gambling by foreigners and wealthy Cubans in casinos and by everyday Cubans through the national lottery, increasing the latter's frequency from weekly to daily drawings. He allowed an illegal numbers game (*bolita*) to flourish; part of the *bolita*'s revenues ended up in the pockets of the police, who protected its organizers. Batista invited foreign "businessmen," many of them associated with the American mafia—who had set up shop in Cuba earlier to buy molasses for U.S. distilleries gearing up to expand liquor production as Prohibition in the United States was coming to a close—to establish gambling operations in Havana (Schwartz 1997, 135).

With Cuba becoming once again relatively prosperous during World War II as world demand for Cuban sugar increased, corruption flourished. Manipulating wartime rationing to their advantage, government officials—including Batista—lined their pockets (Ameringer 2000, 14–15). By the end of Batista's constitutional term (1940–1944), even a citizenry already resigned to public corruption was calling for reforms, with business groups in particular demanding improved services and honesty in government. Spruille Braden, the American ambassador, wrote in an angry cable to the U.S. State Department on May 29, 1943: "corruption has never become so rampant, so organized, or so profitable for those at the top. It has never caused such widespread disgust" (cited in Gellman, 1973, 209–210). Focused on a war being fought in several continents, however, the U.S. State Department was more concerned with Cuba's stability and continued supplies of sugar than with the prevalence of graft and corruption.

Batista benefited greatly from his encouragement of gambling and his connivance with the mafia's management of the country's major casinos. From 1933, when he had an inconsequential net worth and relied on his salary as an army sergeant, to the time he left Cuba voluntarily for Daytona Beach in 1944 upon completing his presidential term, Batista had amassed a $20 million personal fortune (Thomas 1971, 736). Meyer Lanski, a noted mafia figure, allegedly deposited millions of dollars annually into Batista's Swiss bank accounts (Ameringer 2000, 39; Schwartz 1997, 100).

THE AUTÉNTICO YEARS: PRESIDENTS GRAU AND PRÍO

President Ramón Grau San Martín assumed power in 1944, after winning the presidential race against the candidate of Batista's coalition, on the strength of the reputation he had gained in 1933 as head of the post-Machado interim government and his promises to eliminate corruption. Yet the arrival of his Auténtico party to the presidency unleashed a new wave of corruption. In his inaugural address, Grau emphasized the need for the "efficient and honest administration of the Ministries of Treasury, Education, and Health" and called for immediate congressional approval of complementary laws to the 1940 Constitution to establish government institutions with a mandate to improve government financial management and quell corruption, such as the National Court of Accounts, an accounting law, a professional civil service, and a national bank (Ameringer 2000, 18; Vignier and Alonso, 1973, 38–40).

But in 1945 a scandal broke when senior government officials were found to be profiting from commodity barter deals with Argentina and Ecuador, engineered under international auspices to minimize war shortages (Ameringer 2000, 28; Márquez Sterling 1969, 524–525). Although serious, this scandal was but a harbinger of things to come. The Ministry of Education, which received the proceeds of a nine-cent levy on every bag of sugar produced as mandated in 1943 under *inciso K* (paragraph K of Law No. 7) to fund improvements in the educational system, became a prime target of corruption. *Inciso K* funds were diverted by Minister of Education José Manuel Alemán for many purposes, among them undermining the Communist-controlled labor federation (the Confederación de Trabajadores de Cuba, or CTC) and supporting clandestine foreign military ventures, such as the overthrow of military dictatorships in the Dominican Republic and in other Caribbean countries (Ameringer 2000, 32, 46–54). Millions of dollar of *inciso K* funds were diverted to influence electoral outcomes and provide political patronage or were plainly stolen by Grau administration officials. Education Minister Alemán, generally believed to have been the most corrupt Grau associate, arrived "in Miami in 1948 after two years as minister with $20 million in notes in a suitcase" (Thomas 1971, 738).

During the Grau administration, corruption in the Ministries of Education, Treasury and Commerce reached "gigantic proportions" (Márquez Sterling 1969, 526). His administration oversaw the diversion of public funds to armed gangs of political activists, the infamous *grupos de acción,* or action groups (Márquez Sterling 1969, 526–534). The reserves of nongovernmental pension funds, particularly those of the Federación Nacional de Trabajadores Azucareros (FNTA) sugar workers union, fell victim as well to the insatiable thirst for theft of Grau and his associates (Thomas 1971, 746–747).

In the early to mid-1940s, in Cuba's rather tolerant environment, the ugly spectre of illicit activities continued to raise its head, first with the alleged complicity of Batista and then under President Grau. Many Cubans in diverse walks of life benefited from illicit gambling and drug trafficking. Not only were imported illicit drugs consumed in Cuba, where they were easy to find, but Cuba became an important transit point for drug shipments to the United States originating in South America, mainly from Peru. The country assumed its role as an important source of illicit drugs in the Western Hemisphere as European supplies were cut off by World War II. Police and military connivance with the traffickers was reported in the diplomatic correspondence being sent to Washington at the time and in the press (Sáenz Rovner 2005, 67–97). Following the arrival in Cuba in 1946 of Lucky Luciano, a well-known Italian-born American mobster, the illegal drug traffic boomed until Luciano was deported to Italy in 1947 at the insistence of the American government (Ameringer 2000, 39–40).

Just as damaging as the overt acts of graft and corruption were the more insidious entitlements that began with the Machado administration but truly came into their own after his overthrow in 1933. Popular demand for the protection of Cuban over foreign labor was but the initial salvo.

What followed was a rush by special-interest groups to protect their positions through state regulation of the economy. Many of their demands, to a great extent formalized in the 1940 Constitution, responded to a context in which lack of economic diversification undermined economic growth and "Cuban workers and their leaders [were] prey to the anxieties which result from the instabilities, the stagnation, and the chronic unemployment of the Cuban economy" (IBRD 1951, 358). In an overregulated economy, as is keenly appreciated today, opportunities for corruption increase as public officials enjoying discretionary authority exercise it to their own benefit:

> Ever increasing State regulation and control over key sectors, such as the sugar industry, exacerbated the corruption already endemic in Cuban public affairs, turning both politics and business into a fierce struggle for government favors. Corruption from the 1930s on took the form not only of outright kickbacks, bribes, and graft but also of what economists call a 'rent-seeking' mentality that pervaded Cuban society. Instead of concentrating on innovations to improve products or develop new products, Cuban workers, farmers, and industrialists had to compete to secure political benefits and protection. (Speck 2002, 118)

By the end of President Grau's term in office (1948), despite the early expectations of his supporters, the corruption situation had taken a turn for the worse, thus shattering the dream for honest and accountable government and betraying many of the 1933 revolutionaries. Schwartz (1997, 112) describes the scale of disillusionment:

> The presidential election campaign of 1948 found Cubans more cynical than ever about their corrupt politicians. The elected officials who gained power in 1944 proved themselves one more phalanx of greedy officeholders. With high sugar demand and prices sustained by European production shortages . . . money flowed into government coffers. Public payrolls swelled, and lucrative contracts once again filled private pockets. Elected and appointed guardians of Cuba's patrimony embezzled and stole at a level that would have reddened the faces of even the most profligate office holders in Cuba's long history of abuse.

Upon taking office in 1948, President Carlos Prío Socarrás, a protégé of President Grau and prime minister during the Grau term, was forced by partisan considerations to embrace as his first order of business clearing up irregularities in balance sheets of many entities resulting from embezzlements during the preceding administration by absorbing them as part of the fiscal deficits. Massive firings of Grau's Ministry of Education appointees soon led to political fissures within the Auténtico party, as Grau took these actions as a rebuke of his administration (Ameringer 2000, 75–77, 108). Prío had few other choices as he confronted a national cry for administrative transparency and probity in the management of the country's finances. The leading voice against corruption was that of Senator Eduardo R. Chibás, who in numerous press articles and in a popular weekly radio program relentlessly decried corruption with his rallying cry of *vergüenza contra dinero* (decency versus money). In November 1948, after a while as president, Prío publicly reiterated accusations of corruption in the Grau administration, alleging pervasive graft in the education and finance ministries and profiteering in the customs department through foreign exchange controls and the importation of rationed consumer goods.

Chibás lambasted Prío for his role in the Grau administration and accused him of illicit enrichment (Vignier and Alonso 1973, 157–166). He alleged that during the Grau administration under Prío's supervision, the Cuban state had been "captured" by the Compañía Cubana de Electricidad (Cuban Electric Company), the local affiliate of the U.S.-based Electric Bond and Share Company, obtaining a 70 percent rate increase and thus forcing Cubans to pay the highest electricity rates in the Western Hemisphere (Vignier and Alonso 1973, 183).

Despite the allegations of corruption, the Prío administration saw the enactment of several legislative initiatives that had been under discussion to improve management of the country's finances. These included establishing the National Bank of Cuba and the Court of Accounts, along with enacting a national budget law and accounting rules governing the financial affairs of the state, provinces, municipalities, and autonomous institutions, all part of the enabling legislation of the 1940 Constitution that had not been implemented under the Batista or Grau governments. The Prío administration also began institutionalizing in selected government agencies policies to create a professional civil service insulated from politics and whose members would be recruited and promoted on the basis of qualifications and merits. Some of these initiatives began shortly after Prío took office; many of them, while mandated by the 1940 Constitution, were also recommended by a World Bank mission (IBRD 1951) that assessed the state of the Cuban economy in 1950 and noted with concern the contempt with which the average Cuban regarded the government

(Ameringer 2000, 132; IBRD 1951, 453–474). Prío's government was responsible for a vast expansion of the state's regulatory role; under his watch the country enacted the most significant body of laws in Cuba's republican era (Álvarez Díaz 1963, 787).

Despite many promising initiatives and the honorable discharge of their duties by some prominent public officials, corruption soon became unbridled. Nepotism raised its head as the president appointed his brother as treasury minister, a post the appointee used for his—and the president's—enrichment. Corruption scandals plagued Prío's administration. Perhaps the most infamous was the disappearance of a mountain of evidence related to alleged graft committed during the Grau presidency involving *inciso K* funds at the Ministry of Education; the records were stolen from the presiding judge's chamber by several masked and heavily armed men (Ameringer 2000, 111; Vignier and Alonso, 1973, 27). Allegations of illegal enrichment, fueled by U.S. press accounts of large-scale real estate purchases in New York City by Cuban investors, and charges that labor leaders had diverted workers' retirement funds for their own use and to finance political campaigns further exacerbated the perception that corruption was uncontrolled. Adding to the perception of corruption were charges of presidential pardons granted to rich landowners convicted of common crimes in exchange for land deeded to Prío and his relatives (Ameringer 2000, 162–176).

Allegations were frequent that in exchange for government contracts, suppliers had to pay bribes ranging from 20 to 30 percent of contract value to government officials and that considerable graft usually accompanied the negotiation of foreign loans (Vignier and Alonso 1973, 188–193). Finally, a general state of disgust prevailed as armed gangs of activists—the so-called *grupos de acción*—aligned with different political factions were co-opted into remaining at relative peace through payoffs provided by President Prío and his Auténtico administration (Ameringer 2000, 177).

Fidel Castro's earliest claim to fame and a source of political legitimacy despite his violent past (Ros 2003) was his public denunciation of corruption in the Prío administration. Castro published several articles in the magazine *Alerta* exposing the president's private land deals and the life of luxury in his rural retreat, where Castro alleged that Prío exploited soldiers by using them as farm labor. Castro denounced the 2,200 sinecures provided by Prío in several government entities and in the presidential palace to the *grupos de acción* (Ameringer 2000, 176–177; Vignier and Alonso, 1973, 236–249). With Prío, the last vestiges of moral renovation under Auténtico rule were forever buried in 1952 when Batista succeeded in a coup for which he partly justified disrupting constitutional rule by promising to fight corruption and lawlessness (Thomas 1971, 784).

DEVELOPMENT, TOURISM, AND CORRUPTION UNDER BATISTA

The 1952 coup d'état that deposed President Prío installed Fulgencio Batista as president. Batista continued practicing the same corrupt practices of his predecessors and his own, in some instances bringing them to a more sophisticated level. The granting of sinecures to political supporters, profiteering from the lottery, illegal gambling, and some other forms of corruption remained relatively unchanged. Police corruption attained new heights, however, as officers extracted protection payments from legitimate shopkeepers as well as bribes from those engaged in illegal gambling, drugs, and prostitution, with a share of the proceeds going up the chain of command (Schwartz 1997, 138). The military was in charge, and occasional press censorship made it more difficult to publicize abuses, a vastly different situation than under Auténtico rule. New opportunities for grand corruption also emerged during Batista's government. In part this resulted as the state continued its economic activism in infrastructure development, particularly in metropolitan Havana. Significant public works projects were initiated with financing provided by government-issued bonds and foreign loans. These transactions facilitated the consummation of illicit deals between business interests and public officials. As he did not enjoy popular support, Batista tried to enhance his appeal by satisfying the multiple obligations called forth by the redistributive state established by his predecessors.

Just as in the 1920s, when politically well-connected businessmen made fortunes building Havana's western suburbs, during Batista's government of the 1950s the rush was to develop Havana in an easterly direction. While in the 1920s a bridge spanning the Almendares River and government-built roads and utilities had made possible profitable real estate developments west of the city, in the 1950s the Havana harbor tunnel and the Vía Blanca highway were the gateways to neighborhoods and beach resorts to be built in the city's eastern suburbs. The tunnel's construction, a concept initially proposed during the Prío administration, only came to fruition when the Batista government raised the necessary funds through the placement of a bond issue (Schwartz 1997, 151). Inflated infrastructure development cost the country dearly: some estimates suggest that as much as 50 percent of reported costs for these projects went to pay commissions (Pérez-Stable 1999, 54). As in the development of Miramar three decades earlier, land acquisitions made in advance of announcements of infrastructure plans resulted in huge gains for speculators and real estate developers who were willing to share their spoils with well-placed government officials (Sáenz Rovner 2005, 182).

Batista himself benefited handsomely. Sáenz Rovner (2005, 182–183), reviewing accounts culled from several historical sources, cites Batista's former press secretary, José Suarez Núñez, who estimated that at the end of 1958, when Batista fled Cuba, he had a $300 million fortune stashed overseas. Within Cuba, Batista is alleged to have owned several sugar mills, together with several construction and investment firms heavily involved with the largely government-financed construction boom under way at the time. His landholdings included several farms and, most importantly, lots slated for urbanization east of Havana and in other prime Cuban locations, such as Varadero Beach. Batista was also said to be a shareholder in two of Cuba's private airlines and print and electronic media companies and owner of industrial enterprises, several hotels, and a tourist resort development company. An early 1959 official report issued by Felipe Pazos, the respected Central Bank president, claimed that Batista and his cronies had pilfered $424 million in U.S. currency held as reserves to back the value of the Cuban peso.

Gambling became another quick route to illicit enrichment. The 1950s saw the growth of Cuba as an important tourist destination, with large gambling casinos and luxurious hotels that catered to American visitors sprouting in choice locations around Havana. They were managed by well-known tourism facility operators who had gaming know-how and mafia connections. The leading hotels were modernized or built largely with funds provided by national development institutions such as the Banco de Fomento Agrícola e Industrial de Cuba (BANFAIC), the Financiera Nacional de Cuba, and the Banco de Desarrollo Económico y Social (BANDES). The Batista administration redirected BANFAIC's lending away from agricultural and industrial development and "toward hotel projects, specifically those large enough to warrant the granting of casino licenses" (Schwartz 1997, 152). A BANFAIC loan, for example, was used to remodel the Hotel Nacional, a landmark hotel built in the 1920s and managed by the Intercontinental Hotel Corporation, which leased the hotel's casino to a Las Vegas gaming operator. The Havana Hilton, managed by the Hilton hotel chain, was financed with funds from the restaurant workers union pension fund and BANDES. Meanwhile, the

Havana Riviera was bankrolled primarily by U.S. gambling interests, with BANDES participation. Other important hotels included the Capri, whose casino was operated by Americans with ties to the mafia, and the Comodoro, as well as several smaller hotels. Schwartz (1997, 137) elaborates on the connections:

> If prospects for growth required deals with businessmen whose experience recognized political payoffs as legitimate expenses, Batista had no qualms about such transactions. Kickbacks and political patronage, longtime Cuban practices, distributed profits to a broad circle of colleagues but were more lucrative for those at the top. The partnership was as much a marriage of convenience as a love match: casino operation, the key to hotel profitability, required expertise, and the mobsters had it.

There is also documentation that drug trafficking was part of the corruption mix. Countless low-level officials received payments to protect drug traffickers, and some sources alleged that the government studiously ignored requests by U.S. antinarcotics agencies for traffickers to be investigated, apprehended, and prosecuted. Drug smugglers who were intercepted plying their illicit trade often were released upon paying large bribes to high-ranking police authorities. As the 1950s were coming to a close, Cuba was perceived as the most important transshipment route for heroine and cocaine to the United States. Some observers regarded the Cuban court system as the biggest obstacle for effective action against the traffic, as even on those occasions when police authorities were willing to cooperate with U.S. requests to prosecute smugglers, in short order they were released. As during these years the judicial system enjoyed a relative degree of autonomy from the executive branch, the assumption can be made that smugglers bribed their way out of detention by paying judges and other court officials (Sáenz Rovner 2005, 181–197).

As 1958 ended and Batista fled Cuba, several hotels and tourist resorts were under construction and others were in the planning stage (Schwartz 1997, 147–163). The promise of a large-scale windfall from the operation of the hotels and casinos in Cuba, and the profits to be made from real estate developments east of Havana, had only begun to materialize. Cuba's political instability of the late 1950s slowed down tourist traffic to Cuba. With the advent of the 1959 Revolution, the eventual nationalization of private property, and the government's decision to turn away from international tourism as an engine of economic growth, the promise of tourism was set aside, only to be revived in the 1990s. Meanwhile, East Havana failed to reach its anticipated glory and decayed; the only new real estate developments in the area were unattractive socialist-style housing projects built by voluntary labor and assigned by the state to model workers.

A NATIONAL CULTURE OF CORRUPTION

As this chapter has shown, republican Cuba was burdened with a deeply ingrained tradition of corruption forged over four centuries of colonial rule. This tradition rested on governance practices instituted by colonial administrators that placed a premium on rent seeking, permitted the sale of official positions and nepotism, and relied on low compensation for public officials. Within this context, other practices conducive to fraud and corruption emerged as the residents of Cuba, by engaging in contraband, circumvented a highly constricted economic environment imposed by the metropolis, which favored Spanish colonizers over Cuban natives.

With the coming of the Republic and with opportunities for social and economic advancement limited by excessive foreign domination of the national economy, Cubans with ambition turned to politics and the opportunities it created for wealth accumulation. Many less fortunate or skillful Cubans became dependent on political patronage to earn a living. The situation was to become even more dismal as the dominant role of Cuban sugar in international markets diminished and as the sugar industry suffered periodic crises. Within this environment of uncertainty, many organized social groups—from the ranks of labor, the professions, and business—turned to the state for economic security.

One response was to regulate the economy, initially the sugar sector but eventually others as well. The number of sector-specific rules that governed economic activities grew exponentially, from no regulations in 1915 to a few transitory rules enacted during World War I to 159 approved between 1925 and 1934 as Cuba sought to adapt to international economic crises. The next ten years saw the implementation of 325 new rules governing the sugar industry, with the Auténticos adding 190 more. Labor rules became ever more complex (Speck 2002, 125), and so were the laws governing other economic activities. Whether or not this proliferation of rules and regulations achieved its objective, one thing is certain—it encouraged corruption by expanding the discretion of regulators to make economic decisions and to collect bribes. Thomas (1971, 740) notes with dismay that it was not just the president and a few ministers who helped themselves to cash which was not theirs—that was a comparatively minor problem—but everyone, in any official position: mayors, sub-mayors, governors and lieutenant-governors of provinces, treasurers, accountants of small towns . . . school inspectors and school teachers. There was no social stigma to graft. It resembled the non-payment of taxes in Italy.

A mushrooming public sector added to the problem as more and more Cubans gained access to positions on which they depended and from which they could profit. Domínguez (1978, 93–94) explains that

> as more groups participated actively in politics, government corrup-
> tion reflected a broader spectrum of techniques. . . . Sinecures were
> another accepted form of corruption, as were subsidies to private
> enterprises to finance featherbedding or to sustain a near-bankrupt
> company, a policy that was not corrupt according to prevailing
> norms and that was understandable in times of high unemployment.

Republican Cuba's weak political formal organization and governance structures permitted corruption—or worse, abetted it. The low esteem in which Cubans held formal institutions and the lack of recognition by government officials of the virtue of hard, honest work were integral parts of the political culture in republican Cuba.

Writing in the 1920s, essayist and philosopher Jorge Mañach analyzed the personality of Cubans centering on one of its characteristics: the proneness to engage in *choteo,* a generalized mocking and kidding behavior that made light of serious matters. Mañach later associated *choteo* with the rejection of authority commanded by elected government officials, but also the authority of experts and intellectuals. According to Mañach, Cubans, like their Spanish ancestors, were more concerned about violations of individual rights than of collective rights, a characteristic consistent with acceptance of public corruption (1940/1969, 54). They poked fun at government officials and legislators who took their duties seriously, referring to them disparagingly as *románticos* (Mañach 1940/1969, 72). In his view these characteristics contributed to the national culture of corruption that prevailed in republican Cuba.

Another insight about the culture of corruption in Cuba comes from the work of historian Jorge Ibarra (1985). Following several prominent psychosociologists, Ibarra posits that a nation's popular language reflects its psyche, the way a nation's people feel and react to events. Ibarra examined a broad corpus of Cuban popular culture—dictionaries and compendia of popular phrases, humor magazines, satirical plays, novels and other works of fiction, lyrics of popular songs—from the first quarter of the twentieth century to identify key psychological trends in Cuban society. He found that Cubans developed a new vocabulary for institutions and political relations during this period. In particular, Ibarra notes that out of sixty popular terms associated with administrative corruption in use in the 1920s, only eleven were in use during the colonial period. That is, popular terms for corruption multiplied nearly sixfold in the early twentieth century, suggesting an important shift in Cuban culture vis-à-vis corruption. Ibarra further notes that many of the new terms associated with corruption were irreverent, in keeping with *choteo,* for example referring to bribe-taking and other corrupt practices by public officials with the terms *se pegó al biberón* (sucked the nipple) or *al mamey* (fruit), *jamón* (ham), or *teta* (breast) (Ibarra 1985, 279–280).

In the final analysis, during the republican era, Cubans became largely dependent on the state for economic security. The state employed a growing number of poorly paid civil servants, many of them susceptible to corruption or enjoying sinecures obtained through patronage; others protected their often meager labor, professional, or business interests through political lobbying, a process that often involved paying bribes. Few were the Cubans immune from this mentality. An excessively regulated economy not only prevented growth but also paved the way for many forms of corruption, including petty or low-level corruption. Labor legislation, writes Speck (2002, 125), became a

> complex web of benefits, wage controls, job guarantees, un- and under-employment subsidies, arbitration procedures, health and safety regulations plus measures designed to regulate (and, if necessary, repress) labor unions and professional associations. All these new rules, of course, were multiplied by the daily bureaucratic rulings on the requests of individual producers to trade quotas, hire or fire workers, renovate facilities, import machinery and more.

This dependency on the state would be carried to its ultimate expression by the Castro Revolution, which made the Cuban socialist state the final arbiter of the fate of every Cuban, regardless of social and economic status: the jobs they were to fill, where they were to reside, and even the goods and services they were to consume. This legacy of state control over the economy, jobs, and the population's welfare was well established before Castro assumed power. The new level to which socialism has taken state control, however, will have to be taken carefully into account when considering the future direction of the country and the best policy options to minimize corruption in its transition to a new political and economic system.

Four

DETERMINANTS
OF CORRUPTION
IN SOCIALIST CUBA

The extremely high concentration of resources in the state sector and the centralized nature of the management system place a great deal of power into the hands of government officials of a socialist, centrally planned economy. As we discussed in Chapter 1 and as Klitgaard (1988) has posited, the level of corruption is a function of the degree of monopoly exercised by the state over the supply of a good or service, the degree of discretion enjoyed by a government agency or official in making resource allocation decisions, and the degree of accountability of the government (or its agents) to others.

In socialist societies such as Cuba's, with an all-encompassing public sector, most resource allocation decisions are made by government employees who have wide discretion in their activities and are susceptible to using state property for private gain. Corruption is another side of bureaucratic discretion, since delays create the opportunity to take bribes (La Porta et al. 1998, 23). Moreover, public control of resources results in a lack of identifiable ownership and widespread misuse and theft of resources. President Castro has recognized the potential for power to corrupt, although in his view, revolutionary convictions can overcome the human temptation to abuse power and to participate in corrupt activities for personal gain:

> One of the participants [at the conference] asked me . . . whether power is corruptive. I think it is. This is true. Having the power to steal is corruptive. Many have been corrupted by power because they have had the opportunity to rob. I have seen many men with the tendency to abuse power. This happens when they have a bit of power. This is a human weakness. We see ourselves as revolutionaries, and revolutionaries have convictions. Our convictions have remained unchanged throughout time. Convictions must be cultivated. They do not develop by themselves. (Castro 1997)

There is also a tremendous potential for corruption in socialist societies since checks and balances such as rule of law, separation of powers, account-ability systems, transparency, an inquiring press, and a vigilant civil society are very weak or missing altogether. Socialist societies have traditionally controlled public media and restricted—or banned—independent civil so-ciety organizations. The Cuban government has been particularly effective in preventing civil society organizations from being formed and has not hesitated to punish dissenters even at the cost of widespread international repudiation.

The size and structure of the Cuban state, the high degree of discretion that Cuban government officials continue to have over resource allocation, and the lack of public accountability explain the very high level of ad-ministrative corruption that plagues socialist Cuba. This chapter examines the determinants of corruption in socialist Cuba, while the next chapter documents the incidence of corruption on the island based on the best available information.

GOVERNMENT MONOPOLY

Soon after coming to power, Cuba's revolutionary government moved ag-gressively to take over the nation's productive resources. In early 1959 the government issued a series of law decrees that authorized the confiscation of property and funds controlled by the deposed dictator Batista and his collaborators. Accordingly, the state took control of several sugar mills, construction companies, agricultural enterprises, factories, hospitals, and transportation service providers. In May 1959 the Cuban government pro-mulgated the First Agrarian Reform Law, which established an upper limit of about four hundred hectares of landholding by any individual—with some exceptions—and expropriated landholdings beyond this upper limit. The bulk of these expropriated lands were organized into state-controlled production cooperatives, along the lines of the Soviet *kolkhozy*. This was followed in the second half of 1959 by government takeover of key indus-tries, including some owned by foreigners, under the pretext that business executives were mismanaging their firms as a form of economic sabotage.

In 1960 the Cuban government nationalized property owned by U.S. and other foreign citizens and key enterprises owned by Cuban citizens—banks, insurance companies, manufacturing plants, sugar mills, depart-ment stores, private health clinics, pharmacies, laboratories, warehouses.

By 1961 the Cuban government controlled essentially all wholesale and foreign trade, banking, and education and held commanding control over industrial, construction, and transportation activities; the private sector only maintained a significant role in agriculture and retail trade.

It was only a matter of time until the Cuban government acted to eliminate these remaining vestiges of private-sector activity. In 1963 the so-called Second Agrarian Reform Law nationalized landholdings over sixty-seven hectares, doubling the share of land under state control. And in 1968 a "revolutionary offensive" seized virtually all remaining private businesses in the retail sector: corner grocery stores, vegetable and fruit stands, dry cleaners, barber shops, bars and restaurants, clothing stores, auto repair shops. Finally, in the 1970s and 1980s Cuba gradually reduced the number of small private farms by encouraging private farmers to join cooperatives or by acquiring land when owners died or retired from farming.

State Ownership of Productive Resources

Table 4.1 presents rough estimates of the state's share of ownership of productive resources in Cuba over the period 1959–1988. In 1959, prior to the start of the socialist collectivization process, the bulk of the productive resources in the Cuban economy were in the hands of the private sector. Exceptions were education, where there was a heavy state presence via the public education system (at the basic, intermediate, and higher education levels); health, where state and private services providers coexisted; and to a lesser extent construction, transportation, wholesale and foreign trade, and banking. The speed and breadth of the collectivization process is evident by the rapidly rising share of state ownership of productive resources. In 1968 the Cuban state controlled 100 percent of industry, construction, retail trade, wholesale and foreign trade, banking, and education; only in agriculture (74 percent under state control) and transportation (98 percent) was there measurable private-sector presence. By 1988 the state's share of agriculture had risen to 97 percent and of transportation to 99 percent. Thus, by the latter date, with the exception of some private farmers and owners of taxis and other means of transportation, the Cuban state had complete control over the nation's productive resources. In the 1990s ownership of the means of production by the Cuban state remained very high, although it declined in comparison with the end of the 1980s as a result of some economic reforms instituted between 1993 and 1996 (see below).

TABLE 4.1. ESTIMATED SHARE (PERCENTAGE) OF STATE OWNERSHIP
OVER MEANS OF PRODUCTION

Sector	1959	1961	1963	1968	1977	1988
Agriculture	0	37	70	74	79	97
Industry	0	85	95	100	100	100
Construction	10–20	80	98	100	98	99
Transportation	15–20	92	95	98	100	100
Retail trade	0	52	75	100	100	100
Wholesale and foreign trade	5–10	100	100	100	100	100
Banking	5–10	100	100	100	100	100
Education	80	100	100	100	100	100

Source: Mesa-Lago 2000, 347

Employment in the State Sector

Another indicator of the overwhelming control of the state within the Cuban economy is the share of the total civilian labor force it employs. Statistics regarding state and nonstate employment are only available for selected years. Thus, the Cuban state employed more than 85 percent of civilian workers in 1970; this share rose to nearly 92 percent by 1981 and remained roughly at this level through the end of the 1980s. The approximately 8 percent of the labor force that was employed by the nonstate sector in 1981 consisted mostly of private farmers, agricultural cooperative members, self-employed workers, and a small number of salaried private workers.

In the 1990s, with the expansion of legalized self-employment, the establishment of joint ventures with foreign investors, and the creation of agricultural cooperatives, the state's share of total civilian employment declined markedly. In 2002, the latest year for which these data are available, the state accounted for 76.7 percent of civilian employment; the largest share of private-sector workers were in the agricultural sector (private farmers and cooperative members) or self-employed (ONE 2003, 122).

International Comparisons

Precise cross-country comparisons of the share of productive resources under state control are difficult to make not only because of scarcity of data but also because of differences in countries' estimation methodologies. Some estimates rely on share of employment in nationalized enterprises and others on share of the national output produced by such enterprises or on the share of resources (assets) owned by the state. Notwithstanding data availability and methodological problems, available information suggests that in the 1980s the Cuban state's share of ownership of productive resources exceeded that of several socialist countries and was in line with the socialist countries that were considered as the most highly collectivized, namely the former Soviet Union and Czechoslovakia (Pérez-López 1995, 39–42). In fact, writing about the Cuban economy at the end of the 1980s, economist Díaz Vázquez (1998, 27) stated that "based on the degree [of involvement] and role of the State in the management of the economy, it can be affirmed that there was no economy in the planet equivalent to Cuba's, whether the point of reference is within or outside the socialist experiences."

Considering the profound economic reforms in Eastern European nations and the former Soviet Union in the 1990s that promoted privatization of state assets and energized their private sectors, it is evident that contemporary Cuba far surpasses the former socialist bloc countries with respect to control over the means of production. Although data to make the comparisons are not available, it can be argued that Cuba and North Korea are probably the remaining bastions of state ownership of the means of production, as even socialist China and Vietnam have developed forms of land ownership that permit farmers essentially to own the land they till and have opened their economies quite widely to foreign investment.

Reforms of the 1990s

In the early 1990s, at a time when the economy was reeling from the sudden change in economic relations with the former socialist community and the loss of foreign assistance from these nations, the Cuban government took several initiatives to stimulate economic activity that reduced somewhat the role of the state in the economy. These reforms included decriminalizing the use of foreign currencies and enactment of other measures to attract U.S. dollar remittances (1993); expanding legal self-employment (1993); restructuring the agricultural sector by breaking up state farms and converting them into agricultural cooperatives (1993); establishing farmers' and artisans' free markets (1994); and passing a new mining law (1994), a new foreign investment law (1995), and legislation authorizing the creation of foreign trade zones (1996), coupled with more aggressive efforts to attract foreign investment.

DOLLARIZATION

The first market-oriented economic reform measure undertaken by the Cuban government in the summer of 1993 was to decriminalize the holding and use of hard currency. Up to that time, the holding or using of foreign currency by a Cuban citizen was a crime punishable under the penal code. Their decriminalization was designed to stem the booming black market for hard currency and to stimulate hard-currency remittances to Cuban citizens from relatives and friends living abroad.

To give further incentive for remittances, the government established special hard-currency commercial outlets (*tiendas de recaudación de divisas,* TRDs) where Cuban consumers holding foreign exchange could purchase goods not generally available to individuals holding pesos. And in December 1994 the Cuban government created a new form of domestic currency, the convertible peso, valued at par with the U.S. dollar, to increase the hard-currency money supply and facilitate sales at hard-currency stores. Two other actions that stimulated remittances were the decision by the Cuban National Bank in September 1995 to accept hard-currency deposits from individuals and the creation in mid-October 1995 of foreign-currency exchange houses (*casas de cambio,* CADECAs) where Cuban citizens could exchange hard currencies for pesos at rates close to those prevailing on the black market.

SELF-EMPLOYMENT

To legitimize a very active black market for personal services and handicraft production and to absorb the large number of unemployed and underemployed workers dislocated from factories that had to shut down as a result of shortages of imported raw materials, in September 1993 the Cuban government authorized self-employment in about 100 occupations, primarily related to transportation, home repair, and personal services, and subsequently expanded the number of occupations to more than 160. Up to the time this decision was made, essentially all nonagricultural employment in socialist Cuba was in the state sector. Although self-employment was subject to severe restrictions—e.g., self-employed workers could not hire others, were required to pay fees and taxes to the government, were subject to strict rules on how they obtained raw materials and sold the goods and services they produced—the number of self-employed workers increased rapidly, reaching 129,200 workers in 1997 and 156,600 in 1999.

AGRICULTURAL COOPERATIVES

In September 1993 the Council of State broke up large state farms into quasi-cooperatives called basic units of cooperative production (*unidades básicas de producción cooperativa,* UBPCs). The state farms, established in the early 1960s after short-lived experimentation with land redistribution to landless peasants, followed the Soviet agricultural model: large spreads of land, extensive use of machinery, and heavy application of chemical fertilizers; Soviet-style state farms were considered "factories in the field"—their workers were state employees with no property rights to the land they worked, their production plan was determined by the central authorities, and their output had to be sold to the state. In contrast, UBPCs would have the use of the land they worked for an indefinite period of time, own the output they produced, have the ability to sell it to the state or to third parties (after meeting some threshold level of sales to the state), elect their own leadership, manage their own financial affairs, and have their own bank accounts. The rationale for creating the cooperatives was that under this form of organization, workers would have greater incentives to increase production with the least expenditure of material resources.

AGRICULTURAL AND ARTISAN MARKETS

To provide outlets for nongovernment production, in late September 1994 Cuba authorized the creation of farmers' markets, locations at which producers of selected agricultural products could sell a portion of their output at prices set by market forces. Before an agricultural producer—whether a private farmer, a cooperative member, or a state enterprise—could use the new markets, sales obligations to the state procurement system had to be met. Vendors using the agricultural markets had to rent stalls from the state and pay sales taxes. In most respects, the agricultural markets authorized in September 1994 were similar to the farmers' free markets (*mercados libres campesinos,* MLCs) created in 1980 and scuttled in 1986 as part of the "rectification" process launched by Castro after he criticized MLC participants for illicit enrichment. In October 1994 the Cuban government also authorized the creation of special markets for artisans and artists to sell their products to the public.

FOREIGN INVESTMENT AND EXPORT PROCESSING ZONES

Although socialist Cuba first enacted legislation to allow foreign investment in the island in 1982, very little foreign investment materialized until the 1990s when Cuba mounted an aggressive campaign to attract foreign investment and made some changes to the legal framework governing foreign investment.

In 1992 the National Assembly of People's Power (Asamblea Nacional del Poder Popular, ANPP), revolutionary Cuba's legislative body, passed several amendments to the 1976 Constitution clarifying the concept of private property and providing a legal basis for transferring state property to joint ventures with foreign investors. A new mining law that facilitated foreign investment in the exploration and production of oil and minerals was enacted in December 1994. A new foreign investment law was passed in September 1995 that introduced some innovations to the legal framework for foreign investment, such as eliminating the 49 percent maximum foreign ownership limit, simplifying the investment screening and approval system, and allowing foreign investment in real estate. In June 1996 Cuba enacted complementary legislation that created export processing zones and provided incentives for investment that settled in such zones.

The Cuban government also aggressively marketed the island as a location for foreign investment, sending missions to foreign countries and holding seminars for potential investors. Cuba held several auctions of exploration areas to attract foreign oil companies to invest in exploratory drilling and production. Finally, the Cuban government entered into more than four dozen bilateral investment promotion and protection agreements to provide additional guarantees to foreign companies considering investing in the island.

Each of these reform measures tended to stimulate activities by economic actors with some degree of independence from the state—individuals receiving remittances from abroad, self-employed workers, private farmers, agricultural cooperative members, and joint ventures with foreign investors operating on the island and their workers. The reforms opened up a modicum of space for civil society actors as the government reluctantly empowered some citizens as entrepreneurs, consumers, producers, or traders. This is consistent with Kornai's (1992, 369) observation regarding socialist countries:

> Reforming tendencies increase the autonomy of individuals, groups, and organizations in several respects. This applies to independent political movements, associations in society, private businesses, self-governing local authorities, self-managed firms, state-owned firms that become more independent with the idea of market socialism, and so on. Various combinations of autonomy and subordination appear, but within them the weight of autonomy grows as a result of the reform, and as it increases, so the totalitarian power of the central leadership decreases.

It is also consistent with the experience in contemporary China, as Wank (1995, 57) has observed: "private capitalist business in China [was] perhaps the most distinctive aspect of China's civil society in the 1980s."

However, consistent with its deep-seated ambivalence toward markets and economic activities outside of its direct control, the Cuban government froze the reform process in 1996 and since then has taken a number of steps to stifle the growth of economic activity outside of the realm of the state enabled by the reforms:

- Faced with an overwhelming response to the liberalization of self-employment through the creation of home restaurants (*paladares*), the government initially reacted by banning them. It subsequently reinstated the *paladares* but limited their size to twelve customers and instituted aggressive inspections to ensure their compliance with laws and regulations, thereby threatening their economic viability and long-term prospects.
- Imposing very high fees and taxes on self-employed workers, coupled with strict enforcement of rules regarding sources of inputs (to ensure that raw materials are not stolen from state enterprises, since there are no alternative sources of inputs), has severely hampered the economic viability of self-employment. The number of self-employed workers peaked at 156,600 in 1999 and had declined to 152,900 in 2002. (ONE 2003, 122)
- In May 2000 the Committees for the Defense of the Revolution (Comités de Defensa de la Revolución, CDRs) launched a campaign to eradicate "illegal" economic activities throughout the island. Among the illegal activities singled out by the CDRs were the work of porters, valet parking assistants, and nightwatchmen in *paladares* and in private homes; private "banks" renting magazines, books, and videos to the public; rental of rooms in private homes; storage space rentals to individuals participating in the agricultural markets; and even cockfights ("Arremeten" 2000; Vincent 2000).
- The Cuban government increasingly has placed obstacles to incoming foreign investment, including time-consuming screening of individual investments and arbitrary decisions that affect their profitability.
- After initially encouraging foreign investment in real estate, the Cuban government declared a moratorium on the construction of condominiums and apartments financed with foreign capital in May 2000 and took over the sale or lease of units that were already completed.
- In July 2003 the Cuban government banned the use of hard currencies in transactions among state enterprises and between state enterprises and joint ventures, decreeing that they must use convertible

pesos instead, putting into question the long-term convertibility of profits and assets of joint ventures.

- Government-established committees have been created to review and approve hard-currency imports, including imports to be sold by hard-currency stores, sharply reducing the number of state entities that are able to engage in foreign trade.
- In the fall of 2004 the central government took control over key industries such as tourism, which had been permitted to operate in a decentralized fashion through competing state enterprises and joint ventures.
- Effective October 2004, the Ministry of Labor no longer issued self-employment licenses for forty occupations, declaring that the economic recovery required "that the work performed by these occupations be brought under the control of the central government" (Cancio Isla 2004a).
- Effective November 8, 2004, the U.S. dollar no longer circulated on the island. Between October 25, when the measure was announced, and November 8, Cuban citizens were allowed to exchange dollars they held at par with the convertible peso; any dollars exchanged after November 8 were subject to a 10 percent surcharge. This action essentially reversed the 1993 measure that depenalized the circulation and use of the dollar on the island.
- In December 2004 the Cuban Central Bank established a system of foreign exchange controls whereby all hard-currency revenue received by Cuban enterprises would be deposited in the Central Bank and could be spent only with approval of that entity.

State-sector workers who are responsible for making myriad resource allocation decisions in Cuba's state-heavy economic system earn meager salaries. Moreover, because their salaries are paid primarily in domestic currency (pesos), the purchasing power of their earnings is very low, a recipe for absenteeism and corruption. In 2002 the average salary of a worker employed by the state sector was 261 pesos per month, 6.5 percent higher than in 2001 (ONE 2003). The highest average salary was earned by workers in the electricity and gas industry, and the construction industry, with monthly average salaries of 322 pesos and 321 pesos, respectively; at the other end of the scale, workers in wholesale and retail trade, restaurants, and the hospitality industry earned an average monthly salary of 213 pesos. At the unofficial exchange rate of 26 pesos for one U.S. dollar prevailing in official exchange houses in early 2005, the average monthly salary of state workers in 2002 was equivalent to $10 monthly, while the average monthly salary of the highest-paid state workers was about $12.40 and of the lowest-paid workers about $8.20. Considering the very high prices of consumer goods in both peso- and dollar-denominated outlets and the shrinking access to basic commodities in peso-denominated stores, the purchasing power of state workers that earn only pesos is exceedingly low. State workers who earn dollar supplements—because they work in sectors that the government wishes to stimulate, such as tourism, where they can get tips from foreign visitors, or cigar production, which generates foreign exchange—are somewhat better off than their counterparts who earn only pesos, but even these privileged workers have very low purchasing power, meaning that they must find other ways to make ends meet, either stealing property from the state to sell or exchange in the black market or not showing up for work and using that time to engage in legal or illegal activities that generate hard currencies.

To summarize, the state currently controls the bulk of productive resources and directs economic activities. In the mid-1990s some reforms instituted by the government at a time of economic crisis opened up space for Cuban citizens to operate somewhat independently of the state as entrepreneurs, consumers, producers, or traders. Since 1996, the government has closed spaces for independent economic activity, reclaiming some of the ground ceded earlier to the private sector and disenfranchising independent economic actors that could have agglomerated into an emerging civil society. Moreover, as will be discussed below, the Cuban regime has not undertaken concomitant political reforms that would move in the direction of permitting personal freedoms and the establishment of independent organizations.

DISCRETION

Socialist Cuba's all-encompassing public sector has been subject to Soviet-style centralized planning since 1961. Centralization took a quantum leap in 1962 when the government imposed strict controls on prices, put in place a commodity rationing system—which exists to this day, more than forty years later—and set mandatory quotas on the output that farmers were required to sell to the state at fixed prices (*acopio*). Under such a centralized system, government officials make discretionary resource allocation decisions at all levels: which goods and services will be produced; which will be made available to other state enterprises, destined for export, or offered to domestic consumers; where they will be sold and at what prices. Government officials also have a great deal of discretion over decisions regarding housing.

Central Planning

In 1959 the Cuban government set retail prices for certain staple agricultural products and thus began to engage in the practice of controlling prices. Later the government established ceilings on profit margins on wholesale and retail food sales. At about the same time, the state established a mandatory *acopio* system to purchase corn from farmers in the eastern region of the island; this system was subsequently expanded to cover other commodities (e.g., rice and beans) and geographic areas. Purportedly to stem speculation, the state also took over wholesale food businesses and many retail food stores.

In 1961 the Cuban government created a Central Planning Board (Junta Central de Planificación, JUCEPLAN) and charged it with formulating annual and longer-term economic plans. A network of central ministries and agencies was created to manage various sectors of the economy, creating monopolies to control foreign trade, finance, labor, and banking. State enterprises under state control that produced similar goods were merged into trusts (*consolidados*), each controlled by a central entity or ministry.

Behind this veneer of scientific organization of the economy, ideological disputes among key leadership figures about the proper model of socialism to be implemented on the island created a chaotic situation and eliminated many of the (weak) management and financial controls associated with central planning. By the end of 1966 JUCEPLAN's functions had been relegated to research and logistical support, and the central plan had been supplanted by ad hoc programs (referred to as sectorial plans or miniplans) entrusted to loyal revolutionaries. The allocation of resources was done by "superior order," meaning by President Castro and the revolutionary elite. The Ministry of Finance was abolished, and so was a national budget (the country operated without a national budget from 1966 to 1977). The study of economics and accounting also suffered as a result; in 1969 enrollment in economics and management careers at universities and technical schools was one-twelfth that of 1965 (Mesa-Lago 2000, 210–211).

Connected with the emphasis on the development of rural areas brought about by the agrarian reform, the government established a chain of retail stores (*tiendas del pueblo*) to improve the supply of goods available to the rural population. Purportedly to prevent speculation, goods were sold at fixed prices. In November 1961 JUCEPLAN issued regulations freezing all enterprise-level, wholesale, and retail prices at then-prevailing levels. As could have been anticipated, this action led to severe shortages. In response, the government expanded the *acopio* system to all agricultural products in order to channel additional supplies through its distribution system. Under the *acopio* system, each private farmer was required to sell certain volumes of output to the state at fixed prices; fulfillment of *acopio* procurement quotas was a condition for continuing to receive allocations from the state of credit, agricultural services, seed, fertilizer, and other inputs. Output in excess of the *acopio* quota could be used by farmers for self-consumption or disposed of through legal means (e.g., sale at government-sanctioned outlets). Of course, much of it was dealt illegally (e.g., used for bartering, sold through the black market). Determination by government officials of the types of crops or livestock to be produced in a given parcel of land and of the quantities to be sold to the state are eminently discretionary administrative decisions that provide ample opportunities for corruption by government officials.

Rationing

To address shortages of consumer goods and to promote their more uniform distribution, the government instituted a national rationing system in March 1962. The rationing system established monthly physical allocations for a broad range of consumer goods—food, clothing, personal hygiene products—for each citizen. Although initially considered a temporary measure to ease the transition to a socialist economy, it continues in place after more than forty years. As discussed below, the high level of discretion associated with the implementation of the rationing system provides myriad opportunities for government officials to engage in corrupt acts.

Although there have been changes over time to the rationing system in varying the number of products and quota amounts, the mechanics of rationing have changed very little. Each household is annually issued a rationing book—the despised *libreta de abastecimiento*—that contains the names and ages of individuals in the household. Allocations of goods sold at official prices are made on a monthly basis. The head of the household chooses the store where he or she wishes to shop and registers with the National Rationing Board to have his or her household rations sent to that store. The household must shop at the designated store; adjustments may be made to accommodate moves to other locations and changes in household size. Similarly, provisions (e.g., special allocation of goods) may be made to meet the special dietary needs of children, the elderly, or individuals who require special diets. Under the rationing system, processed foods typically are purchased at a grocery store (*bodega*), meat and chicken at a butcher shop (*carnicería*), bottled milk at a dairy store (*lechería*), and fruits and vegetables in season at a vegetable stand (*venduta* or *puesto de frutas*).

Table 4.2 illustrates the continuity in the commodity rationing system by tracing monthly rations of certain staple products from 1962 to 2003. Many other products are subject to the rationing system but are not included in the table because time-series information was not available. Over time, the relevance of the rationing system has declined as the ration amounts have declined and other venues to purchase food products have been created (see below), but the rationing system still constitutes the backbone of the consumption of basic goods by the average Cuban citizen. According to analysts, even if the full allotment of goods subject to rationing were available in a given month, such supplies would last seven to ten days (USDA 2003), forcing consumers to turn to other—more expensive—sources of supplies. Nevertheless, the rationing system continues to play a key role in the nutrition of Cubans. According to Cuban economist Nova González (2000, 146), in the late 1990s food products sold through the rationing system provided around 61 percent of the calories, 65 percent of vegetable proteins, 36 percent of animal proteins, and 38 percent of the fats of the daily intake of the population in Havana.

Other Consumer Markets

In an effort to increase the variety of consumer products and compete with a thriving black market, the government created an official "parallel market" beginning in 1973. The parallel market has been used by the government to sell agricultural and manufactured products not available in sufficient quantities to be distributed to the general public through the rationing system or to make available to consumers additional quantities of rationed products. Prices in the parallel market typically are several-fold higher than rationed prices.

In the 1990s the Cuban government increased consumers' options to purchase essential goods, particularly food. Among these are the following (Álvarez 2001; USDA 2003):

- *Agromercados,* established in 1994, are open-air markets where consumers can purchase fruits, vegetables, and certain meats from private farmers and credit and service cooperatives that have fulfilled their *acopio* quotas and have surpluses to sell. Prices are high, and therefore products are out of the reach of the average Cuban without access to hard currency.

TABLE 4.2. MONTHLY RATIONS PER ADULT (IN POUNDS), SELECTED FOOD PRODUCTS AND YEARS

Item	1962	1963	1965–67	1969	1971–72	1983	1989	1991–94	1998	2003
Rice	6	6	3	4	3–6	5	5	5	6	6
Beans	1.5	1.5	3–9	1.5	1.5–3	1.25	0.625	0.625[1]	1.25[1]	1.25[1]
Sugar	NR	NR	6	4–6	4	4		4	6	2
Cooking fat or oil	2	2	2	2	1.5	0.5		1.5	0.5	0.5
Coffee	NR	0.75	0.375	0.375	0.375	0.25	0.25	0.25	0.375	0.25[2]
Beef[3]	3	3	3	3	3	1.25	0.75	0.75	0.5	0.5

NR Not rationed

[1] Often substituted by peas

[2] Mixed with roasted peas

[3] In the 1990s rationing of protein sources has changed so that different sources of protein are distributed each month, depending on their availability. For example, if beef is not available, chicken may be substituted. Other products that may be substituted for beef are a soy/meat or sausage/soy blend.

Sources: (1962–1989) Pérez-López 1995, 45; (1991–1994) Mesa-Lago 2000, 387; (1998) Álvarez 2001, 309; (2003) USDA 2003

- *Mercados de productos agrícolas con precios topados,* established in 1999, are open-air markets organized by the Ministry of Agriculture that sell agricultural products at prices that cannot exceed a certain level (the *tope* or cap). Prices are normally 25 to 30 percent lower than in the *agromercados.* Problems of quality, assortment, and regular supply of products affect these outlets. Consumers prefer *agromercados* but for the price differential.
- *Huertos* and *organopónicos,* examples of Cuba's urban agriculture, are located on the outskirts of cities. They are under the jurisdiction of the Ministry of Agriculture. Urban gardens and organic gardens sell their output directly to consumers at prices that are typically about 15 percent below those in the *agromercados.*
- *Placitas* are outlets that sell "surplus" products (beyond the needs of the armed forces) originating from agricultural activities of the Workers' Youth Army (Ejército Juvenil del Trabajo, EJT). These outlets have the lowest prices outside of the rationing system and therefore are the preferred option for Cuban consumers. However, the relatively low number of *placitas* limits their impact on the population's consumption levels.
- *Imágenes* chain stores are the closest semblance on the island to a supermarket where a Cuban citizen can shop. They sell processed food products such as vegetable oil, cheese, juices, and other nonperishable food products such as rice and beans. The stores are owned and operated by the government. Prices are very high relative to the earning capacity of Cuban citizens but lower than in hard-currency stores.
- *Ferias agropecuarias* are events organized once a month in Havana by the Ministry of Agriculture that bring together consumers and private sellers of agricultural products. Prices tend to be low compared to other outlets. The fact that they are held so infrequently limits the positive impact of the *ferias* on consumers.
- *Fish shops* are operated by the Ministry of the Fishing Industry. Supply at these outlets is irregular and of low quality. The most popular items carried by the fish shops are fish croquettes, fish burgers, and ground fish.
- *Tiendas de Recaudación de Divisas* (TRDs), also known as "dollar stores," are government-owned and -operated stores that sell a wide assortment of imported products, food and nonfood. The TRDs replaced the stores for foreign diplomats (*diplotiendas*) and for foreign technicians (*tecnotiendas*) that existed in the 1970s and 1980s to meet the needs of foreigners on the island. All transactions in TRDs are

conducted in hard currency and at very high prices. According to analysts, the markup in the TRDs exceeds 200 percent over the import price, placing these stores out of the reach of the majority of Cubans.

The *acopio* system, the rationing system, and the system of government-operated food outlets provide numerous opportunities for discretionary behavior by government officials and thus for bribe seeking and other forms of corrupt behavior. Government employees are responsible for making decisions on the amount of production of certain agricultural products that farmers will have to turn in to the state—at low prices, paid in domestic currency—to meet their *acopio* quota. Needless to say, farmers prefer to have as low an *acopio* quota as possible to maximize the amount of production that they would have available for self-consumption or to dispose of through more lucrative means; thus they are willing to influence the *acopio* official through bribes (in money or in kind) to go along with lower quota amounts. At the next level in the distribution system, government employees responsible for distributing rationed goods to the population have been known to divert some of the goods for their own use or to distribute the best-quality products or the largest amounts to friends and family or to those willing to pay a bribe in the form of money or in exchange for another desired product that is in short supply. The new food outlets operated by the government provide similar opportunities.

To summarize, the combination of a shortage economy and government control over the procurement and sale/distribution of food and other basic consumer goods creates ample opportunities for government officials to provide special benefits for consumers who are willing to make special payments in return for a lower procurement quota to fulfill, a ration to which the consumer was not entitled, or a larger quantity of a rationed good. In a capitalist society, these decisions tend to be made between private parties and are moderated by prices; in a socialist system such as Cuba's, where prices are largely fixed by the state, they involve government officials who can use their discretionary power to engage in corrupt acts.

Housing

The state also plays a very significant role in the housing sector. The Urban Reform Law of 1960 established the concept of housing as a public service and prohibited individuals from renting out their houses. Property owners were permitted to retain their own homes and vacation houses; tenants were allowed to "buy" the property they formerly rented through monthly rent payments to the state for a specified period of time, ranging from five to twenty years depending on the age of the property. The state collected rents and made payments to former owners of property. After more than four decades, the pre-1960 housing stock overwhelmingly is the property of the former tenants. Sale of housing units is prohibited, although swaps (*permutas*) are allowed; the swaps have to be approved by the state to ensure that they are genuine swaps rather than efforts to subvert the ban on private housing sales, but under-the-table payments are common.

From the early 1960s through the early 1980s, all residential housing construction was done by the state, which discouraged (or prohibited) private housing construction. As housing construction was not a high government priority, construction of new housing units lagged substantially behind demand. The state distributed the housing units it built through labor unions or other mass organizations. The General Housing Law of 1984 encouraged individuals to build homes for their own use and facilitated housing construction by individuals and cooperatives. There was a very positive private housing construction response to the 1984 law, but its ultimate impact was thwarted by the general shortage of construction materials, exacerbated by the cutbacks in imports associated with the economic crisis of the 1990s.

Thus, housing construction in socialist Cuba has been grossly inadequate to meet demand, and investments have not been made to maintain the existing housing stock. Mesa-Lago (2004, 96) estimates that the housing deficit surpassed 1.6 million units in 2000; the housing shortage is compounded by the deteriorated condition of a significant share of the existing stock. The very high premium on influencing government decision makers to obtain a new state-built housing unit, the materials to repair or build a unit, or the approval of a *permuta* creates opportunities by individuals to influence government officials through bribes and other illicit arrangements. The premium for doing this has probably risen since the mid-1990s, as housing has become a factor in earning foreign currency—under the umbrella of self-employment—through the rental of rooms in private homes to foreigners or the creation of small businesses such as *paladares*.

ACCOUNTABILITY

Cuba has had a one-party system for more than forty-five years. The Cuban Communist Party (Partido Comunista de Cuba, PCC), the only allowed political party, is an integral part of the Cuban government and so recognized in Article 5 of the Socialist Constitution. Fidel Castro is chief of state with the titles of president of the Council of State and of the Council of Ministers, first secretary of the Communist Party, and commander in chief of the armed forces.

After more than fifteen years of government based only on the executive branch, in 1976 Cuba created a legislative body, the Asamblea Nacional del Poder Popular (ANPP). Among its powers, the ANPP may enact or modify legislation, declare war and make peace, approve the budget and the national economic plan, elect the members of the Council of State, and elect the members of the Supreme Court. The ANPP meets twice a year for a few days essentially to ratify decisions and policies previously decided by the Council of State. It does not perform the accountability and oversight functions that are common for legislative bodies in other nations.

The 601 ANPP deputies are chosen in uncontested elections from lists of eligible candidates developed by the officially sponsored mass organizations from within the PCC. Voters have three choices: vote for the official slate in full, vote for some of the candidates on the slate (but never for an opposition candidate), or cast a blank ballot (Domínguez 2002). The fact that only PCC members may run means that the elections are not competitive and elected officials owe very little accountability to their electors.

Critical to guaranteeing government accountability are the rule of law, freedom for independent civil society organizations (CSOs) to exist and to perform their functions freely, and a press independent of government influence. Socialist Cuba scores very low on all three of these counts.

Rule of Law

The formal institution that is probably most critical for promoting government accountability is the rule of law. This essentially means a sound and predictable legal framework in which rules are known in advance, rules are enforced, there are mechanisms to amend rules when appropriate, and mechanisms for resolution of conflicts are readily available. Particularly important for promoting economic growth are legal frameworks and judicial systems to enforce contracts and property rights. Where there are means for citizens to pursue valid claims, there is government accountability.

There is a vast literature on the Cuban legal system and its shortcomings in providing a rule of law for the nation. Travieso-Díaz (1996, 49–50) summarizes the status of the rule of law in contemporary Cuba:

> During the first two decades of Cuba's revolution (that is, in the
> period extending roughly from 1959 to the enactment of the 1976

constitution), there was a deliberate effort on the part of the Cuban
Government to dismantle the legal system, diminish the importance
of the courts, and replace them with ad-hoc "people's courts" and
"revolutionary tribunals," and discourage the study and the practice
of law. It has been only in the last decade, and particularly since
the collapse of socialism in Eastern Europe, that a significant effort
has been undertaken to upgrade the qualifications and increase the
numbers of those involved in the legal system.

   . . . [L]aw practice in Cuba is constrained by the inadequate
number of legal professionals, the judiciary's lack of independence,
the prohibition against the private practice of law, and the generally
poor training of the practitioners. . . . The situation is not much
better with respect to the laws. By and large, the laws in effect in
Cuba today are obsolete (in that they do not represent currently
accepted legal and business practices throughout the world) and . . .
infused with Socialist dogma.

Cuba's record is among the worst in the world today with respect to
individual property rights and the enforcement of contracts to guarantee
such rights. Thus, the Heritage Foundation and the *Wall Street Journal*
(2004) in their *2004 Index of Economic Freedom,* assign Cuba the lowest possible rating in the category of level of protection of individual property
rights. In justifying this rating, the authors explain:

   Private ownership of land and productive capital by Cuban citizens
   is limited to farming and self-employment. According to the Department of State, "The Constitution . . . explicitly subordinates the
   Courts to the ANPP [National Assembly of People's Power] and the
   Council of State, which is headed by Fidel Castro. The ANPP and
   its lower level counterparts choose all judges. . . . The law and trial
   practices do not meet international standards for fair public trials.

   And in the *2003 Index of Economic Freedom* (Heritage Foundation / *Wall
Street Journal* 2002) the authors elaborate:

   Cuba outlaws private property. Some individuals are allowed to
   operate self-employed businesses, but the government can confiscate all earnings from these activities if these individuals are
   deemed "unduly wealthy." There is no enforcement of contracts,
   and some European and Canadian investors have found their

investments (particularly in the hotel industry) renationalized and resold to other uninformed investors. Cuba does not allow international arbitration of disputes. According to the U.S. Department of State, "The Party controls all government positions, including judicial offices. The judiciary is completely subordinate to the Government and the Communist Party."

Cuba's centralized economy, slow to respond to the needs of the population and perennially short of the most basic consumer goods, has spawned a variety of informal arrangements that permit the population to eke out a living and meet their minimum needs. Cubans usually refer to the broad set of entrepreneurial activities on which they rely to make ends meet as *resolver,* to resolve or get by (Pérez-López 1995, 77). These arrangements are necessary, to a large extent, because formal institutions either do not exist or are ineffective in accomplishing their objectives.

As indicated above, revolutionary Cuba has permitted a limited range of economic activities for private gain. Another legal activity that is common on the island is bartering (*trueque*) of consumer goods obtained from the rationing system in order to accommodate differing household consumption patterns. Bartering of apartments and homes (*permutas*) has been the only way for persons outside of the government elite or *nomenklatura* to adjust the location or size of their dwellings. These forms of exchange are highly inefficient and occur because of the lack of formal institutions (markets) to conduct such exchanges.

Civil Society Organizations

Civil society organizations (csos) are quite varied with respect to their nature and composition, depending on historic origins and country context. Citizens or organizations typically come together to form a cso in order to express the interests and values of their members or of others, based on ethical, cultural, economic, political, scientific, religious, or philanthropic considerations. csos include nongovernmental organizations (ngos), trade unions, business organizations, faith-based organizations, indigenous peoples movements, and foundations. Independence from the state is essential for the existence and operation of csos.

There has been a dramatic expansion in the size, scope, and capacity of civil society around the globe over the past decade, aided by the process of globalization and the expansion of democratic governance, telecommunications, and economic integration. According to the World Bank, csos have become significant players in global development assistance, contributing large volumes of their own resources to promote economic and social development around the world. They have become important channels for delivering social services and implementing other development programs, especially in regions where government presence is weak, in post-conflict situations, or where civil society experience and expertise complements government action. The influence csos have on shaping global public policy has also emerged over the past two decades, exemplified by successful advocacy campaigns to ban land mines, cancel debt of the poorest countries, and enhance environmental protection.

Two prominent types of csos, trade unions and business associations, are incompatible with the political and economic control exercised by the Cuban state. In Cuba, according to the U.S. Department of State (2004),

> established official labor organizations have a mobilization function and do not act as trade unions, promote worker rights, or protect the right to strike. Such organizations were under the control of the State and the Communist Party, which also managed the enterprises for which the laborers worked. . . . The Communist Party selects the leaders of the sole legal labor confederation, the CTC, whose principal responsibility is to ensure that government production goals are met. Despite disclaimers in international forums, the Government explicitly prohibited independent unions, and none were recognized.

In 2004 the International Labor Organization (ILO) Committee on Freedom of Association (CFA) criticized the Cuban government's recognition of a single official union and prohibition of independent trade unions (ILO 2004). Because there are no private businesses to speak of within Cuba, there can be no genuine business organizations either.

Pioneering work by Aguirre (1998), Donate-Armada (1997), Espinosa (1999), Fernández (1994), López (1999), and Puerta (1997), among others, shows that the Cuban state does not permit—more accurately, it actively prevents—the existence and operation of independent organizations. Linz and Stepan (1996, 11–12) posit, based on their study of economic and political transitions:

> On theoretical grounds, our assumption is that at least a nontrivial degree of market autonomy and ownership diversity in the economy is necessary to produce the independence and liveliness of civil society so that it can make its contribution to a democracy. Likewise,

if all property is in the hands of the state and all price, labor, supply, and distributional decisions are the purview of the state in control of the command economy, the relative autonomy of political society required in a consolidated democracy could not exist.

Cuba's Associations Law (Ley de Asociaciones) purportedly guarantees the right of Cuban citizens to associate freely and form independent organizations. In practice,

> the law effectively bars the legalization of genuinely independent organizations. The law requires organizations to "coordinate" and "collaborate" with a state counterpart entity. Fulfilling these conditions necessitates the group's subjugation to the government organization, by allowing a representative of the state entity to attend and speak at any planned or unplanned meetings; requiring the group to notify the government entity in advance of any publications; coordinating with the government entity regarding participation in any national or international event; regularly reporting to the government entity on its activities; and providing prior notice of the date and hour of any meetings or any other activities. (Human Rights Watch 1999)

The Cuban state uses the registration process to thwart the creation of independent organizations. Only organizations that are authorized by the state can operate legally (see Table 4.3).

The Cuban state encourages citizen participation in officially sanctioned mass organizations. The Cuban Socialist Constitution of 1976, in its Article 7, states:

> The Cuban socialist state recognizes, protects and supports social mass organizations, such as the Central de Trabajadores de Cuba [Cuban Workers Central], which includes in its ranks the fundamental class of our society, the Committees for the Defense of the Revolution, the Federation of Cuban Women, the National Association of Small Farmers, the Federation of University Students, the Federation of Secondary Education Students, and the Union of Cuban Pioneers [elementary school students], as well as others that originated from the historical class struggle of our people and that represent specific interests of our citizens and incorporate them in the tasks of building, consolidating and defending socialist society.

TABLE 4.3. SELECTED OFFICIALLY SANCTIONED
NONGOVERNMENTAL ORGANIZATIONS

Mass Organizations
- Committees for the Defense of the Revolution (Comités de Defensa de la Revolución, CDRs)
- Federation of Cuban Women (Federación de Mujeres Cubanas, FMC)
- National Association of Small Farmers (Asociación Nacional de Agricultores Pequeños, ANAP)
- Cuban Workers Central (Central de Trabajadores de Cuba, CTC)
- Union of Cuban Pioneers (Unión de Pioneros de Cuba)
- Federation of University Students (Federación de Estudiantes Universitarios, FEU)
- Federation of Secondary Education Students (Federación de Estudiantes de Enseñanza Media, FEEM)

Academic and "Think Tanks"
- Center for American Studies (Centro de Estudios sobre América, CEA)
- Center for European Studies (Centro de Estudios sobre Europa, CEE)
- Research Center on the World Economy (Centro de Investigación de la Economía Mundial, CIEM)
- Research Center on the International Economy (Centro de Investigación de la Economía Internacional, CIEI).
- Center for Studies of the Cuban Economy (Centro de Estudios de la Economía Cubana, CEEC)
- Center for Studies of the United States (Centro de Estudios de los Estados Unidos, CEEU)
- Center for Studies of Political Alternatives (Centro de Estudios de Alternativas Políticas, CEAP)
- Art Institute (Instituto Superior del Arte)
- Caribbean Studies Association of Cuba (Asociación Cubana de Estudios del Caribe)
- Caribbean House (Casa del Caribe)

Religious and Charitable
- Yoruba Cultural Association of Cuba (Asociación Cultural Yoruba de Cuba)
- House of the Cuban Hebrew Community (Casa de la Comunidad Hebrea de Cuba)
- Caritas
- Martin Luther King Memorial Center (Centro Memorial Martin Luther King)
- Ecumenical Council of Cuba (Consejo Ecuménico de Cuba)
- Masonic Lodge of Cuba (Grande Logia de Cuba de A.L.Y.A.M.)
- Catholic Church (Iglesia Católica)

TABLE 4.3. (*continued*)

Other

- Chamber of Commerce (Cámara de Comercio)
- Union of Cuban Writers and Artists (Unión de Escritores y Artistas de Cuba, UNEAC)
- Pro-Naturaleza
- Pablo Milanés Foundation (Fundación Pablo Milanés)
- Félix Varela Center (Centro Félix Varela)
- Group for the Integral Development of the Capital City (Grupo para el Desarrollo Integral de la Capital)

Sources: Álvarez Gómez 2003; Gunn 1995

The revisions to the Constitution in 1992 maintained the same article but dropped the listing of the specific mass organizations. Participation in these organizations or their activities, del Aguila (1988, 181) clarifies,

> should not be equated either with individual or group autonomy or with genuine mass spontaneity. Participation . . . means discussing local affairs, doing volunteer work, receiving "guidance" from party officials, marching in the street against fellow citizens who choose to emigrate, attending mass rallies, and engaging in other revolutionary duties.

In addition, Cuba recognizes some professional associations that operate in concert with the state, among them the National Union of Cuban Jurists (Unión Nacional de Juristas de Cuba, UNJC), the Union of Cuban Journalists (Unión de Periodistas de Cuba, UPEC), the Union of Cuban Writers and Artists (Unión de Escritores y Artistas de Cuba, UNEAC), the National Association of Cuban Economists (Asociación Nacional de Economistas de Cuba, ANEC), and the Cuban Dental Association (Asociación Cubana de Estomatólogos).

In the 1990s the Cuban government authorized the formation of a large number of nongovernmental organizations (NGOs). According to Gunn (1995, 1), the move to create a large number of government-sanctioned NGOs came about "because the government deemed them useful financial intermediaries [to obtain funds from abroad] and because citizens desired self-help organizations capable of resolving local problems the state was unwilling or unable to address."

Some of these officially sanctioned organizations were existing government-affiliated entities that were "repackaged" as nongovernmental organizations; among them were several research organizations sponsored by the Central Committee of the Cuban Communist Party, such as the Center for American Studies (Centro de Estudios sobre América, CEA) and the Center for European Studies (Centro de Estudios sobre Europa, CEE). Others were relatively new organizations with questionable independence from the state. For example, the leadership of Pro-Naturaleza, purportedly an environmental NGO, consists of employees of the Ministry of Science, Technology, and Environment, the very state organization that is responsible for designing and implementing environmental policies (Gunn 1995).

With the possible exception of some religious and charitable organizations—such as Caritas (the charitable arm of the Catholic Church), the Catholic Church itself, the Yoruba Cultural Association of Cuba (Asociación Cultural Yoruba de Cuba), the Cuban Ecumenical Council (Consejo Ecuménico de Cuba), and a few others—the "nongovernmental" organizations sanctioned by the Cuban government listed in Table 4.3 are in fact government-sponsored entities.

Fernández (2000, 133) has developed a useful typology of organizations operating in Cuba based on their autonomy from the state: (1) CONGOS are government-controlled nongovernmental organizations, such as the mass organizations sponsored by the state or the Communist Party (including academic think tanks like CEA and CEE); (2) GONGOS are government-oriented nongovernmental organizations, such as the Center Félix Varela and the Martin Luther King Memorial Center, which have been approved by the state and meet the requirements of the Associations Law. GONGOS "are headed by individuals with close personal contacts with state and party officials"; and (3) NGOS, the familiar nongovernmental organizations known outside Cuba, are a relatively new phenomenon. Government-approved NGOS tend to be religious and fraternal organizations, such as the Catholic Church or the Masons. Using Fernández' typology, nearly all of the officially sanctioned organizations in Table 4.3 fall into the first two categories.

In contrast with the organizations sanctioned by the state are myriad truly independent civic organizations seeking recognition to operate legally on the island. Álvarez García (2003) identified some 470 opposition organizations in Cuba in April 2003, including civic, labor, and environmental organizations, independent libraries, and others. Earlier work by del Castillo et al. (1996) had identified 360 dissident, opposition, and human rights organizations as of the end of 1996. A partial list of these independent organizations is given in Table 4.4. Common threads running through these organizations are that they are very small, command very few resources, and operate illegally since they have not sought the required registration from the state or, if they have sought such registration, have not received it. Thus, members of these organizations risk the possibility of harassment, fines, and arrests at any time for breaking the law. The fact that these organizations are illegal also hinders their ability to receive resources from abroad.

Examples of the difficulties faced by independent organizations in Cuba include:

- Independent agricultural cooperatives. The movement began in 1997 with the establishment of the Transición cooperative in Loma del Gato, Santiago de Cuba Province, followed by a few others, and the attempt to establish the National Alliance of Independent Farmers of Cuba (Alianza Nacional de Agricultores Independientes de Cuba, ANAIC). ANAIC has not received legal status from the government. According to news reports, the first Congress of ANAIC, scheduled for 1998, was disrupted by government-inspired Rapid Response Brigades, the State Security Police, and the regular police forces and was aborted (Álvarez 1999).
- Independent labor organizations. The government has refused legal recognition for independent labor organizations, among them the Confederation of Democratic Workers of Cuba (Confederación de Trabajadores Democráticos de Cuba), the United Council of Cuban Workers (Consejo Unitario de Trabajadores Cubanos), and the Cuban Institute for Independent Labor Studies (Instituto Cubano de Estudios Sindicales Independientes). These organizations have been applying for legal recognition since the mid-1990s. There are numerous allegations of detentions and harassment of labor rights activists by the Cuban government (Human Rights Watch 1999). In 2003, seven independent trade union leaders were arrested (see below) as part of a crackdown on the opposition and sentenced to a combined 150 years of imprisonment (Brito and Sabatini 2003, 129). The International Confederation of Free Trade Unions (ICFTU) and the World Confederation of Labour (WCL) have filed several complaints before the International Labor Organization (ILO) against the Cuban government alleging violations of workers' rights, including the lack of recognition of independent trade unions, raids and searches of trade unionists' homes, and arrests of trade unionists. In June 2003 the International Labor

TABLE 4.4. SELECTED INDEPENDENT NONGOVERNMENTAL
ORGANIZATIONS

Human and Civic Rights
- Lawton Foundation (Fundación Lawton)
- Christian Liberation Movement (Movimiento Cristiano Liberación)
- Democratic Solidarity (Solidaridad Democrática)
- Máximo Gómez Civic Movement (Movimiento Cívico Máximo Gómez)
- University Students Without Frontiers (Universitarios sin Fronteras)
- Cuban Youth Movement for Democracy (Movimiento Cubano Jóvenes por la
  Democracia)
- Civic Forum (Foro Cívico)
- Cuban Council (Concilio Cubano)
- About 350 other organizations as of the end of 1996

Labor
- Independent National Workers Confederation of Cuba (Confederación Obrera
  Nacional Independiente de Cuba)
- United Council of Cuban Workers (Consejo Unitario de Trabajadores Cubanos)
- Cuban Workers Union (Unión Sindical de Trabajadores de Cuba)
- Christian Workers Central (Central Sindical Cristiana)
- Confederation of Democratic Workers of Cuba (Confederación de Trabajadores
  Democráticos de Cuba)
- Cuban Institute for Independent Labor Studies (Instituto Cubano de Estudios
  Laborales Independientes)

Agriculture
- Cooperativa Agropecuaria Independiente Transición, Loma del Gato, Santiago de
  Cuba Province
- Cooperativa Agropecuaria Independiente Progreso I, Bejuquera de Filipinas,
  Guantánamo Province
- National Alliance of Independent Farmers of Cuba (Alianza Nacional de Agriculto-
  res Independientes de Cuba, ANAIC)
- Cooperativa Agropecuaria Independiente Progreso II, San José de las Lajas,
  La Habana Province
- Cooperativa Agropecuaria Independiente Portadores del Futuro, Vázquez, Puerto
  Padre Municipality, Las Tunas Province

Libraries
- Biblioteca Félix Varela, Amancio Rodríguez, Las Tunas Province
- At least 100 others throughout the island

Media
- CubaPress
- Cuban Independent Press Bureau (Buró de Prensa Independiente de Cuba)

TABLE 4.4. (*continued*)

Other

* Green Path Ecopacifist Movement (Movimiento Ecopacifista Sendero Verde)
* Cuban Environs Environmental Agency (Agencia Ambiental Entorno Cubano, AAMEC)
* Cuban Independent Economists Institute (Instituto de Economistas Independientes de Cuba, INEIC)

Sources: Álvarez Gómez 2003; Pax Christi 1998

> Conference adopted a resolution condemning the government of Cuba for its violation of internationally recognized workers' rights such as unjustly imprisoning independent trade unionists and urging the government to reform law and practice to come into compliance with such rights and to recognize independent unions. The ILO requested that the government of Cuba accept the visit of a direct-contacts mission from the organization to more thoroughly investigate the workers' rights situation on the island (Brito and Sabatini 2003, 132).

* Independent libraries. The first independent library in Cuba was the Biblioteca Independiente Félix Varela, established in March 1998 in Las Tunas Province by economist Berta Mexidor. The independent library movement spread quickly throughout the island despite government harassment, imprisonment of librarians, and seizure of materials. As of the end of 2002, the Independent Libraries in Cuba Project had 103 branches in all fourteen provinces of the nation and about a dozen others were planned; the holdings of the libraries included more than 40,000 books and 57,000 magazines and other materials, and 182,715 readers had registered (Leiva 2003). The Committee on Free Access to Information and Freedom of Expression of the Inter-national Federation of Library Associations and Institutions (IAFLA/FAIFE) has documented numerous reports of government actions against the independent libraries, including threats, intimidation, harassment, eviction, short-term arrests, and confiscation of incoming book donations or book collections (http://www.ifla.org). Among the dissidents apprehended and convicted in March 2003 were ten members of the island's independent library movement; the ten librarians were sentenced to a total of 196 years in prison ("Librarians sentenced" 2003).

- Environmental organizations. Founded in the late 1980s, the Green
  Path Ecopacifist Movement (Movimiento Ecopacifista Sendero
  Verde) sought to restructure the Cuban political system to enhance
  ecological principles; among the specific policies proposed by
  Sendero Verde were returning land to individual farmers and using
  solar rather than nuclear energy for electricity generation, a position that put the organization at odds with the Cuban government's
  push to promote nuclear power on the island. The leaders of
  Sendero Verde were arrested several times for their activities and
  left the island in 1991. It is not clear whether the organization still
  exists (Díaz-Briquets and Pérez-López 2000, 276).

Mass Media

All mass media organizations in Cuba are owned and operated by the
Cuban government, the PCC, or government-affiliated organizations (Nichols 1982, 75). The Cuban revolutionary government took over most
newspapers and broadcast stations in 1959 because they became insolvent
(having lost advertising revenue after the government nationalized private
businesses), they published news or commentaries "which might tend to
impair the independence of the nation or provoke the non-observance of
the laws in force," a crime since 1959, or the workers of a particular institution denounced the management as counterrevolutionary (McGaffey and
Barnett 1965, 332). In February 1961 only six daily newspapers were being
published in Havana, compared to sixteen in 1959 (McGaffey and Barnett
1965, 333). After 1963, *Granma,* the organ of the Central Committee of the
PCC modeled after the Soviet Union's *Pravda,* became the only newspaper
in the country (Nichols 1982, 77). Other government-run newspapers were
created in the 1970s and 1980s to address special groups (youth, farmers,
workers, military personnel) or geographic regions, but most of these were
shut down in the 1990s when the economic crisis brought about a severe
reduction in the importation of newsprint. The government also owns and
operates all broadcast stations (radio and television) on the island as well as
access to the Internet. Since 1960 the Cuban government has tightly controlled the information that is available to Cuban citizens.

In the 1990s independent journalists within the island began to challenge the government's monopoly over information. Although they were
unable to disseminate their dispatches within the island since the official
media outlets (newspapers, radio, and television stations) are all owned
and controlled by the government, these independent journalists filed

their reports with the foreign press mostly through telephone communication with collaborators in other countries (Ackerman 1997). Reports by
Cuban independent journalists are disseminated through the Internet by
CubaNet, an organization established outside of Cuba for this purpose,
and regularly appear in different media around the world (*Desde Cuba*
1997). CubaNet also disseminates dispatches from outlawed independent
groups in the island such as environmental and labor organizations.

In March 2003 the Cuban government arrested seventy-five peaceful dissidents and subjected them to summary trials. In a matter of a few days, they
were tried and sentenced to prison terms up to twenty-eight years. Among
them were twenty-six independent journalists, including nine who were the
editors of news agencies. While the government's action did not altogether
silence the independent press movement, the jail terms coupled with the
intimidation factor dealt it a severe blow (Reporters Without Borders 2003).

Reporters Without Borders, an international organization devoted to
defending journalists and other media contributors and professionals who
have been imprisoned or persecuted for doing their work, supporting
journalists who are being threatened in their own countries, and fighting
to reduce the use of censorship and to oppose laws designed to restrict
press freedom, in 2003 released its Second World Press Freedom Ranking
(Reporters Without Borders 2003). To compile this ranking, the organization designed a questionnaire with fifty-three criteria for assessing the state
of press freedom in each country. It included violations directly affecting
journalists (such as murders, imprisonment, physical attacks, and threats)
and news media (censorship, confiscation of issues, searches, and harassment). It registered the degree of impunity enjoyed by those responsible
for these press freedom violations. It took account of the legal and judicial
situation affecting the news media (such as penalties for press offenses,
the existence of a state monopoly in certain areas, and the existence of a
regulatory body) and the behavior of authorities toward the state-owned
news media and international press. It assessed the main obstacles to the
free flow of information on the Internet. The questionnaire was sent to
persons with deep knowledge of the state of press freedom in a country
or a number of countries: local journalists or foreign reporters based in a
country, researchers, jurists, regional specialists, and the researchers working for Reporters Without Borders' international secretariat. A total of 166
countries were included in the ranking (as against 139 in the first report);
Cuba ranked 165 out of 166 countries, only ahead of North Korea.

In its annual report of press freedom around the world for 2004, Reporters Without Borders concluded that 2003 was a grim year for press

freedom in Cuba, with twenty-seven journalists arrested and sentenced to long prison terms and held in conditions that their families described as inhumane. Independent journalists who avoided arrest ran the risk of suffering the same fate (Reporters Without Borders 2004a).

Internet

Consistent with its policy of controlling the population's access to information, the Cuban government has placed significant restraints on the average citizen's Internet access. Internet access is governed by Decree Law 209 of 1996. It states that access would be granted "in a regulated manner . . . giving priority to the entities and institutions most relevant to the country's life and development" (Kalathil and Boas 2001, 11). Thus, Internet access is only allowed to businesses, foreign entities, and certain state entities. The sale of computer equipment is strictly regulated; authorization from the Ministry of Domestic Commerce must be obtained prior to purchasing computers or peripherals, and the sale of modems to the general public has been banned (Reporters Without Borders 2004b). At the close of 2003 Cuba reportedly had 270,000 computers in operation throughout the island, 65,000 of which could be connected to the Internet, and 480,000 email accounts ("Sólo 750 sitios" 2004), a several-fold increase over two years earlier (Kalathil and Boas 2001, 12). However, the vast majority of the connections were to a national intranet, tightly controlled by the government, with no access to the World Wide Web.

In January 2004 the government issued a decree prohibiting Internet access over the peso-denominated telephone service for Cubans lucky enough to have home telephone service. To implement the ban, the state telephone company, ETECSA, indicated it would use technical means and block access to the Internet to those not authorized to have access ("Cuba cracks down" 2004). Amnesty International expressed concern about the impact of the new law on freedom of expression and information in Cuba, stating that the new measures limiting unofficial Internet use "constitute yet another attempt to cut off Cubans' access to alternative views and a space for discussing them" (AI 2004). Since then, Cuban authorities have imposed new restrictions on the use of the Internet, for example notifying enterprises that the "indiscriminate use" of electronic mail and of the Internet by its employees (for example, using free accounts such as those provided by Yahoo or Hotmail or the extensive use of search engines to navigate the Internet) could lead to the termination of service (Cancio Isla 2004c).

While restricting Cuban citizens' access to the Internet, Cuba has capitalized on the commercial benefits of this new technology to promote the island's tourism industry and business opportunities, from the sale of cigars, rum, books, music CDs, and art to investment opportunities. The Cuban government website, www.cubaweb.cu, reportedly is the product of foreign entrepreneurs and is hosted on servers outside the island.

CONCLUSION

For the past forty-five years, Cuba's government has actively sought to eliminate the institutions that prevailed in republican Cuba and to replace them with institutions that supported a socialist, centrally directed economy. Cuba's socialist regime undermined the institutions it inherited: it eliminated private property, disassembled the legal framework that enabled private enterprise and that decentralized economic decision making, shackled the free press, and repressed civil society. That it has not fully succeeded in obliterating the institutions it inherited from the Republic is a tribute to the latter's resilience and to the fact that wide-scale institutional change takes time.

An eager convert to socialism since 1959, Cuba has adopted the key institutions of socialism. Among these, the ones most directly connected with corruption are government control over the nation's resources, central planning, and monolithic political control, including a single political party, a government-controlled press, and lack of independent civil society organizations. These characteristics of socialist societies make them fertile ground for petty corruption and for the political elite to enjoy privileges few others have as uncontested rulers of the state. Following Klitgaard (1988), the level of corruption in a socialist society such as Cuba is high given the overwhelming monopoly power exercised by the state over the supply of goods and services, the free hand that government officials enjoy in making resource allocation decisions, and the very low degree of accountability of government officials for their actions, mediated by a controlled press and a ban on independent civil society organizations. The commodity rationing system that characterizes socialist societies provides a welcoming environment for myriad corrupt acts associated with the purchase, sale, and distribution of consumer goods.

From 1993 through 1996, under pressure from a deep economic crisis, Cuba enacted some measures that somewhat reduced government's control over the nation's resources and provided some space for private-sector economic activity, although not providing any space in the political arena. Since 1996 the Cuban government has undermined the economic liberalization measures, and by the end of 2005 Cuba had returned to a very high degree of economic centralization, bringing the tourism industry under closer state control, limiting self-employment, reversing foreign trade decentralization measures that allowed some enterprises to engage directly in importing and exporting, limiting the use of foreign currencies (dollars) in transactions between state enterprises, establishing foreign exchange controls, and banning the use and circulation of the U.S. dollar. At the same time that economic centralization returned, the government stepped up repression, harassing opponents of the regime and sentencing dissidents to prison terms.

Five

CORRUPTION IN
SOCIALIST CUBA

There is very little systematic information on the level or spread of corruption in socialist Cuba. This is not surprising, since corruption is extremely difficult to measure. Corruption is illegal everywhere, and therefore, participants in corrupt activities have an incentive to conceal their actions. In this sense, measuring corruption presents challenges similar to measuring unobserved economic activities that are illegal or verge on illegality, such as the informal, second, underground, or shadow economies.

A complicating factor is what is meant by "level" of corruption. Does it mean more frequent instances of corrupt behavior? Or corrupt behavior that affects larger amounts of goods or money? Or corrupt behavior that has the largest corrosive impact on the public trust or on the effectiveness of government? And in measuring the level of corruption, does it matter whether corrupt behavior is generalized and many participate in it or it is tightly controlled by an elite? Finally, are all acts of corruption—from "grease" payments to expedite administrative action to patronage abuses and to grand theft of government resources—all the same and therefore should be weighted equally when measuring the overall level of corruption, or are they different and should weights commensurate with their relative importance be used in arriving at an overall level of corruption (Johnston and Kpundeh 2002, 34)?

Several methods have been proposed in the literature to assess the extent or spread of corruption in a society: measuring the general or target-group perception concerning corruption; directly or indirectly measuring the incidence of corruption activities; using expert estimates about the level of corruption; and associating corruption with the absence of good governance or of economic freedom and inferring corruption level from these proxies (Hungarian Gallup Institute 1999; Johnston and Kpundeh 2002).

The population's general perception of corruption is shaped, to a large extent, by how frequently citizens are exposed to corrupt acts and by reports they hear from others about the occurrence of corruption. How the media report corruption also has a bearing on public perception. If the media are unbiased, the relative weight of corruption issues in media coverage should signal the relative importance of corruption within society at large. If the media are biased—either underreporting or overreporting incidents of corruption—the public's general perception of corruption may not reflect the actual occurrence of corruption in a society.

Cuba presents a particularly challenging case in this regard. As discussed in Chapter 4, the Cuban government has had a near-absolute monopoly over the island's media for more than forty-five years and thus has controlled the formation of public opinion. The regime's curtain of control over public opinion is pierced only by radio transmissions from abroad (by U.S. government-funded Radio Martí and by other radio and television stations from neighboring countries), but listening to foreign broadcasts is a punishable offense and Cuban citizens do it only surreptitiously. The reporting by independent journalists living on the island is essentially for consumption abroad, as none of the government-controlled news outlets in Cuba carries their work, although some trickles back in the form of transmissions from foreign radio stations or in foreign newspapers that enter the island. The March 2003 government crackdown on peaceful dissidents dealt a serious blow to the incipient independent journalism movement on the island but did not eliminate it.

The official Cuban press does report on corruption, but when it does so, it is at the direction of the government or the PCC and with a certain objective in mind. For example, in the mid-1980s, when President Castro was waging an ideological campaign (called the Rectification Process) to eliminate vestiges of market-oriented behavior and root out entrepreneurship and consumerism, he criticized corrupt government officials who were enriching themselves. At that time, the Cuban press carried numerous articles exposing petty corruption that had allowed some individuals to use government resources for their own gain. The intent of the reporting was to lend support to Castro's rhetoric and actions. On occasion, the Cuban press also has reported on high-visibility corruption cases (see below) involving individuals who have fallen into political disgrace. The Cuban press is silent, however, on the many perquisites and the special treatment enjoyed by the *nomenklatura*. Thus, official reporting underestimates corruption and is not a reliable indicator of the nature and extent of corruption on the island.

The foreign press is also biased, probably in the opposite direction, overemphasizing instances of corruption, abuse, and inequities on the island. Because reporting from independent journalists rarely filters back to Cuba and is mostly consumed abroad, it probably has very little influence in shaping the average Cuban citizen's perception of corruption. Bias also may seep into foreign correspondents' reporting because they tend to base their reporting on the frames of reference of their home countries and may implicitly impose on Cuba the higher standards of their own countries. In contrast, some foreign reporters might underplay instances of corruption in order not to displease the Cuban government to be allowed to continue reporting from the island.

One way in which the wall of secrecy concerning corrupt acts in Cuba has been pierced is through the accounts of defectors, particularly since the late 1980s. On a number of occasions it has been possible to ascertain the truthfulness of defectors' testimonies, as they tend to agree with each other. Through the accounts of defectors the world has learned of the connivance of officials at the highest levels of government, often with what appears to have been official sanction, in a plethora of corrupt activities tantamount to serious violations of international law. These reports have ranged from smuggling numerous products into Cuba to international narcotics trafficking to large-scale money laundering. The findings of judicial proceedings in the United States and other countries, and the reports of allegedly illicit international financial operations, as happened with a case involving a major Swiss bank, add credibility to defectors' allegations.

MEASURING CORRUPTION

Measuring the incidence of corruptive activities—not necessarily actual corruption, but attempts to carry out corrupt acts—centers on surveys of persons who potentially have bribed government officials or who have heard of incidents of corruption, or of government officials who may have been bribed. An example is the "victimization survey" in which respondents are asked if they have personally experienced or have heard of individuals who have experienced corruption. Sometimes assessments of perception are combined with reports of victimization. The World Bank Institute, for example, has developed a methodology whereby three parallel surveys—of households, public officials, and private enterprises—are conducted to assess governance and corruption perceptions from three different but interrelated perspectives. The responses to these surveys permit experts to infer the frequency of corruption in different types of transactions and to devise anticorruption programs. This method is unfeasible, as the government does not permit independent public opinion surveys to be taken on the island.

Another approach to measuring corruption relies on evaluations by experts. The most prominent and most cited example is the Corruption Perceptions Index (CPI) developed by Transparency International. The CPI is a synthetic measure that combines experts' evaluations of a country's incidence of corruption and capacity to combat corruption into a single metric. Not only does the CPI provide a measure of the level of corruption in a given country on a standardized scale, but its proponents also posit that it permits cross-country and, with some caveats, time-series comparisons. The CPI has the appeal of simplicity, providing a single metric that allows journalists to write catchy stories about which country is cleanest (least corrupt) or dirtiest (most corrupt), and presumably it can be used to assess how corruption rises or falls in a given country. CPI data have been used by social scientists in a number of quantitative corruption studies.

Still another approach, in some respects similar in methodology to the CPI, relies on interviews of relatively large numbers of business representatives to develop quantitative and qualitative indicators of the extent to which they are exposed to corrupt practices, including whether or not they are willing participants and how they react to such practices. The World Bank has pioneered some of these methodologies particularly to study corruption in transition and developing countries.

Finally, some analysts indirectly infer levels of corruption on the basis of the empirical finding that high levels of corruption are strongly correlated with weak institutions and poor governance or with the lack of economic freedom (Chafuen and Guzmán 2000; Vinod 1999). That is, the stronger the institutional base or the higher the level of economic freedom in a country, the lower the likelihood of encountering corrupt practices. The leading source of information on the quality of institutions is the set of governance indicators developed by the World Bank. With regard to economic freedom, the leading sources of information and analysis include the Heritage Foundation (in collaboration with the *Wall Street Journal*) and the Fraser Institute. Also relevant is the index of political rights and civil freedoms prepared annually by Freedom House.

In this chapter we attempt to provide a notion of the nature and extent of corruption in contemporary Cuba. We do this by culling examples of corrupt acts from the literature (official documents, the work of independent journalists residing on the island, the international press, defector tales, and academic studies) and by examining Cuba's performance in international measures of corruption, governance, and economic freedom developed by reputable organizations. We are aware of the limitations of this methodology, in that individual reports of corruption may represent exceptions to the rule rather than systemic problems; we recognize, too, that some of the international measures of corruption, governance, and economic freedom may be biased against the Cuban regime because of political animosity on the part of respondents. With these two caveats in mind, in what follows we provide our best estimates of the extent and nature of corruption in socialist Cuba.

PERCEPTIONS ABOUT CORRUPTION IN CUBA

As we discussed in Chapter 4, it stands to reason that corruption on the island would closely follow the patterns in other socialist, centrally planned economies whose ideologies and political and economic systems Cuba has emulated under Castro. Corrupt activities for which some concrete evidence can be found in the national or international media include misappropriation of state resources, misuse of office, and special perquisites extracted by the Cuban *nomenklatura*.

Misappropriation of State Resources

The Cuban state's overwhelming control over the island's resources and the shortage economy that prevails because the socialist model of organization is unable to generate sufficient volumes of goods to meet the demands of consumers and producers translates into ubiquitous black markets. There are black markets for food and consumer goods (including items under the rationing system), construction materials for home repairs, spare parts for appliances and motor vehicles, and so on. Periodically the state orchestrates large-scale police raids that snag some black-market operators and employees who misappropriate state property, but the practices are so generalized that enforcement activities have a very limited effect on them.

A chronic form of petty misappropriation of state resources is work absenteeism. As discussed in Chapter 4, one of the characteristics of socialist, centrally planned economies is overstaffing of state enterprises and the state bureaucracy in order to pursue full employment. A problem that plagues Cuba as well as other socialist countries and developing countries is workers on the government payroll who do not show up to work, take unauthorized leave during the day to pursue their own interests, or carry out unauthorized personal business while on the job. The cumulative impact of such absenteeism is very large given the large share of the labor force employed by the state sector and the lack of incentives for workers to perform on their jobs.

Misappropriation of state resources by government employees is perhaps the main source of goods traded on Cuban black markets. Although illegal, it is widely practiced, and there is no stigma attached to it. An interviewee reported to sociologist Clark (1990, 296) that "the majority of the people believe that stealing from one's employer, the state, is not a crime." In Garve (2001) a common Cuban worker explains, "Here, one has to steal to survive. The system itself forces you to do it. They are opening new dollar stores all the time. They sell everything in dollars." Despite periodic crackdowns and heavy sentences imposed on black marketeers and their suppliers, these illegal markets have remained important sources of consumer and industrial goods and services. Because prices in the black market are substantially higher than in official markets, there is a significant incentive for black marketeers to ply their trade and for corrupt government officials to provide goods to supply this market. Misappropriation of government resources takes different forms.

THEFT

This is the crudest form of misappropriation and probably the source of most products that enter the black market, such as food, tools, construction materials, and spare parts for domestic electronic appliances and automobiles. The example below, related to the expansion of self-employment in the mid-1990s, illustrates the nature and importance of theft of government resources.

As discussed earlier, pursuant to legislation adopted in September and October 1993, Cuba authorized self-employment in about 120 occupations. The number of self-employed workers increased rapidly thereafter, reaching nearly 209,000 persons in December 1995. Particularly impressive was the growth of home restaurants, called *paladares,* that sprang up throughout the island—an estimated 1,000 to 2,000 such restaurants in Havana alone and 4,000 nationwide. Since markets for intermediate products either do not exist or are very limited, self-employed workers generally obtain inputs from the black market, which in turn is largely fed by theft from the state sector:

> Cuba has no wholesale distributors. The Cuban government has not opened up supply markets. Intermediaries are not only illegal, but unwanted. . . . When Jorge [a self-employed shoemaker] is asked about where he has been buying the little equipment he uses to work, he answers coyly, "little by little I have been collecting it," but his smile seems to say, "Why are you asking such a dumb question?" And it is, in fact, a silly question. Everybody knows that there are no free markets for any of the instruments used by Jorge; nor are there supplies for most of the products the artisans make. They either take them from their workplaces (in other words, steal them) or they buy them in the black market. Where do the products in the black market come from? From other workers who do the same thing. Everyone has to steal in Cuba for survival. (Jatar-Hausmann 1999, 108–109)

An attorney for a cigar factory in Havana described the magnitude of the workplace theft problem in mid-2002 as follows: "Faced with shortages of food and basic consumer products, workers steal from the workplaces where something is made in order to ease their needs. It doesn't matter what is produced at the factory or the workshop. The important thing is *resolver* [to get by, to solve] today's food problem. Tomorrow is another day, and we'll see what to do" (in Gálvez 2002). Henken (2003, 354) has concluded, "By and large, Cubans do not go to work in state jobs out of a sense of revolutionary obligation or loyalty (*conciencia*) or moral incentives, and much less for any material incentives. They work in state jobs because such a job provides them with access to state goods that can be 'liberated' and resold on black markets."

The following are recent examples of theft of government resources documented by the official and independent press:

- Theft of high-quality rum by workers at the Havana Club rum factory in Santa Cruz del Norte for sale in the black market was detected by agents of the Special Protection Service. Among the creative techniques for stealing the rum discovered by the special agents were a truck used for delivery of products to the factory that had been fitted with a hidden tank with capacity of 260 liters of rum; a hoe that a worker brought in and out each day whose

handle had been hollowed to carry 6 liters of rum per day or
144 liters per month; containers concealed in a wheelbarrow; fake
oxygen tanks used by welders; auto batteries; a bicycle tire that a
worker carried around his waist under his clothes; and condoms
("Revelan" 2003).

- In Güines, Province of La Habana, law enforcement authorities
  arrested nineteen managers of state cafeterias and a high-ranking
  official of the municipal restaurant agency for their involvement in
  a scheme to steal eggs, rum, and bottled beer to sell on the black
  market (Izquierdo 2003).
- In Los Palacios, Pinar del Río Province, two members of the
  Municipal Committee of the Communist Party were arrested and
  expelled from the party. The first, employed by a transportation
  company, stole beer for sale on the black market. The second, employed in a restaurant, stole food items for the same purpose.
  The two thieves were turned in by a disgruntled former employee
  who used to transport the stolen goods to the black marketeers. In
  searches carried out in Los Palacios, the police also found airplane
  fuel stolen from the local airport by two pilots and other airport
  workers ("Escándalo" 2003).
- Law enforcement agencies broke up a ring of about eighty individuals in Camagüey Province who stole cattle from state feeding
  lots, slaughtered them, and sold the meat on the black market. The
  ring included several state officials. The illegal activities started with
  butchers from government packing houses who slaughtered the
  stolen cattle in the field; the meat was then stored in government-
  owned refrigerated warehouses, transported to Varadero or Havana
  in refrigerated government trucks, and sold in large quantities to
  tourism hotels. All of the transactions were conducted in dollars. The thieves were so well organized that they even demanded
  receipts from the tourism hotels that purchased the black-market
  meat (Morán 2002).
- Four workers were dismissed from a cigarette factory in Ranchuelo,
  Villa Clara Province, and charged with stealing cigarette paper from
  the plant. Cigarette paper is highly sought by artisan cigarette makers who sell their product—called *tupamaros*—in the black market
  (Reyes Gutiérrez 2005a, 2005b).
- Interior Ministry officials arrested a ring composed of several dozen
  workers of the pharmaceutical industry—production line operators, technicians, managers, warehouse and transportation workers,

hospital and retail pharmacy employees, security guards—who operated a sophisticated scheme whereby they stole pharmaceuticals for sale on the black market and even produced bogus medicines from stolen raw materials (Alfonso 2005a).

SHORT-CHANGING CUSTOMERS

The chronic shortage of consumer goods and the lack of markets for intermediate products (raw materials, inputs, supplies) mean that government officials who control the supply of consumer or intermediate goods are well placed to benefit personally from their positions. Workers in the state distribution sector often skim a portion of the goods they sell to consumers for their own use or to sell on the black market. For example, restaurant employees might decrease the size of portions they serve, bartenders might skimp on liquor in a mixed drink, or butchers might snip an ounce or two of meat from each customer to sell on the black market. So ubiquitous and accepted is this practice that it is known in the island as a fine (*multa*) imposed on consumers. Independent journalist Lázaro González (2002) reports that the multitude of miniscule thefts add up to large losses:

> Cuban consumers must always be ready to be pinched. You can be sold a tube of toothpaste inflated with air or a ham and cheese sandwich without ham. The most typical and generalized situation is not that the tube is empty or the sandwich is without ham altogether but rather that the tube is missing a little of the toothpaste and the sandwich a few grams of protein. The problem with this example—or with the million of examples that occur every day—is that these little bits are missing from nearly all products sold on the island. . . . The worst is that society accepts this situation as the norm. There is collective acceptance that the kilogram has 900 grams, the pound 13 ounces and the liter 920 milliliters.

Another common form of cheating occurs when state workers impose a "fine" on consumers by charging higher prices for goods than authorized and pocket the difference. Corporación Cimex, perhaps the largest operator of dollar stores on the island, has vowed to root out overpricing in its nearly 1,300 retail outlets. A Cimex official is quoted as saying that "fining" customers (*multando al cliente*), that is, charging higher prices for products or services rendered, "continues to be the sick obsession of a few *mala-cabezas* [rotten apples] in our dollar retail stores throughout the country.

And such conduct reflects poorly on the image of our corporation. It brings about lack of confidence, lack of prestige and lack of security in our stores" (cited in Castellanos 2002). This practice also manifests itself in the transportation sector. For example, an individual traveling from Santa Clara to Havana without a reservation on a high-demand train was able to secure a seat by paying the conductor two and one-half times the normal fare of ten pesos; the traveler observed that the employees of the train worked as a team in carrying out the illicit activity, allowing on board only those passengers willing to pay the higher price (Maseda 2003a). The condition of the public transportation system in Havana is so poor and the service so unreliable that bus riders are regularly being charged one peso per ride while the official rate is forty centavos. In one documented instance passengers were charged five pesos for a ride to Alamar because no other transportation was available (Pesant 2004).

Since 1999 the National Association of Cuban Economists and Accountants has conducted an annual exercise whereby some percentage of retail outlets are inspected to ensure compliance with pricing regulations. From 1999 through 2001 a total of 36,000 unannounced inspections were carried out, of which 42 percent revealed violations in the form of "fines" imposed on consumers through higher prices and other irregularities (López 2002). These problems continued unabated in 2002. The Ministry of Finance and Prices reported that 55 percent of the inspections of enterprises and establishments that it conducted in 2002 revealed violations of pricing regulations (López 2003). The leading violations in 2002 were failing to post prices in an area visible to the customers, altering weight scales (always to the detriment of consumers), mislabeling products offered for sale to indicate higher quality, and offering products for sale after the last date they were slated to be sold (Maseda 2003b). According to official sources, 16,000 cases of violations of rules by employees of state enterprises primarily in the areas of public health, food preparation and sale, and tourism were prosecuted in 2002 to 2004; the violations ranged from illegal sale of goods and services to padding of budgets and improper use of bank accounts ("La Fiscalía" 2005).

Tourists who are not familiar with the ways and means of the Cuban economy are particularly vulnerable to price overcharging. One common scam occurs in cafeterias that sell at prices set in domestic currency. Often, operators of such cafeterias charge tourists the price in foreign currency; for example, a cup of coffee that sells for one peso is sold to a tourist for a dollar, about twenty-six times the peso price, with the employee pocketing the difference (Díaz-Marzo 2002). At the Villa Tortuga Gret Resort in

Varadero, investigators found that corrupt managers overcharged tourists about US$7,000 for lodging and other expenses (Linares 2001).

DIVERSION OF STATE RESOURCES

Another form of misappropriation of state resources common in Cuba is through diversion (*desvío*). The objective of the diversion is typically personal gain for the government official, to the detriment of the activity for which the resource was intended. Examples follow.

- The manager of an *acopio* center might understate the quantity of a certain item that is procured from farmers and divert the difference for personal use or for sale in black markets.
- A trucker delivering certain products might drop off additional amounts in certain stores in cahoots with the store keepers to be sold under the table.
- The manager of a store might report a higher percentage of goods damaged in transit or spoiled and divert the difference for personal use.
- The manager of an enterprise might divert construction materials from his workplace to build or repair his own home or that of family and friends.

And the following two examples are gleaned from the independent press:

- The manager of the Antonio Guiteras sugar mill in Puerto Padre, Las Tunas Province, used construction materials from the mill to build a pen in the back of his residence to raise pigs; reportedly, the quality of the construction of the pigpen was superior to that of many of the homes of workers at the Antonio Guiteras mill (Hernández 2002).
- A radio transmitter and eight receivers destined for the ambulance service of a province to establish links between mobile units and hospitals were instead diverted for the use of high-level public health officials; the receivers were installed in the autos used by the head of the public health service of the province and his immediate subordinates ("Desvío" 2002).

Another common form of diversion is the use of government vehicles or equipment for personal use. For example, a high-level local government official in Aguada de Pasajeros, Cienfuegos Province, who was assigned a government car to perform his official duties was turned in to law enforcement authorities by a citizen who accused the official of turning down an (illegal) offer of ten pesos for a ride to Havana; according to the report, the government official demanded twenty pesos for a ride in his state-owned car (Medina 2001). Another example involves two passenger vehicles and a microbus donated by the Spanish region of Utrera to the municipality of Consolación del Sur, Pinar del Río Province. These vehicles, intended to be used to transport patients from the towns of Alonso de Rojas and Herradura to the city of Pinar del Río for dialysis treatments, were diverted by municipal employees for their own use and for that of the local government and party (Arroyo 2002).

Although somewhat dated, the classic example of diversion of state resources for personal use was given by an unimpeachable source, President Castro himself, in a speech in 1987:

> We know about the problems caused by *desviaciones* [diversions of state property]. Not too long ago I was visiting a certain zone of the country, taking a look at some problems related to the economy. I found a crane in the area. A person was putting a cement roof on a house and had gathered a sixteen-ton Kato crane, made in Japan, a Japanese concrete mixer, a truck to carry the cement mixer, and a tank truck, all property of the state. He had bought a pig, beer, etc., for those who were helping him. The three trucks came from different enterprises. . . . As I was telling this story to the head of the Central Planning Board, he tells me: "On Sunday I found a crane doing the same thing, but it was a forty-ton crane." (Castro 1987, 4)

Misuse of Government Office

The extremely high concentration of resources in the state sector, the centralized nature of decision making, the very general nature of laws, and the lack of means to contest arbitrary enforcement actions place a great deal of power in the hands of government officials and hence create ample opportunities for corruption. A generalized form of misuse of government office associated with favoring family and friends generally is referred to as *sociolismo*. Paying bribes as a way to influence a government official is commonplace; bribes are also common as a means to persuade government officials to turn a blind eye toward illegal behavior. Finally, the dollar-related areas of the economy, particularly tourism, have become a magnet for corruption, and several high-visibility cases of corruption have been reported by the official press.

SOCIOLISMO

Corruption in socialist Cuba sometimes takes the form of a generalized "I'll scratch your back if you'll scratch mine" system that rewards friends and family of government officials; this is known as *sociolismo,* a take-off on *socio* (buddy) and *socialismo.* General Prosecutor of the Republic Ramón de la Cruz Ochoa told a journalist in 1991 that Cuba's corruption problem was *sociolismo organizado,* "sometimes used to solve enterprise problems and other times to solve personal problems. These corrupt practices tend to build on each other and bring about a lack of respect for rules and laws" (Carrasco 1991, 27).

In a provocative book about Cuban politics and culture, Fernández (2000) analyzes informal relationships in the Cuban economy and society. He uses the term *lo informal* to refer to patterns of behavior that break the rules and challenge the establishment's emphasis on hierarchy, collective harmony, and regulations. *Lo informal* is based on *simpatía* (likability), *confianza* (familiarity that leads to trust), and *ser buena gente* (being a nice person).

> *Lo informal* is composed of groups of individuals who know and like each other, the networks of affection through which the politics of affection are manifested. These groups bring together peers, superiors, and subordinates. . . . Informality depends on the possibility of bending the rules and bypassing legal norms. . . . Its capacity to rationalize each and every action on the basis that what is most important is to satisfy one's needs and those of our loved ones seems infinite. Precisely because of its immense capacity to justify what could be considered self-serving, the normative foundation of informal behavior usually suffers from civic myopia; it fails to see what is beyond the networks of affection and disregards in the process the significance of institutions for the common good. (Fernández 2000, 29–30)

Participation in *lo informal* "socializes individuals in a culture of illegality. It accustoms them to break the law" (Fernández 2000, 32) and fosters corruption.

BRIBES

A common form of corruption is for government officials to take bribes
in return for conferring benefits. The following examples of bribes are
documented in the recent literature.

- Cuban citizens who do not have access to the dollar-denominated
  health system often must make "gifts" to physicians to get medical
  care or access to scarce medications; in some instances, admission to
  a hospital requires payment of a bribe ("Crisis en la salud" 2003).
- At the Manuel Piti Fajardo Hospital in the municipality of Plaza
  in greater Havana, at least twenty doctors were dismissed and had
  their degrees revoked because they were found selling certificates
  prescribing special diets for diabetics (persons under medically prescribed special diets can qualify for extra rations under the rationing
  system); there are also reports of employees of medical laboratories
  receiving payments for false laboratory reports that would justify
  special diets (Pedroso 2002).
- Musicians regularly pay bribes to government officials and booking
  agents to be able to perform at locations where they can earn
  convertible currency (Cancio Isla 2001).
- In Pinar del Río, meter readers working for the Union of Electric
  Enterprises overlooked illegal electric intakes and rigged electric
  meters in return for the payment of bribes ("Robo" 2002).

Fidel Castro, in an address at the end of 2002 to foreign students enrolled
in the Latin American Medical Sciences School, acknowledged corruption
problems in general and in the medical services sector in particular.

> We know a lot of things. Don't believe for a minute that we do
> not know about some of the things that have been going on. The
> Special Period brought upon us shortages of many products . . .
> one person would say to another: "I will get this item for you if you
> take care of this other problem that I have, if you bring me a gift."
> We hope that the awareness of our workers, and particularly of our
> physicians, will make them reject from the bottom of their soul the
> entreaties of mercenaries who seek to corrupt our physicians, our
> health care workers, and those who will want to get under-
> the-table payments for providing a dental or eye consultation or
> some other service. (Castro 2002a)

An analyst who conducted field research on the island found that "all manner of illegalities, low-level corruption, and bribery are commonplace within the private, self-employed sector" (Henken 2003, 350). Thus, Henken writes,

> because the law is often unclear, inspectors have broad power to interpret and apply it arbitrarily. Interviews with private renters [of rooms in private homes to international tourists] indicate that the threat of fines and even closure is often used by inspectors to elicit bribes. Field studies among private entrepreneurs in Havana have found that very few feel that they have any input in the decisions that affect their livelihoods and that the appeal process for contesting an unjust fine is a sham. . . . These perceptions are likely to increase a homeowner's propensity to pay bribes, since one may conclude that there is no other effective recourse. (ibid., 11)

Some large-scale *paladares* tend to be egregious lawbreakers, not only exceeding the legal maximum of twelve diners at a given time, but also violating the ban on employment of third parties—that is, people who are not family members—as cooks, servers, security personnel, entertainers and musicians, taxi drivers, and so forth. The owners do this through "special arrangements with the inspector corps" in the form of bribes (Henken 2002b, 15). Clandestine *paladares* are particularly vulnerable because the better-known they become, the more likely their unlawful operation will be detected by authorities, resulting in more and higher bribes, blackmail, or outright closure (Henken 2003, 350). Successful *paladar* owners contend that "their success derives from their ability to corrupt low-level police officers and inspectors" (Henken 2003, 354).

MISUSE OF OFFICE AND THE DOLLAR ECONOMY

The very visible rise in corruption associated with misuse of office and bribe-taking associated with the international tourism industry and other sectors of the economy that operate with foreign currencies has triggered steps within the Cuban government and the Cuban Communist Party to address the most blatant excesses. According to the Cuban press in 1998, the Cuban Communist Party conducted 1,159 investigations, including allegations of "diversion and misuse of state resources" (439 investigations), "lack of economic controls, irregularities and lax management" (247), and "social conduct unbecoming of a Party militant" (170); these investigations resulted in sanctions for corruption against 1,500 party members

(Rousseau 1999). According to another source, in 1998 the Cuban Communist Party reportedly received 21,828 complaints regarding misappropriation of public goods, lack of management controls, abuse of power, and conduct unbecoming a party member; 77 percent of the complaints were at least partly justified (Tamayo 1999a).

Since employment opportunities are not advertised anywhere, the lack of labor-market information encourages corruption and arbitrariness in hiring (Pumar 1996, 107). There are numerous reports of government officials "selling" jobs that provide workers with access to hard currencies. Unemployed tourism workers in Ciego de Avila, affected by the closing of the Tryp Cayo Coco hotel, complained about not being able to land jobs in other tourism facilities under construction because of the corruption and *sociolismo* that prevailed in the hiring agency (Cruz Lima 1997). Independent journalists reported that in 2001 officials of the Ministry of Tourism were demanding US$500 to US$800 from job seekers trying to secure jobs as taxi drivers, hotel bellboys, front-desk employees, or hotel security officers ("Empleos" 2001). Two military officers in Trinidad subjected tourism taxi drivers to very rigorous inspections and evaluations with the intent of firing them and selling their slots, in dollars, to other prospective drivers ("Two military" 1997).

Officials of several government entities and of *sociedades anónimas* (S.A.'s), similar to limited-liability corporations in other legal systems, operating in the dollar economy have been implicated in corrupt activities and either removed from their jobs or arrested. The tourism industry has been the focus of several high-profile investigations and dismissals, but corruption has also plagued other sectors of the economy.

- In 1995, Abraham Maciques, at the time president of tourism enterprise Cubanacán S.A., was dismissed in the midst of a US$20 million corruption scandal (Amuchástegui 2000a; Tamayo 1999b).
- In June 1999 Andrés Soberón, head of the hotel division of Cubanacán S.A., and several executives of Rumbos, an enterprise that operates tourism facilities such as golf courses and cafeterias and provides other services, were dismissed; among them was María Elena García, wife of then-Minister of Foreign Relations Roberto Robaina (Tamayo 1999b).
- In what may have been a related development, in late August 1999 the Cuban media reported that Minister of Tourism Osmany Cienfuegos had been replaced by former Minister for Foreign Investment and Economic Cooperation Ibrahim Ferradaz ("Council of

State" 1999). Cienfuegos reportedly was involved in an Internet prostitution ring run by a Mexican company (Bardach 2002, 281).

- In December 2003 Juan José Vega, president of Cubanacán S.A., was dismissed and reportedly held under house arrest on suspicion of corruption. Allegedly, millions of dollars were missing from the hotel, restaurant, and travel agency operations of Cubanacán ("Top Cuban" 2003). Vega reportedly also had a credit card given to him by entrepreneur Enrique Martiñón, the head of Spanish hotel chain Sol Melía and a significant investor in the island ("Raúl Castro supervisa" 2004). The Cuban government subsequently confirmed that in addition to Vega, the directors of two non-hotel divisions of Cubanacán and of a subsidiary had been dismissed, but they denied that the dismissals had to do with corruption, claiming instead that they were related to management errors and laxities ("Nota Informativa" 2003).

- Also in December 2003 it was reported that the hotel chain Horizontes had been dissolved because of "serious administrative problems," and its activities were to be taken over by hotel chains Islazul and Gran Caribe (Alfonso 2003).

- In February 2004 Tourism Minister Ibrahim Ferradaz was dismissed from his post and replaced by a young colonel, Manuel Marrero, who had formerly managed Gaviota S.A., the tourism arm of the armed forces (San Martin 2004a; "Toma control" 2004). According to press reports, Marrero's mandate was to root out corruption and reorganize the tourism sector ("Más control" 2004; "El Ministro" 2004). Vice President Raúl Castro reportedly assumed more direct control over the tourism industry, centralizing decision making and presumably reducing opportunities for corruption among managers (Alfonso 2004; Rivero 2004).

- Also in February 2004 several high-level officials of conglomerate Corporación Cimex S.A. were dismissed for involvement in a financial scandal centered on the duty-free shops in Cuban airports operated by Cimex in conjunction with foreign corporations (Cancio Isla 2004a, 2004b).

Reports of high-profile corruption in other sectors of the economy include the following examples.

- In 2003, audits of "dollar stores" revealed widespread financial irregularities, including understating inventories, theft, overpricing items, and conducting sales off the books. Among the implicated stores were those run by the chain TRD Caribe, part of the Minis try of the Armed Forces. The audits resulted in the replacement of management officials at different levels (Cancio Isla 2004d).

- In March 2001 Minister of the Fishing Industry Orlando Rodrí-guez Romay was dismissed as a result of allegations of corruption in his ministry. An investigation cleared the minister but not his two brothers, who were also high-ranking ministry officials (Frank 2001).
- Three top officials at the Hermanos Ameijeiras Hospital, run by the PCC, whose services are only available to party members and foreigners able to pay with hard currency, were dismissed in mid-1999 because of allegations of corruption and of misuse of foreign currencies (Tamayo 1999a).
- Allegations of corruption and excessive travels abroad to meet with foreign capitalists surfaced with regard to the dismissal in July 1999 of Dr. Manuel Limonta, long-term head of the Center for Genetic Engineering and Biotechnology (Centro de Ingeniería Genética y Biotecnología), one of Fidel Castro's pet science and technology projects ("Cuba ridicules" 1999; Tamayo 2000).
- A Canadian investor stated that three Cuban civil aviation officials took a US$200,000 bribe from a Canadian firm involved in an airport construction project and subsequently defected in Ottawa (Tamayo 1999a).
- An army colonel controls an attractive multistory apartment build-ing where he lives in a plush penthouse unit, close to the American Embassy in Havana. The apartments are rented to foreigners in dollars, and the colonel pockets the payments. Before the building was renovated, its Cuban former residents, lacking high-level connections, were evicted despite the country's severe housing shortage (Latell 2005, 242–243).

Privileges and Abuses of Power by the Ruling Elite

As in the former Soviet Union and other socialist countries, Cuba has a system of special privileges for members of the *nomenklatura,* whose mem-bers are referred to on the island as *pinchos, pinchos grandes,* or *mayimbes.* These perquisites, which are not available to the general public, include total or partial exemption from the rationing system, the ability to obtain

imported food and other consumer goods, good housing (including vacation homes), use of government vehicles, access to special hospitals and
imported medications, admission to special schools for their children (the
so-called *hijos de papá*), and the ability to travel abroad, to name a few.

PERCEPTION OF PRIVILEGES AND ABUSES OF POWER

Seminal work by Clark (1990, 1999) based on interviews with émigrés has
documented the Cuban population's perceptions regarding corruption on
the island. Surveys conducted in 1971 and 1986 revealed a high degree of
awareness of the special privileges enjoyed by the elite. In the 1971 survey,
nearly 90 percent of respondents indicated that the ruling elite enjoyed
privileges; when questioned about the group or groups that received such
privileges and the degree of privilege, the respondents overwhelmingly
(86 percent) indicated that the *comandantes* and the top leaders of the PCC
and of the government received the highest degree of privileges, followed
by top leaders of the armed forces (Clark 1990, 439). In the 1986 survey,
97 percent of the respondents indicated that there were privileged groups
in Cuba; 80 percent of the respondents identified top government officials and PCC leaders as the main recipients of such special treatment,
followed by top leaders of the armed forces and top administrators (ibid.,
439–440).

Subsequent interviews of émigrés conducted by Clark (1999, 222)
identified a new privileged group: individuals who interact with foreign
investors, particularly foreign investors in the tourism sector, and who
have access to hard currency. Interestingly, this new group is not necessarily composed of top party or government officials; their privileges and
opportunities for abuses of power relate to their contacts with foreigners
and access to hard currency.

DOCUMENTED CASES OF ABUSE OF POWER

Abuses of power and perquisites by the ruling elite can be traced back to
the early years of the Revolution. In the mid-1960s, Fidel Castro led a
drive against privileges and extravagant lifestyles he dismissively referred to
as *la dolce vita*. Glimpses of the excesses of some members of the ruling elite
during this period—control over several residences, access to imported
automobiles, high living on government expense accounts, purchases of
foods and other imported luxury goods, heavy drinking and partying—
are documented in the work of eyewitness Llovio Menéndez (1988).

Comandante Efigenio Ameijeiras, one of Castro's early associates who
participated in the 1956 expedition from Mexico aboard the *Granma,* was

stripped of his military rank and removed from his position as deputy minister of the armed forces in March 1966 because of "irresponsible" conduct and abuse of power; Ameijeiras was accused of using his position to protect friends and to facilitate their access to power (Domínguez 1978, 230–231). Interestingly, after many years of relative anonymity, Ameijeiras was reinstated to the rank of brigadier general and recognized as a Hero of the Republic in 2001 for his participation in repelling the Bay of Pigs invasion in 1961.

The first member of the Cuban *nomenklatura* to be publicly accused of abuse of power, dismissed from his official duties, and sent to prison was Luis Orlando Domínguez. In June 1987, when his case was made public, Domínguez was president of the Cuban Institute of Civil Aeronautics (Instituto de Aeronaútica Civil de Cuba, IACC); prior to this, he had been first secretary of the Union of Communist Youth (Unión de Jóvenes Comunistas, UJC) and a member of Fidel Castro's personal staff. President Castro himself appeared on national television to present the bill of particulars indicting Domínguez: renovations made at the home of Domínguez' relatives with work crews from the Ministry of Construction; use of government resources in renovating Domínguez' home (which Castro referred to as a "Garden of Eden," occupying an entire city block in a Havana suburb); failure on the part of Domínguez to follow rules to obtain permits to perform home repairs; and importation of goods for personal use using hard currency to which he had access through his official position. A more in-depth investigation carried out after Domínguez' dismissal revealed further irregularities:

- Purchase of automobiles (in hard currency) for the use of his family using public funds;
- Travel to Panama by one of his subordinates to purchase imported goods such as electronic equipment, ceramic tiles, outboard marine engines, and other goods for Domínguez' use;
- Very large cash holdings, both in pesos and in foreign currencies.

The investigation further revealed that Domínguez embezzled funds the UJC had set aside for a program to encourage youth camping. The prosecution accused Domínguez of embezzlement, abuse in the exercise of his position, improper use of public resources, abuse of authority, and forgery of public documents and sought the maximum sentence of twenty years in prison.

The 1989 trial of General Arnaldo Ochoa and several high-level accomplices for drug trafficking and other offenses brought into the open
evidence of the privileges enjoyed by the ruling elite and how this group
used its power for private benefit. The Cuban government's official version
of the case (*Causa 1/89* 1989) is peppered with references to black-market
activities, misappropriation of funds, purchases of imported items for personal use, and "gifts" given and received.

Carlos Aldana, the PCC's chief of ideology and foreign affairs and at
the time reportedly the third person in the Cuban hierarchy after Fidel
and Raúl Castro, was unceremoniously sacked in October 1992. Allegations against Aldana of improper behavior centered on his relationship with foreign businessman Eberto López Morales, director of Aero-
visuales Caribbean S.A. López Morales was accused of violating tax, customs, and currency laws; Aldana reportedly protected López Morales and
accepted gifts from him of electronic equipment, cash, and use of a credit
card ("Aldana-linked" 1993).

Roberto Robaina González, a former president of the Federation of
University Students and first secretary of the UJC, was dismissed as foreign
minister in 1999 and subsequently expelled from the Cuban Communist
Party. Robaina's double dismissal was reportedly connected to his relationship with foreign businessmen and the acceptance of gifts of furniture for
his home from foreign contacts. Allegedly he also had a close relationship
with, and accepted money from, Mario Villanueva Madrid, former governor of the Mexican state of Quintana Roo, accused in Mexico of having
links with the Juárez drug cartel ("Cuba's Communist Party" 1999).

Several leaders of the Union of Communist Youth were dismissed from
their posts in early 2005. They were found to be appropriating funds for
personal use that were intended to promote the so-called Battle of Ideas,
an ideological program intended to demonstrate the superiority of Cuban
socialism over capitalism and democracy. The dismissed leaders were accused of embezzling public funds and using a dozen state-owned automobiles for their private use (Alfonso 2005b).

The corruption charges against Ochoa, Aldana, Robaina, and other
members of the elite were pursued, at least partially, for political reasons.
The real or perceived lack of political loyalty by these officials prompted
their dismissals from the key posts they held and the corruption charges
against them. This suggests that probably countless other cases go unreported of abuse of power and privileges by government officials who
remain loyal to the regime.

NEPOTISM

Nepotism is a factor in attaining leadership positions and joining the Cuban *nomenklatura*. Fidel Castro's brother Raúl is minister of the armed forces, first vice-secretary of the PCC, and first vice-president of the Council of Ministers and of the Council of State, giving the two Castro brothers inter-locking roles in top party, state, military, and executive echelons. Another Castro brother, Ramón, has been the manager of important agricultural projects and a major force behind the country's agricultural policy. Vilma Espín, Raúl Castro's wife, has been the head of the Federation of Cuban Women (Federación de Mujeres Cubanas, FMC) since 1959 and a member of the Political Bureau of the PCC. Fidel Castro's son Fidel Castro Díaz-Balart was the executive secretary of the Cuban Nuclear Energy Commission until 1992, when he was dismissed. Luis Alberto Rodríguez López-Calleja, married to Fidel Castro's niece (Raúl Castro's daughter Deborah), is the director-general of a very large business enterprise controlled by the armed forces, as discussed below (Alfonso 2002b, 2002c; Fogel 2003). Marcos Portal León, minister of Basic Industry, member of the Council of State, and member of the Political Bureau of the PCC, is married to one of Fidel Castro's nieces. Portal was dismissed from his ministerial post in October 2004 for what the government called mismanagement that led to a crippling energy crisis (San Martin 2004b). José Antonio Fraga Castro, another nephew of the Castro brothers, is the head of the Grupo Empre-sarial de Laboratorios Farmacéuticos (Labiofam), an important biotech-nology enterprise ("Bajo el ala" 2001).

Numerous instances of nepotism practiced by the *nomenklatura* have been documented, including a new variant whereby *nomenklatura* mem-bers secure business or schooling opportunities abroad for their children in anticipation of regime change. Montaner (2000, 210) explains that

> these government officials capitalize on their contacts with foreign visitors and their access to the national patrimony. One of the high-est-ranking revolutionary leaders sent paintings valued at more than one-half million dollars out of the island and used the money to set up a restaurant for a son in Europe. Others find scholarships for their children or jobs in companies that have commercial relations with the island. Plain influence peddling. The children leave the island with valuable books or artworks in their suitcases that they later sell to foreigners. Sometimes, since they have access to dollars, they "buy" a foreign destination for their children. For eight or ten

thousand dollars they are able to get an Italian or a Spanish citizen with the right connections to provide their son or daughter with a job or the opportunity to enroll in a foreign university to pursue a mysterious "master's" degree. In some instances, in a clear case of corruption, the foreign lover of a daughter and future lifeline for the family is rewarded with a consultancy paid in dollars by the Cuban state.

Alfonso (2002c) gives the following examples of entrepreneurship in foreign countries being practiced by children of the Cuban *nomenklatura*.

- Javier Leal, son of Eusebio Leal Spengler, historian of the city of Havana and head of the commercial enterprise Habaguanex, owns a shop specializing in Cuban art and antiques in Barcelona, Spain.
- Juan Antonio Almeida and Juan Juan Almeida, sons of General Juan Almeida, are businessmen living abroad. Juan Antonio operates a restaurant in Madrid and Juan Juan is a businessman in Cancún, Mexico.
- Lourdes Argivaes, former wife of Che Guevara's son Ernesto Guevara March and niece of deceased Castro confidante Celia Sánchez Manduley, operates a restaurant in Marbella, Spain.
- Ramón Castro, grandson of Fidel's and Raúl's brother Ramón, manages a restaurant in Tenerife, Canary Islands, reportedly owned by his great-uncle Raúl Castro.

Numerous relatives of members of the *nomenklatura*, including close relatives of Fidel Castro, reside abroad and study in foreign universities.

Many former officials of the Ministry of State Security and relatives of *nomenklatura* members have been placed by the Cuban government into highly sought jobs abroad. These jobs result in salaries that are many-fold higher than those earned in Cuba. Even if these workers are forced to turn over a significant (in some cases fifty percent) of their salaries to the Cuban government, they are nevertheless much better off than if they stayed on the island. In mid-2002 the enterprise Cubatécnica had placed approximately four hundred handpicked professionals in jobs in Mexico, Panama, Chile, Venezuela, Italy, Canada, and France (Tamayo 2002).

Some of the entrepreneurial activities by children of the *nomenklatura* and their associates have created controversy. Mexican authorities discovered in December 2003 a network based in Cancún, headed by Juan Juan Almeida, that sold real and counterfeit Cuban passports and Mexican visas to Cuban women and men intending to travel to Mexico to engage in prostitution; other children of *nomenklatura* members were supposedly also involved in the network (Montaner 2003). And Dashiel Torralba, a former girlfriend of Fidel Castro's son Antonio, told reporters of the U.S.-based Univisión TV network that she was involved in selling exit visas to Cubans who wanted to emigrate to Spain; when questioned by Cuban authorities, she told them that Castro's son was her accomplice and that they had earned US$30,000 from visa sales. According to Ms. Torralba, the case against her was dropped by Cuban authorities when they learned that Antonio Castro was involved ("Piden a España" 2002).

"Spontaneous" Privatization

Although the Cuban leadership has stated unequivocally that it will not stray from the path of socialism and privatization is out of the question,[1] the latter is in fact already occurring through a process similar to the one that preceded the transitions in Central and Eastern Europe and the republics of the former Soviet Union and has been deemed "the very essence of corruption, being the outright theft of public assets by politicians and/or enterprise directors associated with the *nomenklatura*" (Kaufmann and Siegelbaum 1997, 439).

The Cuban leadership has spawned a new class of "Cuban entrepreneurs," composed of PCC officials, current or past members of the armed forces, and sons, daughters, and other relatives of Cuban *nomenklatura* members. They have already appropriated state assets through a sort of "spontaneous privatization," transferring state property through the paper reorganization of state-owned enterprises into "private" corporations of which the *nomenklatura* members are owners or directors. The "owners" and managers of the *sociedades anónimas* are predominantly high-level military officers and PCC officials (Alfonso 1999b).

The rise of this new "capitalist" class is full of ironies. Ramiro Valdés, a participant in the 1953 attack on the Moncada Barracks, a member of the expeditionary force led by Fidel Castro that landed in Cuba in 1956 aboard the *Granma,* a *comandante* in the rebel army, and a feared former minister of Interior, is the head of the Grupo de la Electrónica, a holding group that controls the production, sale, and imports of electronic products and services and of computer hardware and software. Valdés reportedly lives in Cuba in luxury and travels frequently to Spain, where he stays in first-class hotels, dines in "five-fork" restaurants, and has purchased expensive properties, including a large farm in Asturias ("Un señorito" 1999).

Víctor Bordón, a guerrilla leader in Las Villas province who rose to the rank of *comandante,* is head of Grupo COMETAL, an enterprise that manufactures metal products such as construction panels, covers for refrigeration units, and elevators and provides equipment maintenance services (de la Rosa Labrada 2002).

For Hungarian political scientist Agh (1993, 15), spontaneous privatization is a phenomenon that occurs at a time when state socialism has weakened but there are still legal gaps and uncertainties in property regulations. Sik (1992, 158) finds that in such a period of uncertainty, "those possessing economic power carve out for themselves and their clients valuable pieces of the state-owned cake." In contemporary Cuba, there is evidence not only that spontaneous privatization has been occurring but also that these new so-called entrepreneurs have begun to flex their muscles and increasingly are influencing state decision making for their current and future benefit.

CUBA'S SOCIALIST ENTREPRENEURS

In the 1970s the Cuban government established about a dozen small corporations abroad (mostly in Western Europe and Panama) to facilitate foreign trade and circumvent the U.S. economic embargo on the island (Amuchástegui 2000a, 6). The corporations were organized under the legal figure of *sociedades anónimas.*

In 1979 the Cuban government established the first domestic S.A., Corporación de Importación y Exportación S.A. (Corporación Cimex S.A. or Cimex S.A.), piercing the monopoly over foreign trade that theretofore had been held by the notoriously slow and inefficient Ministry of Foreign Trade. Consistent with its mandate to act surreptitiously to circumvent the U.S. embargo, Cimex S.A. was initially controlled by intelligence and military officers and concentrated on filling priority needs of the government and generating revenue to finance such exports.[2] Other S.A.'s were created in the 1980s and authorized to engage directly in international economic activities, among them Corporación Copextel S.A. (import of high-technology products and computer hardware and software and export of Cuban software); Unión de Empresas Constructoras del Caribe, Uneca (construction projects abroad using Cuban design and manpower), Cubanacán S.A. (promotion of Cuba to foreign tourists), and Cuba al Servicio del Exterior S.A., Cubalse (hard-currency services to the diplomatic corps in Cuba).

Most of these S.A.'s grew over time to become business conglomerates, expanding into different areas of the economy, and many others were established. By the end of 1992 reportedly sixty-three S.A.'s were operating in Cuba (Gunn 1993, 13). More than a decade later, precise information is unavailable on how many S.A.'s may be in operation, but the number is probably in the hundreds. Table 5.1 lists ninety-seven S.A.'s that were active in 2005, as obtained from a cursory Internet search; undoubtedly, more extensive research could identify additional such enterprises. The breadth of activities of the S.A. is illustrated in Tables 5.2 and 5.3 with respect to two of the leading S.A.'s, Cubanacán S.A and Corporación Copextel S.A.

- Established in 1987, Cubanacán S.A. was created to develop the tourism industry in collaboration with foreign partners. Over the years Cubanacán S.A. has evolved into a conglomerate of enterprises that serve the tourism industry. According to promotional materials in its website accessed in 2005, 48 percent of foreign tourists traveling to Cuba were serviced by Cubanacán. Cubanacán operates nine branch offices in Europe and the Americas and eighteen companies. In addition to numerous joint ventures (see below), in 2003, Cubanacán directly managed some thirty hotels (under the brand names Cubanacán, Brisas, Club Amigo, Cubanacán Boutique, and Carrusel), fifty-two restaurants (under the Palmares brand name), a chain of retail stores catering to tourists (under the Universo brand name), three marinas, thirteen scuba-diving centers, thirty-eight health clubs and health tourism hotels, a full-service tour agency, a ground transportation system, and a convention cen ter in Varadero (Table 5.2; Amuchástegui 2000a).
- Established in 1985, Copextel brought together several electronics and computer-related companies and subsequently expanded through joint venture and "cooperated production" agreements with foreign partners. According to its promotional materials, Copextel's fifty operating units are engaged in the production, assembly, repair, or sale of the following products and services: (1) restaurant and hotel equipment, refrigeration equipment, professional audio and lighting equipment, recreation equipment, furniture, and elevators; (2) computer hardware and software; (3) engineering and automation services; (4) home electronics; (5) telecommunications; (6) energy, electricity, and electronics; and (7) project engineering (Table 5.3; Amuchástegui 2000a).

The S.A.'s tend to operate in the more dynamic segments of the economy, generally referred to by Cuban economists as *mercado de frontera*

TABLE 5.1. SELECTED CUBAN *SOCIEDADES ANÓNIMAS* (S.A.'S)

Aerocaribbean S.A.	Cubanacán S.A.
Agencia Aduanal y	Cubanacán Naútica S.A
Transitaria Cubanacán Express S.A.	Cubanacán Viajes S.A
Always Travel S.A.	Empresa Logística de Carga Aérea
Antex S.A.	de Cuba S.A.
Arandia S.A.	Empresa de Telecomunicaciones
Artex S.A.	de Cuba S.A.
Aseguradora del Turismo, La Isla S.A.	Emprotur S.A.
Asistur S.A	Expedimar S.A.Financiera Nacional S.A.
Banco Financiero Internacional S.A.	Fimel S.A.
Banco Internacional de Comercio S.A.	Finagri S.A.
Banco de Inversiones S.A.	Financiera Cimex S.A.
Banco Metropolitano S.A.	Gaviota S.A.
Bravo S.A.	Geominera S.A
Bufete Lex S.A.	Gran Caribe S.A.
Caribe International Tours S.A.	Grupo Nueva Banca S.A.
Caribex S.A.	Habaguanex S.A.
Casas de Cambio S.A.	Habanos S.A.
Comercializadora NACARI S.A	Havanatur S.A.
Compañía Fiduciaria S.A	Havanatur Celimar S.A.
Compañía Contratista de	Havanatur Celimar S.A.
Obras para la Aviación S.A.	Horizontes Hoteles S.A.
Compañía Taday Marine S.A	Increfin S.A.
Conavana S.A	Labiofam S.A.
Consultores Asociados S.A	La Isla S.A.
Copextel S.A.	Malfi Marine Corp. S.A.
Coral Container Lines S.A.	Marinter S.A.
Corporación Alimentaria S.A.	Motores Internacionales del Caribe S.A.
(CORALSA)	Panafin S.A.
Corporación Financiera Habana S.A.	Pérez S.A.
Corporación Turística del Caribe S.A.	Prensa Latina S.A.
Cubacel S.A.	Producciones Abdala S.A.
Cubadeportes S.A.	Sermar S.A.
Cubalse S.A.	Servimed S.A
Cubamar Viajes S.A.	S.I.S. Cubacontrol S.A.
Cubatel S.A.	Suchel S.A
Cubamar Viajes S.A.	Telefónica Data Cuba S.A.
Cubana de Aviación S.A.	Transtur S.A.

Source: Internet search

TABLE 5.2. OPERATING UNITS OF CUBANACÁN S.A.

28 hotels under five trademarks:
Cubanacán, Brisas, Cubanacán Boutique,
Club Amigo, and Carrusel

Cubanacán (4-star quality)
    Cubanacán Comodoro (Havana)★
    Cubanacán Marina Hemingway (Havana)
    Cubanacán El Viejo y el Mar (Havana)
    Cubanacán Tarará
    Cubanacán La Pradera (Havana)
    Cubanacán Hotel del Río (Sancti Spíritus)
    Cubanacán El Colony (Isla de la Juventud)
    Palco (Palacio de Convenciones, Havana
Brisas (4-star, all-inclusive)
    Brisas Trinidad del Mar
    Brisas del Caribe (Varadero)
    Brisas Guardalavaca
    Brisas Santa Lucía
    Brisas Sierra Mar-Los Galeones (Santiago de Cuba)
Cubanacán Boutique (4-star)
    Cubanacán Boutique Chateau Miramar
    Cubanacán Boutique La Unión (Cienfuegos)
Club Amigo (3-star)
    Club Amigo Plus Varadero
    Club Amigo Faro Luna (Cienfuegos)
    Club Amigo Mayanabo (Santa Lucía)
    Club Amigo Carisol-Los Corales (Santiago de Cuba)
    Club Amigo Atlántico-Guardalavaca
    Club Amigo Marea del Portillo (Manzanillo)
Carrusel (2- and 3-star)
    Carrusel Mariposa (Havana)
    Carrusel Bello Caribe (Havana)
    Carrusel La Granjita (Santa Clara)
    Carrusel Rancho Hatuey (Sancti Spíritus)
    Carrusel Morón
    Carrusel El Yarey (Granma)
    Carrusel Versalles (Santiago)
    Carrusel Sierra Maestra
    Carrusel El Saltón (Santiago)

TABLE 5.2. (*continued*)

Miscellaneous holdings

52 restaurants

3 marinas

13 scuba diving centers

38 health clubs and hotels specializing in health tourism

A chain of shops catering to tourists

A full-service tour agency

A transportation agency offering transfers, car rentals, and taxicabs

A convention center at Varadero Beach

---

*Note: Location of hotel given only when not evident from the name.
Source: http://www.cuba.tc/cubanacan.htm

("border" or "frontier" market), market niches where transactions are carried out in hard currency, companies can attain high profit margins, and foreign investors are willing to come in (Peters 2001). S.A.'s tend to have a significant presence in areas such as tourism, transportation, commercial real estate, and financial services.

According to Cuban Minister of Foreign Investment and International Cooperation Marta Lomas, at the end of 2002, there were 403 active joint ventures between Cuban companies and foreign investors. Foreign countries with the largest participation in joint ventures were Spain (105), Canada (60), and Italy (57) (Lee 2003). Minister Lomas also reported that at the end of 2002, there were 270 "cooperated production" associations—akin to assembly operations for export—with foreign partners (Pagés 2003). More recent information suggests that the number of joint ventures had declined to 342 at the end of 2003 ("Menos empresas" 2004; Spadoni 2004), as some of the joint ventures lapsed and were not renewed by the Cuban government, while others were terminated by the foreign investors because they failed to meet commercial objectives. S.A.'s were often the Cuban entity in joint venture or cooperated production associations.

Another set of economic actors with some independence from the state are enterprises within the Revolutionary Armed Forces (FAR). Particularly in the 1990s the FAR has been at the forefront of experimentation with management techniques to improve enterprise efficiency and has taken on an increasing role in generating revenue to fund the military establishment. Ratliff (2004, 166) likens the role of the FAR to that of China's People's

TABLE 5.3. OPERATING UNITS OF COPEXTEL S.A.

Restaurant and Hotel Equipment, Refrigeration Equipment, Professional Audio and Lighting Equipment, Recreation Equipment, Furniture, Elevators

Audiomax	Tegos Servicios Técnicos
Elevadores EVC	Visionica
Reclisah	Desic
Tegos Clima (refrigeration equipment)	

Computer Hardware and Software	**Engineering and Automation Services**
LTel	Giga
Conet	Publicidad Gong
Lambda	PCmax
Mayorista Equipos de Cómputo	Datec
Mundo Ofimatico	Daisa
Helposs	Sis
Mghelposs	Maxso
Hiper	Columbus
Standard Computer	PCnet
	Technostar

Telecommunications	**Energy, Electricity, and Electronics**
Antel	Ecosol Eficiencia
Antsys Radiocom	Ecosol Electric
Antsys Sistemas	Ecosol Hidraulica
Itelcom	Ecosol Matelec
LG Telecomunicaciones	Ecosol Solar
Tecxo	Seitron
Telocel	Electronica General
TVS	
Le Atiendo	

Project Engineering	**Home Electronics**
Capitel	Electrohogar
Coordinacion de Proyectos	S-Tec
Gerproyect	LG-Vince
	GSTB

*Excludes staff organizations, i.e., those providing financial services, economic control and supervision, information services, accounting and financial controls, insurance, human resource management, investments, exports, internal and external communications, advertising, and legal services. Also excludes sixteen regional offices: Pinar del Río; Playa–Vedado; Cerro; San Francisco; 10 de Octubre; Matanzas; División Centro; Cienfuegos; Sancti Spíritus; Camagüey; Ciego de Avila; Las Tunas; Holguín; Granma; Santiago de Cuba; Guantánamo.

Source: http://www.copextel.com.cu

Liberation Army (PLA) in the 1980s, when Chinese leaders encouraged PLA involvement in commerce and economic activities to earn money to pay for its supplies and personnel. The FAR has been particularly active in the area of tourism. For example, tourism enterprise Gaviota S.A. is reportedly controlled by current and former officers of the armed forces. Among the operating units of Gaviota S.A. are Hoteles Gaviota, Aerogaviota S.A., Gaviota Tour, Arcoiris, Marinas Gaviota, Via (auto rentals), Transgaviota (helicopter and small aircraft rentals), Tiendas Gaviota, Parques Naturales Gaviota, Inversiones Gaviota, and Comercial Gaviota (Amuchástegui 2000b; Espinosa 2001; Mastrapa 2000, 431).

Although in theory S.A.'s are owned by the state, many managers reportedly act as if they were privately owned, and in fact, there is some ambiguity about their legal ownership. Zimbalist (1994, 233) succinctly sets out the ownership issue:

> [F]or most purposes, [S.A.'s] are allowed to operate independently of the central state apparatus. They behave as profit-maximizing entities and engage in joint ventures inside and outside of Cuba. In part to facilitate trade insurance and to diminish the perceived foreign exchange risk to trading partners, the Cuban state has arranged for most of these corporations to be owned privately by individual Cubans.

Gunn (1993, 13) states that shareholders in S.A.'s are trusted individuals in good standing with the government. They are permitted to contribute capital and earn dividends on their investments, in effect constituting a state-sanctioned domestic capitalist sector.

Notwithstanding the arguments that these corporations are privately owned, they are in fact instruments of the Cuban state. Their "owners" have not purchased assets from the state, nor have they contributed intellectual property, invested any savings, or incurred any risks. Instead, they are individuals loyal to the Cuban government who have been given control over state assets illegally in a manner reminiscent of the systematic theft of property by the Sandinistas in Nicaragua known as *la piñata* or spontaneous privatizations in the former socialist countries of Eastern Europe.

The "owners" and managers of the S.A.'s are predominantly from the *nomenklatura,* i.e., high-level Cuban Communist Party and military officers (Alfonso 1999b; Hidalgo 2004). As mentioned earlier, former Minister of the Interior Ramiro Valdés for many years has controlled computer hardware and software company Copextel S.A. Meanwhile, Gaviota S.A. is led by Division General Julio Casas Regueiro and General Luis Pérez Róspide (Espinosa 2001, 24); the latter is one of the key architects of management reforms that began in the late 1980s known as *perfeccionamiento empresarial*.

One of the few studies of the behavior and perceptions of Cuban managers was conducted by Gerardo González (1999), who administered a standard survey instrument to sixty-two managers and interviewed an additional twenty-nine, for a total sample size of ninety-one managers. These managers worked for enterprises associated with the external sector but with different degrees of subordination to the state's central apparatus: centralized enterprises, typically the trading arm of specific ministries, highly subordinated to the state; decentralized enterprises, typically enterprises serving the internal economy and sometimes also involved in foreign trade, with some autonomy over decision making; and "private enterprises" in the foreign trade and tourism industries essentially with complete autonomy from the state and oftentimes legally established in foreign countries as non-Cuban corporations.

Particularly relevant are the views of managers of "private enterprises," that is, S.A.'s operating at home or abroad. Gerardo González (1999, 473) observes that these managers tended to think and act with substantial independence from the Cuban state, so much so that he tentatively refers to them as *empresarios,* or entrepreneurs, with full knowledge that in a capitalist setting, "entrepreneur" also implies ownership. Managers of "private businesses" on average tended to attribute the nation's economic ills to internal factors (e.g., failure in domestic economic policy making, exhaustion of the socialist model) rather than to external factors (e.g., the U.S. embargo) as does the official Cuban government line. Despite the lower intensity of control they faced from the central authorities compared to other enterprises, managers of "private enterprises" advocated deeper reforms that would enhance their autonomy of enterprises from the state. Finally, these managers also expressed concern about the methods through which high-level management is chosen and evaluated, in no small part because these affect their own performance and rewards:

> Many enterprises are managed by persons who were placed in such
> positions because of their history, their political career, but they do
> not have management expertise. Their own history allows them to
> make decisions about matters that may or may not be covered by
> rules, allows them to be bold; they are not afraid to make a mistake

because their trajectory and loyalty to the revolution supports them. However, at a similar enterprise, a manager without the authority gained by a political trajectory may not take a decision because of fear. (González 1999, 475)

Managers of "private enterprises" expressed concerns about the status of their firms—and their own status and prerogatives—in the future as the Cuban economy and society undergo change. For example, they expressed concern about the entry of foreign corporations or joint ventures into the (protected) domestic market (González 1999, 475). This concern became even sharper when managers were quizzed on their views on privatization. While the majority of managers favored additional enterprise autonomy, their enthusiasm fell short of advocating privatization. Managers feared that privatization would result in the loss of state protection for enterprises; managers have grown and developed within a paternalistic system, where the state ultimately is responsible for bailing out loss-making enterprises and there is no threat of bankruptcy (González 1999, 476).

There is some evidence of Cuban enterprises "capturing the state," influencing rules and regulations in the tourism area to improve their economic positions. For example, rentals of rooms in private homes (*casas particulares*) became a permitted activity with the expansion of self-employment in the early 1990s. As this practice became more popular and some of the landlords more sophisticated,[3] private room rentals began to compete with the lodging services offered by the state (either state-owned hotels or hotels operated by joint ventures with foreign investors). As a new housing law was being drafted in 2003, which, inter alia, would regulate room rentals, representatives of the established hotel chains and foreign investors lobbied intensely to place further limitations on private room rentals in order to maintain their monopoly over the lodging industry, reportedly by increasing fees and taxes on room rentals, limiting the number of rooms that can be rented in a dwelling to two, revoking the right to rent an entire apartment, and requiring that one of the renters always be at home (Henken 2003, 350–351). In 2003 and 2004 the government cracked down on *casas particulares,* and eighty-nine landlords who were found not to be in compliance with regulations faced loss of license to operate or even confiscation of their properties; in the city of Havana, nearly one-fifth of the 3,339 licenses that had been granted to *casas particulares* were cancelled because they made unauthorized home improvements ("El gobierno" 2004).

Foreign firms are central to key industries such as tourism and natural resources extraction (nickel, oil, natural gas). Since 2004 the Cuban government has been systematically allowing small joint venture agreements to lapse and dissolving poorly performing associations with foreign investors, thereby somewhat reducing foreign presence on the island. However, personal relationships between Cuban managers and representatives of foreign firms formerly operating in Cuba could be quickly reestablished once a transition gets under way and shady deals negotiated if both parties agree that the opportunity is ripe to do so.

The Economic Wealth of the Castro Family

The magnitude of Fidel Castro's wealth and that of his immediate family has been the subject of considerable speculation. Needless to say, analysts' estimates are probably quite off the mark, given the secrecy that surrounds Castro's personal affairs. In the rest of this section, we present some of the estimates that are available to inform the readers about their range, but we do not endorse them. In fact, there is considerable merit in Yáñez's (2005) argument that the toolbox of techniques generally used in market economies to measure the wealth of individuals is not applicable to a figure such as Castro, who, although strictly speaking may not hold title to assets, has the unchallenged ability to use them at his whim.

In July 1997 U.S. business magazine *Forbes* estimated Fidel Castro's personal wealth at US$1.4 billion, ranking him seventh (just behind Saddam Hussein, who was ranked sixth on the basis of wealth estimated at US$5 billion) in the category of wealthiest royals and dictators, i.e., those among the super-rich who came into their wealth by circumstance of birth or political activity but did not earn their wealth. The methodology of the calculation of Castro's wealth was not spelled out, but it seems to be based on an assumption that Castro controlled 10 percent of Cuba's GDP, anchored on investments in the sugar and nickel industries. In 2004 *Forbes* recalculated Castro's wealth at a much lower US$150 million, indicating that Castro personally earned approximately US$20 million per annum from the sale of Havana Club rum through a joint venture with the French firm Pernod Ricard ("Varios latinoamericanos" 2004).

In 2005 *Forbes* estimated Castro's personal wealth at $550 million, attributable to his control of the earnings of a web of public corporations, among them the Havana Convention Center, the chain of retail stores operated by Cimex, and Medicuba, an entity that markets vaccines and other pharmaceuticals produced by Cuban laboratories ("Castro es cinco"

2005). Castro reacted angrily to the *Forbes* story, calling it "infamy," and retorted: "Do they think that I am (former Zairian President) Mobutu (Sese Seko) or one of the many millionaires, those thieves and plunderers that the empire has suckled and protected? . . . What they should be doing is looking for the money of all of those people" ("Castro angry" 2005).

Former Cuban official Jesús M. Fernández, who left Cuba in May 1996 after holding important government positions in the management of international financial resources, has described a set of accounts controlled personally by Fidel Castro that are separate from those of Cuban government entities (Fernández 1997; see also Soler 2002). These accounts, generally known as the Commander's Reserves (Reservas del Comandante), reportedly have existed since 1959 and been used by Castro throughout his more than forty-five years in power to finance deeds or projects that catch his fancy without having to resort to the official budgetary mechanism. Initially Castro used the reserves to make small gifts to needy citizens during his frequent trips throughout the island, but they eventually became a source of funds for other undertakings, including financing insurrections in Latin American countries.

Although Fernández (1997) does not make an estimate of the magnitude of the reserves, he suggests that they are considerable: since the 1980s, the main sources of income feeding the reserve accounts originate from quasi-private businesses operated outside of the central planning system (e.g., Corporación Cimex S.A., Cubanacán S.A., Cubalse S.A., the Havana Convention Center), commissions paid by foreign businessmen and investors, diversion of foreign assistance, and possibly proceeds from money laundering and drug trafficking. The reserves are held in untraceable accounts in the Banco Financiero Internacional and the Banco de Inversiones. In addition, there are reports of bank accounts in the names of Fidel and Raúl Castro in secretive Swiss banks, and there may be others in Spain and Panama (Fernández and Menéndez 2001).

A story published in June 2001 in a Madrid newspaper (Fernández and Menéndez 2001) based on extensive interviews with Delfín Fernández, a.k.a. Agente Otto, a former member of Cuba's counterintelligence services, provides details on the organizational structure and activities of Grupo de Administración Empresarial S.A. (Grupo Gaesa), a conglomerate of enterprises operated by the Cuban military from which Fidel and Raúl Castro allegedly benefit directly. The organizational structure is reproduced in Figure 5.1.

The increased role of the military in the Cuban economy, particularly since the 1990s, has been well documented by several researchers

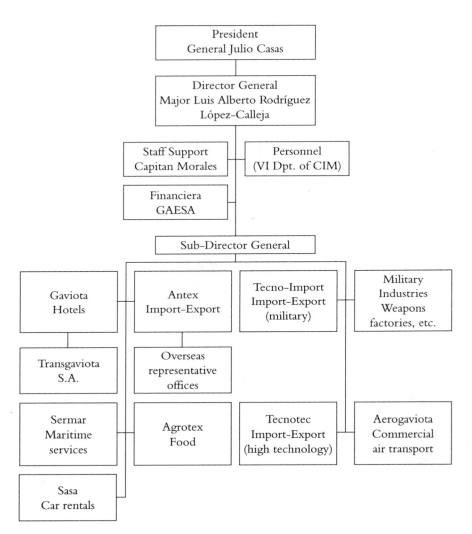

FIGURE 5.1
Organizational Structure of GAESA.
Source: Fernández and Menéndez 2001

(Amuchástegui 2000b; Espinosa 2001; Mastrapa 2000). Thus, General Julio Casas, first deputy minister of the armed forces, is the president of Grupo Gaesa. However, the conglomerate is reportedly run by Director General Major Luis Alberto Rodríguez López-Callejas, son-in-law of Minister of the Armed Forces and Vice President Raúl Castro. Gaesa is such a large enterprise (revenue in 1997 estimated at US$1 billion; probably quite a bit higher by now) that it has its own subsidiaries—finance (Financiera Gaesa) and human resources (VI Departamento de la Contra Inteligencia Militar, CIM). The latter is actually closer to a security department to ensure the loyalty of employees and is drawn mostly from the armed forces. Gaesa controls numerous manufacturing plants throughout the country (*industrias militares*) producing weapons, uniforms, and other military supplies as well as an extensive network of farms and food processing enterprises (Agrotex) to meet the needs of the armed forces. In addition, Gaesa owns and operates several enterprises that generate hard currency revenue and have relationships with foreign businessmen. Among these are:

- Tourism company Gaviota, the second largest on the island in terms of the number of hotel rooms it controls; Gaviota directly owns and operates a dozen tourism hotels in Havana, Varadero, Caibarién, Topes de Collantes, Holguín, Santiago de Cuba, and Baracoa and leases another two dozen to foreign hospitality companies, among them Club Med, Blau Hoteles, Meliá, Occidental Hoteles, LTI, and Accor;
- Tourism-related companies Aerogaviota (domestic air transportation for tourists), Transgaviota (road tourism and transfers), and Servicio Automotriz S.A., or Sasa (auto rentals for tourists, auto repairs, gasoline stations);
- General export-import company Antex, with offices in ten foreign countries, also a provider of Cuban manpower for assignment abroad;
- Technology products export-import companies Tecnoimport (military goods) and Tecnotex (general purpose);
- Maritime services company Sermar S.A., also involved in underwater salvage operations, including the search for treasures from shipwrecked Spanish galleons.

Not shown in the figure but also reported as Gaesa subsidiaries are Almest S.A., a real estate company that builds hotels and tourism facilities managed by foreign companies; Almacenes Universal S.A., an import-export company that also operates the Wajay, Mariel, Cienfuegos, and Santiago de Cuba industrial zones; TRD Caribe, a chain of more than four hundred dollar stores (TRDs) located throughout the island; and Geocuba, a company that produces and sells maps and geographic information.

As has been discussed above, further enhancing the role of the military in the economy, in February 2004 Colonel Manuel Marrero, at the time president of Gaviota S.A., was appointed minister of Tourism (San Martin 2004a; "Toma control" 2004). In addition to Minister Marrero, several other former military officers associated with Gaviota also moved over to the ministry ("Tourists" 2004).

In a major address in June 2002, President Castro felt compelled to make the point that while Cuba has welcomed foreign businesses and foreign investors to promote economic development, the Cuban leadership does not extract bribes or benefits personally from these activities. Curiously speaking in the third person, Castro (2002a) said,

> Not a single cent winds up in the pockets of Castro or his followers. Not a single top revolutionary leader has a dollar in a bank account, personal accounts in foreign currency within or outside Cuba, or front men who have accounts on their behalf. They are not corruptible. This is well known by the hundreds of foreign companies that do business with Cuba. Not a single one of them is a millionaire.

Journalist Alfonso (2002a) has commented that Castro's claim of poverty and protestations about corruption are disingenuous and ignore high-publicity prosecutions of corruption by his regime against such top-level officials as Aldana, Domínguez, and Ochoa.

Narcotics Trafficking

Since the early 1980s there have been credible allegations that Cuba has served as a transit point for the international narcotics traffic, claims not easily dispelled given Cuba's geography astride the most important sea and air routes linking South American cocaine- and marijuana–producing countries and the United States. The fact that Cuban airspace and waters are frequented by smugglers as transshipment points is not challenged; what is in question, however, is the extent to which Cuban government officials, if not the government itself, are or have been willing and active participants in the international narcotics trade. While Havana has acknowledged on at least one occasion the direct involvement of high government officials in the narcotics trade (the Ochoa affair in 1989), some observers see a preponderance of evidence indicating that the Cuban government has either tacitly approved numerous narcotics operations or has been a willing partner or instigator of others, generally with a nod from the country's top political leadership (Fuentes 2002).

Why Cuba may have chosen this course of action is open to dispute. It is often alleged that by condoning or actively participating in narcotics operations, Cuba has been able to advance its internationalist agenda, as when the Cuban security forces have provided safe passage to South American smugglers in exchange for the delivery of clandestine arms shipments to leftist guerrillas in Colombia and elsewhere. Military interventions in countries like Angola were also accompanied by illegal trading operations, as financially hard-pressed Cuban commanders in the field had to rely on "creative" approaches to satisfy some of the logistical needs of their troops. During the 1970s and 1980s smuggling operations were performed as part of broader strategies to foil the effects of the U.S. trade embargo and acquire scarce foreign exchange with which to purchase badly needed imports, in particular technological equipment not available from Soviet bloc suppliers (Del Pino 1999; Friedl Zapata 2005; Office of Research and Policy 1992; Oppenheimer 1992). Details about the nature of these operations were vividly displayed for the whole world to see in the summer of 1989 during the famous trial leading to the conviction of General Arnaldo Ochoa and three of his associates under charges of conniving with the Colombian cartel to use Cuba as a transshipment point for smuggling cocaine into the United States.

Allegations by Cuban authorities that Ochoa and his confederates were acting on their own, absent knowledge and approval from the leadership, have been repeatedly challenged by defectors with firsthand knowledge and understanding of the workings of Cuba's political system. Operations of that magnitude and significance, they maintain, could not have been undertaken without acquiescence from the leadership since they involved breaching highly sensitive and tightly controlled national security systems (small airplanes securing passage through Cuban airspace, landings in military airports, access by speedboats to Cuban naval bases). Their conclusions are also based on clandestine testimony provided by still-imprisoned close associates of General Ochoa (e.g., General Patricio de la Guardia) and recollections of defectors who directly or indirectly were privy to some of these clandestine but officially condoned operations (Alarcón Ramírez 1997; Fuentes 2002).

Close associates of well-known leaders of drug cartels, such as the notorious Pablo Escobar, have provided firsthand accounts of official Cuban connivance—at the highest level of government—with the illegal international narcotics trade. Jhon Jairo Velásquez Vásquez, Escobar's right-hand man, relates how the Medellin Cartel smuggled cocaine into the United States by first having it shipped to Mexico and from there to Cuba. He claims that through intermediaries Escobar sent frequent missives to Fidel Castro and enjoyed doing business with Raúl Castro, whom he considered serious and entrepreneurial (Legarda 2005, 219–224).

Many observers have suggested that Ochoa's show trial was adroitly staged with two purposes in mind: to cover up incontrovertible evidence gathered by U.S. authorities linking the Cuban government with international drug trafficking and to send an unmistakable message to high-ranking military officials discontent with Cuba's political and economic situation and sympathetic to liberalization measures at the time being implemented in the Soviet Union by Mikhail Gorbachev. The U.S. allegations were to have followed on the heels of the 1983 indictment of several high-ranking naval officers, including Vice Admiral Aldo Santamaría Cuadrado, the commander of the Cuban navy, accused of conspiring to smuggle drugs into the United States (for details see Cuban-American National Foundation 1983).

Some observers have posited that since the early 1990s, possibly as a means to cope with the severe economic hardships Cuba endured following the end of Soviet subsidies and the beginning of the Special Period, Cuba embraced the clandestine narcotics trade and related money-laundering activities as high-stakes, intrinsic elements of its economic survival strategy. While evidence to substantiate this viewpoint is spotty and fragmentary, it includes the continued interdiction of sea smugglers with alleged connections to Cuba, the confiscation of several containers loaded with cocaine destined from Colombia to Spain via Cuba, and a 2005 exposé of a cocaine deal brokered in Havana between alleged Cuban government-sponsored traffickers and an undercover investigation by a journalistic team from Madrid's Telecinco TV channel, conducted in the early 2000s and eventually broadcast and published as a book (Botello and Angulo 2005). In Botello and Angulo's view, no operation of that sort would be possible in Cuba's totalitarian state without the knowledge and approval of the country's security services. The authors of the report furthermore stated that their alleged cocaine suppliers claimed to be working for the Cuban government.

Despite repeated denials by the Cuban government to charges of narcotics trafficking and alleged efforts to reduce smuggling around its waters

("Declaran" 2005), the U.S. State Department claims that Cuba's territory continues to be an attractive Caribbean smuggling route ("Afirman" 2005). The official position of the United States is that Cuba chooses not to allocate the necessary resources to effectively interdict drug smugglers, selecting instead to assign enforcement resources to the internal apparatus of political repression.

Money Laundering

Some analysts have questioned the veracity of Cuban balance of payments statistics and estimates by economists that suggest annual emigrant remittances in the range of $800 million to $1 billion. Betancourt (2000) has argued that these levels of remittances far exceed the capacity of the Cuban community abroad to remit and probably hide income of the Cuban government attributable to drug trafficking and money laundering. Betancourt (2000, 160) argues that some portion of these alleged remittances are probably moneylaundering proceeds associated with drug-trafficking operations in the Caribbean region.

Lending credence to Betancourt's hypothesis was the revelation in 2003 that Swiss financial institution UBS had violated an agreement with the Federal Reserve Bank of New York and exchanged U.S. banknotes held by Cuba, Libya, Iraq, and Yugoslavia, four countries expressly prohibited from participating in the program because they are (or were, in the case of Iraq) subject to U.S. economic sanctions (Baxter 2004). UBS exchanged $3.9 billion over seven years from Cuban sources and credited them to accounts controlled by the Cuban government; while U.S. authorities have not revealed the source of the funds, money laundering is one possibility (Reyes 2004a).

Cuba reacted strongly to the investigation of UBS practices and the fine levied against the bank by the New York Federal Reserve Bank, blaming it on the policy of sanctions of the Bush administration and claiming that the U.S. currency exchanged through UBS was legitimately obtained from tourism and emigrant remittances ("Cuba acusa" 2004). Former Castro associate Ernesto Betancourt—the first director of Radio Martí, the U.S.-financed service established to broadcast news to Cuba—meanwhile responded in an opinion column to Cuba's arguments, again raising allegations of illegal behavior and money laundering (Betancourt 2004). The investigation of the sources of the currency exchanged by Cuba and of the accounts that were credited with the cash is continuing (Reyes 2004b).

GOVERNMENT EFFORTS
TO STEM CORRUPTION

Another indication of the level of corruption in socialist Cuba is the level of government effort to curb it. Prior to the 1990s, effective management of the national economy was not a policy priority of socialist Cuba. Generous Soviet subsidies, which lasted through the end of the 1980s, served to mask the regime's inefficiency and misuse of resources. In fact, in the mid-1960s Cuba went so far as to abolish the Ministry of Finance, eliminate a national budget, and do away with concepts such as cost of goods sold and interest payments; the study of economics as well as the career of public accountant disappeared from the university during this time (Batista Odio 1986, 239–240). Then-Minister of Industries Ernesto "Che" Guevara, an influential voice in economic decision making, proposed the organization of all state enterprises as simple branches of a central government agency (a ministry, for example), to be financed through the so-called budgetary financing method in which individual state enterprises would receive interest-free loans from the state to meet their needs and would transfer all of their revenues to the state. The plan called for eliminating mercantile relations among state enterprises and eventually eliminating the use of money in the nation (Mesa-Lago 1981). In the 1970s most radical economic policies were gradually reversed as, under Soviet prodding, Cuba began to adopt an orthodox socialist economic management and planning system. As part of the Rectification Process in the mid-1980s, Castro railed against mid-level corruption, misuse of government property, and inefficiency of government officials in preventing illicit enrichment. Justifying the shutdown of farmers' free markets in May 1986 after six years of operation, Castro said,

> In the search for economic efficiency, we have created a culture
> medium for a host of evils and deformations and what is worse,
> corruption. These practices blunt the strength of the Revolution
> politically as well as militarily. A working class that prefers money,
> that is guided by monetary pursuits is not an optimal defender of
> the Revolution and of the fatherland. (Castro 1986, 32)

The economic crisis that enveloped socialist Cuba in the 1990s brought about changes in the form and visibility of corruption. Some of the economic policies implemented during this period—particularly after

1993 — that created some space for the private sector in the absence of well-developed property rights and legal institutions also created new opportunities for corruption. The legalization of the use of foreign currencies and the enthusiastic pursuit of foreign investment in order to ease very serious balance of payment problems have been among the policies most directly responsible for the government's concern that corruption is rampant and threatens the socialist system. In 1995 Castro warned that corruption played a significant role in the demise of the former Soviet Union and could pose a potential threat to Cuban socialism as well unless measures were taken to curb it ("Cuba creates" 2001). The government set into motion a series of anticorruption actions, among them new laws, a code of ethics for officials and state managers, the creation of a Ministry for Auditing and Control, improvements in accounting practices, and more recently, campaigns to root out corruption.

Anticorruption Legislation

In May 1994 the Council of State approved a statute (Decree-Law No. 149) granting the government sweeping powers to confiscate cash, goods, and income of individuals who had obtained them through "undue enrichment" (*enriquecimiento indebido*). The purpose of this law was to penalize individuals who were profiting from a booming black market (Pérez-López 2001, 48). Decree-Law No. 150, approved by the Council of Ministers in June 1994, modified the Penal Code (Law No. 62 of 1987), explicitly making "illicit enrichment" (*enriquecimiento ilícito*) a criminal offense subject to seizure of cash, goods, and income, plus fines and prison sentences. Decree-Law No. 150 explicitly addressed illicit enrichment committed by state employees and authorities (corruption) as well as by ordinary citizens (Lafita 1994).

Decree-Law No. 175, approved by the Council of State in June 1997, amended the penal code by increasing the punishment for "white collar" crimes, promotion of prostitution, and abuse of minors and by adding the crimes of influence peddling, tax evasion, and conduct of illegal business activity by public officials ("Corruption Law" 1997). Under this decree-law, managers of state companies for the first time could be held legally accountable for the actions of the companies they managed. Penalties for white-collar crimes were increased to include sentences of up to twenty years in prison for crimes that resulted in serious damage to the economy. Along the same line, Decree-Law No. 232, approved by the Council of State in January 2003, authorized confiscation of property—including housing—associated with drug trafficking and acts of corruption ("Decreto-Ley No. 232" 2003).

Code of Ethics

In 1997 Cuba issued a Code of Ethics for Cuban State Employees (Código de Ética de los Cuadros del Estado Cubano), reportedly the result of a process of study, analysis, and discussion by managers of state enterprises involved in both commercial activities and public administration (Colombié Santana 2001). The code consists of twenty-eight principles related to ethical behavior of government officials ranging from being sincere and combating half-truths, lies, and fraud, to contributing to defend, preserve, and be faithful to the principles of the fatherland, the Revolution, and socialism. The principles in the *Código de Ética* (1997) most relevant to combating corruption are:

- The official should administer state resources in the proper manner and be an example of honesty, modesty, and austerity at work as well as in personal life, so that such a positive image is conveyed not only to direct subordinates but also to all who come in contact with him or her in the work environment and in the social arena (Principle 12).
- The official should use prerogatives and power of position, means, and resources only to fulfill the requirements of the job and ensure that direct subordinates do the same (Principle 13).
- State administration does not confer any rights or preferences over and above those conveyed to all citizens. State managers should not reap benefits or confer benefits upon friends or family or in exchange for other benefits. The purpose of holding a state management job is to represent, defend, and serve the people, the legitimate owners of state resources (Principle 16).
- Corruption denigrates not only those involved in it but also those who condone it. Corruption is a crime against socialist society. It must be denounced and combated through example and continual self-analysis (Principle 17).

According to Cuban officials, the code of conduct is more than just a set of principles that Cuban managers should observe. Decree-Law 196/96, issued in October 1999, regulates the activities of high-level managers in state and government administration, including their relations with subordinates ("Decreto-Ley No. 196/99" 1999). Article 6(b) requires managers to comply, and make subordinates do the same, with the Code of Ethics for Cuban State Employees. Article 37 sets forth that managers shall comply with the principles of the Code of Ethics in their professional and private lives. Article 40 states that failure to comply with the Code of Ethics shall lead to warnings, censure, suspension, or removal, depending on the gravity of the offense and that violations of law shall be handled as disciplinary or criminal matters, as appropriate.

Ministry for Auditing and Control

In May 2001 the Cuban government announced the creation of a new Ministry for Auditing and Control (Ministerio de Auditoría y Control) ("Creado el Ministerio" 2001). Its mandate is to promote integrity and better discipline with regard to the use of government resources and to prevent and combat corruption. In essence, the action elevated to ministerial rank the existing National Auditing Office in the Ministry of Finance and Prices.

Speaking about the new ministry, Vice President Carlos Lage stressed the need to be more vigilant about corruption in an environment of economic reforms and closer relations with capitalist countries. Lage stated that there was no corruption at the highest levels of the Cuban government, but some instances had been identified at intermediate levels. Thus, the creation of the ministry was an effort to err on the side of being too aggressive about eliminating corruption. According to Lage, "Corruption is intrinsic to the capitalist system—it could be described as the sap that nurtures it—but totally contrary to socialism" (Vicent 2001).

Modern audit and control systems depend on principles of transparency and accountability, largely absent in today's Cuba. Modern systems of audit and control also rely increasingly on the use of technology to promote transparency and to facilitate public access to documents. This does not appear to be the case in Cuba, where the tendency has been to treat budgetary and financial information as privileged and where lack of transparency has been notorious in the operation of the public sector.

Improvements in Accounting Practices

Deficient accounting practices and inadequate financial controls have plagued Cuban state enterprises for many years. In 2000, for example, in 54 percent of three hundred state enterprises of economic significance subject to special audits, accounting procedures were poor and resources inadequately controlled (Espinosa Chepe 2001).

The government has expanded training for accounting and audit personnel in Cuba and abroad to support *perfeccionamiento empresarial,* a new management system for state enterprises intended to enhance their efficiency within the context of continued state ownership and control. One of the main impediments to the implementation of *perfeccionamiento empresarial* has been the inadequacy of accounting and financial control systems.

Despite these efforts, it is clear that deficient accounting practices and inadequate financial controls continue to be significant problems that provide opportunities for corruption to flourish. At the end of 2002, 85 percent of the firms participating in the *perfeccionamiento empresarial* process had serious accounting and financial management problems that needed to be resolved before they could advance within the *perfeccionamiento* process to the higher levels. Among these problems were lack of systematic control over budgeted revenue and approved expenditures, failure to use accounting data to ensure fulfillment of the plan, failure to conduct periodic audits, failure to disaggregate budget data in order to allow for analysis of performance of individual firms within an industrial union, lack of standards on which to base analysis, tendency of firms not to complete projects in which significant levels of resources had been invested, failure of plans to adapt to changing economic conditions and directives from the central government, and heavy indebtedness of firms (Cosano Alén 2002).

The Ministry for Auditing and Control reported that in the first quarter of 2002 more than 2,900 audits of state enterprises were conducted. In 39 percent of the enterprises, accounting and financial control systems were deemed deficient or poor. Among the main problems identified were lack of control over inventories, basic inputs, and accounts receivable; inadequacies in contracting between state enterprises; and improper use of bank accounts and banking services. Other chronic problems were the practice of "fines" (*multas*) that workers in state enterprises imposed on consumers through higher prices than authorized (with the individuals pocketing the difference); sale of products that did not meet quality standards; short-changing customers; sale of products to consumers after their expiration dates for safe consumption; and very high levels of absenteeism, as workers pocketed the state-provided salary and used their time and energies in pursuing other, more lucrative endeavors, such as engaging in unregistered self-employment activities or participating in illegal black-market activities.

The bleak financial management and control situation continued in

2003. The Ministry for Auditing and Control reported that 36 percent of the 5,917 audits conducted in 2003 found that the enterprises had poor or deficient accounting and financial controls; diversion of products to the black market was the most prominent form of "irregularity" identified ("En auge" 2004). In 2004 the ministry implemented a program of unannounced inspections in workplaces and warned of severe sanctions against enterprises that destroyed documents to hamper the ministry's auditing work (Cosano Alén, 2004).

Likewise in 2003, the Ministry of Finance reported that 35 percent of the 316,000 inspections of retail businesses conducted in 2003 revealed violations of price regulation, most of them occurring in restaurants and cafeterias; these violations extended to businesses operating in pesos as well as in dollars ("En auge" 2004). Finally, the National Office for Tax Administration (Oficina Nacional de Administración Tributaria) reported that in 2003 it conducted a very successful campaign to root out tax cheats, focusing on the self-employed, transportation-sector workers, and participants in agricultural markets, as part of a national effort to improve financial management and control and identify and prevent corruption at all levels (Pérez Navarro 2004).

Anticorruption Campaigns

In the aftermath of the high-profile changes in the upper echelons of the tourism industry that began in late 2003, the PCC launched a crackdown on corrupt "socialist entrepreneurs." According to press reports, in 2004 members of the PCC's Political Bureau began making the rounds of local party offices to discuss the rise in corruption and to warn party militants that they needed to clean up their acts or face repercussions, including expulsion from the party or worse.

The moving force behind the crackdown appears to be First Vice President and Defense Minister Raúl Castro, who reportedly has made combating "corruption and illegalities" a high priority. A government official who attended a closed-door meeting with the vice president said, "Raúl was adamant that the Revolution is threatened not just by the United States, but [by] corruption and liberal attitudes that give space for it to grow" (Frank 2004a). Complaining about the serious rise in corruption, particularly with respect to the tourism industry, Raúl Castro has been quoted as saying that "corruption will always be with us, but we must keep it at our ankles and never allow it to rise above our necks" (Frank 2004a), suggesting that corruption was getting out of control.

One of Raúl Castro's closest collaborators, ideological hard-liner José Ramón Machado Ventura, reportedly has criss-crossed the island to bring the anticorruption message to PCC members. In a meeting with party leaders in Matanzas Province in May 2004, Machado Ventura complained that socialist entrepreneurs have not only "copied capitalists' management techniques, [but] also their methods and style." He criticized "those who have copied capitalist methods so well that they have become capitalists themselves" (Frank 2004a). According to a press report, Machado Ventura is in charge of the National Commission to Fight Corruption and Illegalities, a body created recently to combat ideological tolerance and corruption and to strengthen cadre discipline (Frank 2004b).

In March 2005, in a special address to the Cuban people to announce rare good economic news—particularly, anticipated stable electricity supplies and distribution to the population of cooking equipment and of additional quantities of basic food items—President Castro called on the members of the Committees to Defend the Revolution, militants in the Union of Communist Youth, members of the armed forces, and the Ministry of the Interior to get involved in rooting out corruption to avoid maldistribution of goods and services obtained by the government at great cost (Mayoral 2005). Perhaps in recognition of the chronic practice by retail shop workers of short-changing consumers, Castro stated that coffee and chocolate supplies would be distributed in sealed packages—no doubt more costly than if distributed in bulk but less vulnerable to tampering by those involved in the distribution system. Similarly, a major housing improvement and new construction plan announced in September 2005 included as a key element an effort to involve local governments and citizens in preventing corrupt practices in distributing construction materials and housing from negating the benefits of the housing program to the general population (Mayoral 2005a).

In October 2005 all gas station attendants in Havana were sent home for forty-five days and replaced by hundreds of young social workers as part of a campaign to curb generalized theft of gasoline and its sale in the black market. According to authorities, social workers would operate the stations for thirty days in order to estimate the amount of gasoline stolen by gas station attendants each month. It was anticipated that the government would expand the campaign to the rest of the island ("El gobierno inicia" 2005).

Castro raised the level of anti-corruption rhetoric in November, proclaiming the start of a battle against theft, immoral conduct, and misuse of government resources, focusing on corrupt gas station attendants, wasteful consumers of electricity, government employees who misuse state resources, and black market operators. Castro promised to show no mercy in dealing with these miscreants, using measures with the force of a Category 5 hurricane (Sanchez 2005).

CUBA IN INTERNATIONAL MEASURES OF CORRUPTION

As interest in corruption as a development factor has increased, so has the attention devoted to quantifying levels of corruption in individual countries and comparing corruption levels across nations. Lacking a means for measuring corruption directly (e.g., through common questionnaires administered uniformly across countries), several international organizations began in the 1980s to develop indirect measures of corruption, quality of governance, and economic freedom that for the first time allow for some international comparisons. While these measures are still in their infancy and methodological refinements are continuously being made, they provide a corpus of information that permits analysts to make some judgments about the nature and extent of corruption across countries.

Because of the restrictions the Cuban government places on carrying out surveys on the island and concerns from the international community about the reliability of official Cuban statistics, Cuba often has been excluded from international quantitative studies about many social and economic issues, including governance and corruption. However, some international measures of corruption and governance do include Cuba. Although these measures have to be interpreted with caution, they provide a useful yardstick to examine the nature and extent of corruption in socialist Cuba and permit some inferences about potential corruption in the transition if explicit actions are not taken to avert it.

Corruption Perceptions Index

Since the mid-1990s Transparency International has been publishing an increasingly comprehensive Corruption Perceptions Index (CPI) that is compiled for TI by researchers at the University of Göttingen in Germany. The CPI is a "poll of polls" that draws upon surveys of expert and general public views of the extent of corruption in countries around the world (Schloss 2002, 19). The CPI for 2004 draws upon eighteen surveys originating from twelve institutions, among them the World Bank, the World Economic Forum, the Economist Intelligence Unit, Gallup International, and Freedom House. Individual survey results are standardized so that their values range from 0 (highest perception of corruption) to 10 (mostly clean, lowest perception of corruption) and aggregated into an overall CPI. TI annually publishes the composite CPI for each covered country as well as the standard deviation of the raw survey scores and ranks the countries according to CPI levels (Lambsdorff 2003).

The 2004 CPI covered 146 countries, up from 133 in 2003 and 102 in 2002 (Transparency International 2003, 2004a). One of the requirements for inclusion in the CPI is that data from at least three surveys be available. Cuba met this threshold for the first time for the 2003 CPI and therefore was included in official indexes. (Information on Cuba was provided in the TI database for previous years for the two surveys then available.) Cuba was included again in 2004, when data were available from the following four sources.

- The Country Risk Service and Country Forecast for 2004 by the Economist Intelligence Unit (EIU). This forecast is based on assessments by EIU experts (expatriates). The experts provided an assessment of pervasiveness of corruption (misuse of public office for private or political party gain) among public officials (politicians and civil servants).
- The Risk Ratings of the World Market Research Center. These are assessments by staff regarding red tape, corporate fraud, and the likelihood of encountering corrupt officials who take small-scale bribes or larger-scale kickbacks.
- The State Capacity Survey conducted by Columbia University. This survey on the severity of corruption within the state is conducted among U.S.-based country experts (policy analysts, academics, and journalists).
- The Grey Area Dynamics index computed by the Merchant International Group based on inputs from expert staff and correspondents. The index covers corruption ranging from bribery of government ministers to inducements paid to clerks.

Cuba's CPI level in 2004 was 4.6, compared with a "clean" score of 10; the raw scores ranged from 2.2 to 4.7. Overall, Cuba ranked 62 in corruption perception among the 146 countries covered by the TI measures, with 1 the best perception and 146 the worst, suggesting a moderate perception of corruption among politicians and government officials. It should be noted, however, that these estimates by and large do not tap the dimension of petty administrative corruption to which the citizens of Cuba are subjected, practices that are ubiquitous on the island, as discussed earlier.

CUBA IN INTERNATIONAL MEASURES OF GOVERNANCE AND ECONOMIC FREEDOM

As we noted previously, empirical studies have found that high levels of corruption are highly correlated with weak institutions, poor governance, and lack of economic freedom (Chafuen and Guzmán 2000; Vinod 1999). Thus, the stronger the institutional base and the higher the level of economic freedom in a country, the lower the likelihood of encountering corrupt practices.

Governance Indicators

World Bank researchers have developed a set of indicators that track the quality of governance, defined as "the traditions and institutions by which authority in a country is exercised." The World Bank developed the indicators by dividing governance into six categories aimed at capturing how governments are selected, monitored, and replaced; a government's capacity to formulate and implement sound policies; and the respect of citizens for the state and for the institutions that govern them. Released every two years since 1996, the most recent set of indicators—for 2004—covers more than two hundred countries. The indicators are based on several hundred individual variables drawn from thirty-seven data sources constructed by thirty-one organizations, among them Gallup International, the Economist Intelligence Unit, DRI/McGraw Hill, Columbia University, Freedom House, and Reporters Without Borders. The following are the World Bank's six categories of indicators.

- Voice and accountability: Measures the independence of the media and the extent to which citizens of a country are able to participate in the selection of governments.
- Political stability: Measures perceptions of the likelihood that the government in power will be destabilized or overthrown by possibly unconstitutional and/or violent means, including terrorism.
- Government effectiveness: Combines perceptions of the quality of public-service provision, the quality of the bureaucracy, the com-

petence of civil servants, the independence of the civil service from political pressures, and the credibility of the government's commitment to policies.

- Regulatory quality: Includes measures of the incidence of market-unfriendly policies such as price controls and inadequate bank supervision, as well as perceptions of the burdens imposed by excessive regulation in areas such as foreign trade and business development.
- Rule of law: Combines measures of the extent to which agents have confidence in and abide by the rules of society. These include perceptions of the incidence of violent and nonviolent crime, the effectiveness and predictability of the judiciary, and the enforceability of contracts.
- Control of corruption: Measures perceptions of corruption, conventionally defined as the exercise of public power for private gain.

The governance indicators are expressed around a mean of 0, with a standard deviation of 1, and range from −2.5 to 2.5; the higher the values, the better the outcome.

Table 5.4 presents Cuba's scores for each of the six governance indicators for 1996 through 2004. Generally speaking, Cuba scores relatively high with respect to political stability, consistently scoring above the 50th percentile, meaning that Cuba ranks higher than 50 percent of the more than two hundred countries included in the study with regard to this indicator. At the other extreme, Cuba scores low with respect to voice and accountability, regulatory quality, and rule of law. With respect to voice and accountability, for instance, Cuba's score is abysmally low: single-digit percentiles and lower than the second percentile in 2004—meaning that over 98 percent of the countries in 2004 performed better than Cuba vis-à-vis this indicator. With regard to two other indicators, government effectiveness and control of corruption, Cuba's performance is mixed, ranging from the 30th to 59th percentiles with significant weakening in 2004.

These results generally coincide with perceptions of analysts about the nature and functioning of Cuba's political regime. Cuba's favorable performance with regard to political stability and control of corruption are largely explained by more than forty-five years of control by the same regime, a record unmatched in the hemisphere and perhaps in the world, and the nature of a totalitarian state that can enforce its rules to control the forms of corruption it wishes to control through effective govern-

TABLE 5.4. GOVERNANCE INDICATORS FOR CUBA, 1996–2004

Governance Indicator	Year	Percentile Rank (0–100)	Estimate (−2.5 to +2.5)	Standard Deviation	Number of surveys/polls
Voice and	2004	1.9	−1.89	0.15	8
accountability	2002	3.3	−1.77	0.17	7
	2000	3.1	−1.72	0.23	4
	1998	3.1	−1.68	0.23	4
	1996	8.4	−1.31	0.21	4
Political	2004	52.9	+0.18	0.22	8
stability	2002	51.9	+0.22	0.22	6
	2000	46.1	−0.03	0.27	5
	1998	53.3	+0.16	0.28	4
	1996	50.0	+0.11	0.34	4
Government	2004	36.1	−0.47	0.19	8
effectiveness	2002	49.0	−0.26	0.18	5
	2000	48.9	−0.18	0.24	4
	1998	31.7	−0.48	0.31	3
	1996	39.1	−0.41	0.28	3
Regulatory	2004	3.9	−1.81	0.21	7
quality	2002	10.8	−1.21	0.20	5
	2000	8.1	−1.47	0.37	3
	1998	14.7	−1.06	0.40	3
	1996	18.8	−0.72	0.29	4
Rule of law	2004	11.6	−1.12	0.14	10
	2002	16.5	−0.94	0.15	8
	2000	34.6	−0.62	0.21	7
	1998	36.2	−0.50	0.24	6
	1996	24.1	−0.70	0.18	6
Control of	2004	33.0	−0.62	0.7	7
corruption	2002	55.2	−0.13	0.18	6
	2000	45.7	−0.34	0.22	5
	1998	53.6	−0.29	0.26	4
	1996	59.3	+0.01	0.24	4

Source: Kauffman, Kraay, and Mastruzzi 2003, 2005

ment repression. With regard to corruption, the relatively favorable score reflects the ability to presently minimize corrupt transactions with foreign private firms. Representatives from these firms are usually the respondents to business surveys. The arbitrariness of a totalitarian state and a very weak civil society explain Cuba's poor performance with respect to voice and accountability, regulatory quality, and rule of law.

Index of Economic Freedom

Since 1995 the Heritage Foundation and *The Wall Street Journal* have collaborated in an index of economic freedom across countries that permits international comparisons. The index is based on metrics regarding ten factors,[4] which receive scores from 1 to 5; the index is the unweighted average of the scores on the ten factors (Eiras, Schavey, and Kim 2004). Countries receiving overall scores between 1 and 2 on the economic freedom index have the freest economies; those with a score of 3 have economies that are less free; those with a score of 4 have economies that are excessively regulated and would need significant economic reform to achieve sustained increases in economic growth; and those with a score of 5 have the most repressed economies.

The 2004 Index of Economic Freedom numerically graded and ranked 155 countries (Heritage Foundation / *Wall Street Journal* 2004). Hong Kong topped the list as having the freest economy, with a composite score of 1.34; the United States ranked 10th with a score of 1.85. Cuba's composite score of 4.08 ranked it 144th, indicating a repressed economy but ahead of Belarus, Tajikistan, Venezuela, Iran, Uzbekistan, Turkmenistan, Burma, Laos, Zimbabwe, Libya, and North Korea. North Korea, with a perfect score of 5, has the dubious distinction of having the most repressed economy in the world.

With regard to the ten components of the index (Table 5.5), Cuba scored at the most repressed level (score of 5) with regard to wages and prices (very high level of government intervention), banking and finance (very high level of restrictions), property rights (very low level of protection), and informal markets (very high levels of activity). Cuba scored at the 4.5 level with regard to government intervention in the economy (government intervention has declined with respect to earlier years as a result of changes that broadened self-employment), at 4.3 with regard to fiscal burden of the government (reflecting very high levels of government expenditure and high tax rates), and at 4.0 with regard to foreign investment and capital flows (Cuba allows foreign investment although subject

TABLE 5.5. CUBA IN THE INDEX OF ECONOMIC FREEDOM, 1996–2004

Category	1996	1997	1998	1999	2000	2001	2002	2003	2004
Overall index	4.85	4.85	4.85	4.85	4.75	4.75	4.75	4.45	4.08
Trade policy	5.0	5.0	5.0	5.0	5.0	5.0	5.0	3.0	3.0
Government intervention	3.5	3.5	3.5	3.5	3.5	3.5	3.5	4.0	4.5
Foreign investment	5.0	5.0	5.0	5.0	5.0	5.0	5.0	4.0	4.0
Wages and prices	5.0	5.0	5.0	5.0	5.0	5.0	5.0	5.0	5.0
Regulation	5.0	5.0	5.0	5.0	4.0	4.0	4.0	4.0	4.0
Fiscal burden	5.0	5.0	5.0	5.0	5.0	5.0	5.0	4.5	4.3
Monetary policy	5.0	5.0	5.0	5.0	5.0	5.0	5.0	5.0	1.0
Banking and finance	5.0	5.0	5.0	5.0	5.0	5.0	5.0	5.0	5.0
Property rights	5.0	5.0	5.0	5.0	5.0	5.0	5.0	5.0	5.0
Informal markets	5.0	5.0	5.0	5.0	5.0	5.0	5.0	5.0	5.0

Source: Heritage Foundation / Wall Street Journal 2004, at http://www.heritage.org

to many bureaucratic red tape) and regulation (some decline in government bureaucracy as a result of the growth of the private sector). Cuba scored 3.0 with regard to trade policy (relatively low import tariffs and some decentralization of foreign trade). With regard to monetary policy, Cuba jumped remarkably from the worst score, a 5, a year earlier to the best score, 1, because of a significant reduction in inflation. With this one exception, it is clear from Table 5.5, Cuba's scores in individual measures did not change significantly over the period 1996 through 2004.

Political Freedom Index

The Freedom in the World survey conducted by Freedom House (2004) provides an annual evaluation of the state of global freedom. The survey, which includes both analytical reports and numerical ratings of countries and select territories, measures freedom in two broad categories: political rights and civil liberties. Political rights enable people to participate freely in the political process. This includes the right to vote and compete for public office and to elect representatives who have a decisive vote on public policies. The evaluation of political rights is based on responses to questions in three areas: electoral process, political pluralism and participation, and functioning of government. Civil liberties include the freedom to develop opinions, institutions, and personal autonomy without interference from the state. The evaluation of civil liberties is based on responses to questions in four areas: freedom of expression and belief; associational and organizational rights; rule of law; and personal autonomy and individual rights.

A country or territory is assigned a numerical rating on a scale of 1 to 7 based on the total number of raw points awarded to the political rights and civil liberties checklist questions, with 1 representing the most free and 7 the least free. Each pair of political rights and civil liberties ratings is averaged to determine an overall status of "Free," "Partly Free," or "Not Free." Countries whose ratings average 1–2.5 are considered Free, 3–5.5 Partly Free, and 5.5–7 Not Free.

In the 2004 survey, relying on events in 2003, Cuba was assigned rating of 7 with regard to political rights and civil liberties, for an overall ranking of Not Free; this is the same rating that Cuba has had since 1989. In describing the status of political rights and civil liberties in Cuba, Freedom House (2004) included the following assessment.

- Cubans cannot change their government through democratic means.
- All political and civic organizing outside the PCC is illegal.
- The educational system, the judicial system, labor unions, professional organizations, and all media remain state-controlled.
- The executive branch controls the judiciary. The 1976 Constitution concentrates power in the hands of one individual: Fidel Castro, president of the Council of State. In practice, the council serves as a de facto judiciary and controls the courts and the judicial process as a whole.
- The press in Cuba is the object of a targeted campaign of intimidation by the government. Independent journalists are subjected to continued repression, including jail terms at hard labor and assaults by state security agents while in prison.
- Freedom of movement and the right to choose one's residence, education, and job are severely restricted. Attempting to leave the island without permission is a punishable offense.

- In the post-Soviet era, the rights of Cubans to own private property and to participate in joint ventures with foreigners have been recognized. Non-Cuban businesses have also been allowed.
- In practice, there are few rights for those who do not belong to the PCC. Party membership is still required for good jobs, serviceable housing, and real access to social services, including medical care and educational opportunities.

CONCLUSION

As should be expected in a socialist, centrally planned economy with overbearing government presence in the economy and nearly forty-five years of commodity rationing, administrative corruption is rampant in Cuba. Corrupt activities for which some concrete evidence is available from the national or international media include misappropriation of state resources, misuse of office, and special perquisites extracted by the Cuban *nomenklatura*.

The Cuban leadership has spawned a new class of "Cuban entrepreneurs" composed of PCC officials, current or past members of the armed forces, and sons, daughters, and relatives of *nomenklatura* members. They have already appropriated state assets through the paper reorganization of state-owned enterprises into "private" *sociedades anónimas* which they own or control. There is evidence of some of these enterprises attempting to "capture the state," that is, seeking to influence rules and regulations to improve their long-term economic positions.

Six

THE EARLY TRANSITION
AND CORRUPTION

I n this chapter we address the conditions likely to shape the early period
of the transition, defined as the time span during which the socialist,
command economy is being transformed into a more politically open
and market-oriented economy. We also speculate on the potential consequences of various transition scenarios on corruption and discuss several
economic policy levers and potential interventions that, depending on the
nature of the transition, could serve to dampen corruption in Cuba over
the short term. The next chapter presents long-term policy initiatives,
including those associated with institution building, essential for Cuba to
avert corruption during its transition. These initiatives are drawn from the
experience of countries that have managed to minimize corruption and
from practices being implemented (with varying degrees of success) in
transition and developing countries around the world.

The short-term outlook for a Cuban transition with modest levels of
corruption is less than promising. Based on history and close to a half-
century of socialism, there are few reasons to anticipate that Cuba will
face conditions conducive to good governance and prevent state capture
and other forms of grand corruption. However, during the early transition, measures to activate the market should help reduce many forms of
petty administrative corruption. The same will be the case with much of
the corruption associated with Cuba's centrally planned economy as the
economy is privatized and bureaucratic discretion is reduced.

Of particular concern is the spontaneous privatization of state-owned
assets by the Cuban equivalents of the infamous Russian "oligarchs," ex-
Soviet officials who, based on their political power, managed to illicitly
acquire national assets by manipulating privatization procedures. Equally
likely is the prospect that current elites (e.g., the military) may seek to
preserve privileges by retaining control of selected state-owned enterprises, as has occurred in many transition countries and, as we have shown

in the previous chapter, may have started already in Cuba. Thus, spontaneous privatizations and effective control by particular groups over state-owned assets, two forms of appropriation of state assets described by the World Bank (Gray, Hellman, and Ryterman 2004) as "more subtle" and not involving bribery are likely to dominate the early transition. Beneficiaries of these arrangements can be expected to express their influence in attempting to manipulate rules in their favor, engaging in what has been called "state capture" (e.g., bribes or favors provided to public officials by "captor" firms to influence decisions) as the private sector—of domestic and foreign firms—becomes firmly entrenched.

During the early transition, when rule of law and institutions are weak, the only means of controlling state capture and other forms of grand corruption will be external actors, namely by the international development community (financial institutions and multilateral and bilateral development agencies) and by the business sector, including multinational corporations. Options to prevent channeling of state-owned assets to individuals associated with the former regime appear to be far more limited.

Coordinated actions by external actors and the fact that at the onset of the transition asset ownership claims will still have to be validated could help limit the misappropriation of state property. For this process to work, of course, citizens must be educated about ownership rights and provided with the tools to throw a light on state capture attempts. In many cases, years will pass before legal challenges to ownership claims are resolved. And even under the best circumstances, verification procedures will not prevent all corrupt transactions, although at least they should minimize the most egregious forms of spontaneous privatizations.

THE CORRUPTION CHALLENGE

The transition from a totalitarian state to a more politically open form of government with a market-oriented economy will entail a vast transformation of Cuba's institutions. In thinking about a transition path, a priority should be to avoid the eruption of corruption that followed the transitions in the former Soviet Union and Eastern Europe and the electoral defeat of the Sandinista government in Nicaragua. If a government committed to good governance were to lead the Cuban transition, corruption could be mitigated through short-term measures to deter administrative corruption and state capture. For reasons discussed below, we are not optimistic that this will be the case.

As in so many countries around the world—particularly those transitioning from socialism—it is unreasonable to expect that Cuba will be able to tackle effectively the corruption problem over the short term. At the particular historical juncture when the transition will get under way, three historical corruption currents will converge and fuse in Cuba to produce a dangerous and potentially destabilizing and reform-retardant amalgam: the proclivity to engage in traditional corrupt practices, akin to those prevalent in Cuba during its colonial and republican past; the corrupt practices shaped by the ideological underpinnings of more than four decades of socialist rule; and the corrupt practices that can be anticipated to emerge, if in fact they are not already there, as the command economy is dismantled and privatized.

The first current broadly corresponds to the corruption prevalent in contemporary Latin America and common in republican Cuba (Chapter 3), usually associated with lack of transparency and of accountability, nepotism, collusion between private- and public-sector actors, abuse of authority, and an ineffective state overall. The genesis for the second (Chapters 4 and 5) is the totalitarian state and particularly the overregulated command economy, which converted routine commercial transactions into potentially corrupt acts. This was aggravated by vesting discretionary authority in a bureaucratic army burdened by endless rules and contemptuous of the public's right to know about its government, and a political system that conferred privileges to a politically reliable *nomenklatura*. With the transition, finally, another form of corruption has the potential to run rampant as the country's economy, once among the most heavily state-owned in the world, is reformed and at least partially privatized. In fact, as we discuss in Chapter 5, some of these corruptive practices in the form of property grabs seem to have materialized already.

Even before the Revolution, as noted in Chapter 3, Cubans approached corruption rather cavalierly. Politicians, businesspeople, lowly bureaucrats, and even average citizens felt little compunction about paying or accepting bribes and, if the opportunity arose, of taking advantage of positions or circumstances to profit from the national patrimony. With the Revolution, this unfortunate tradition was elevated to a new height: privileges attendant on political loyalty were legitimized, and the informal economy and the black market proliferated—fueled by *sociolismo* and goods illicitly obtained from government farms, factories, and stores. Not that these practices posed a particularly difficult ethical dilemma, as in the egalitarian society privileges were not equally shared, and few hesitated to benefit from the misfortune of others. From the early days of the Revolution, many eagerly took advantage of the jobs, housing, farms, and factories vacated by those abandoning the country. With the Special Period and Cuba's impoverishment, many "moral vices" reappeared with a vengeance. Since then, the dividing line between what an individual owns and what he or she can get has become even fuzzier. In short, in today's Cuba, corruption has become the norm rather than the exception. With this normative framework and facing an uncertain future, it will be nearly impossible during the early transition to prevent a corruption frenzy like the one that afflicted other transition countries.

EXPERIENCE OF OTHER TRANSITION COUNTRIES

In the former Soviet bloc, political and economic liberalization saw if not a resurgence of corruption, at least its transformation and intensification. With the transition came the dismantling of the old economic institutions and the privatization of state-owned assets, a process unevenly implemented across countries. Some countries (e.g., Hungary, Poland, Estonia) managed to substantially reduce administrative corruption while also limiting grand misappropriation of state assets during transition. Others, such as Azerbaijan and Ukraine, still experience high levels of both types of corruption. What factors determined the divergent paths are only imperfectly understood, but it is generally believed that initial conditions at the time of the start of reforms (quality of institutions, human capital, social and natural resource endowments) had much to do with eventual outcomes. The structure of the economy also played a key role; countries whose economies were dominated by a few sectors were more prone to fall victim to state-capture attempts and other forms of grand corruption. The oil-rich countries of Azerbaijan and Russia are prime examples of this (World Bank 2000).

Institutional development appears to have been a determining factor as well. Countries with well-developed administrative capacities and strong civil service traditions, as well as those with less orthodox communist systems and more developed civil societies, were better equipped to manage the transition and restrain corruption.

A related element was whether policies for the break from socialism were radical or less so. Countries that took tentative and partial steps toward reforms created a combination of capitalism and planned socialism that proved most conducive to corruption: in semi-reformed systems, government agents continued to exercise control over resources, but the potential for collaboration with private actors, and hence of corruption, was enhanced (Lotspeich 2003, 83). The countries with the most sweeping transitions not only did better in terms of economic outcomes but also curtailed corruption more successfully.

> In countries whose beneficial institutional legacies pushed them toward a transition path marked by a sharp break with the previous system, greater state capacity, and a civil society strong enough to promote change and accountability, we find a level and pace of political and economic reforms that have contained the worst excesses of corruption relative to other transition countries. State capture has been limited by stronger political competition and a civil society better able to constrain the power of concentrated economic interests. Administrative corruption has been limited by such a higher level of accountability, as well as by the more developed public institutions associated with a more advantageous historical legacy.
>
> In contrast, countries that started the transition with greater continuity between the old and new systems, less developed public administrations, and weaker civil societies tended to adopt a path of partial political and economic reforms that intensified a wide range of rent-generating economic distortions and placed only minimal mechanisms for accountability on public officials. This has proven to be fertile ground for the growth of state capture and administrative corruption. (World Bank 2000, xxi)

Based on its extensive experience working in former socialist countries undergoing transitions and analysis of results of a 1999 survey of private sector firms in twenty-four countries, the World Bank (2000) has posited that the mix of corruption types and their prevalence within a given transition scenario can suggest the policy interventions to pursue to minimize corruption. In its typology, the World Bank identifies four types of transitional corruption scenarios based on the relative prevalence of administrative corruption and state capture, both of which the typology assumes will be present in all transition situations. While the typology is static, it can be approached from a dynamic perspective, as countries may shift from one type to another with relative ease, although not always in a positive direction. The policy focus under each type, together with challenges and priorities, are summarized in Table 6.1.

Even within the most favorable transition environment, corresponding to medium administrative corruption and medium state capture, corruption would be a considerable concern due to its propensity to induce political instability and slow economic growth. Under these circumstances, the reform focus ought to be placed on institutional reforms to promote political accountability and transparency and on building strong partnerships with civil society. The high administrative corruption/medium state capture scenario presupposes a more limited management and regulatory capacity of the state and a weak civil society. The policy prescription to respond to this situation would rest on enhancing the state's administrative capacity. While state capture is not initially overpowering in this scenario, the weakness of the state offers the potential for state capture to increase as the economy grows.

Countries facing medium administrative corruption/high state capture are characterized by having strong rule of law and administrative systems before communism took over. The priority under this scenario would be reinforcing political accountability and diffusing economic power to combat state capture. With highly concentrated economic power, political and economic interests are closely intertwined, resulting in limited political accountability. Some of the countries falling into this category (Latvia, for example) were prone to state capture because of their desirable geographic location for business transactions.

Finally, arresting corruption is particularly difficult in countries facing high administrative corruption/high state capture. Weak institutional capacity facilitates administrative corruption and, with few restraints, creates ample opportunities for vested interests to engage in state capture. Stemming corruption requires severing the policy-making and regulatory power of vested interests while gradually developing accountability mechanisms and awakening constituencies to the dangers and costs of corruption. Technocratic solutions established in isolation are condemned to failure, given the weak institutional context.

SCENARIOS FOR A CUBAN TRANSITION

When a Cuban transition gets under way, a substantial change is likely in the governance indicators identified in Chapter 5. We can expect significant deterioration in two of the indicators in which Cuba performed relatively well, political stability and control of corruption. We would

TABLE 6.1. TYPOLOGY/GUIDELINES FOR COUNTERING
CORRUPTION IN TRANSITION COUNTRIES

Type	Medium State Capture	High State Capture
Medium Administrative Corruption	Key focus: Capitalizing on favorable conditions for strengthening political accountability and transparency through further institutional reforms. Challenges: Risk of complacency and backstepping. Close ties between economic interests and political institutions. Cronyism and conflict of interest in public-sector appointments. Priorities: Promote further reforms in civil services, public finance, procurement, and judiciary. Introduce greater transparency into political financing. Develop strong partnerships with civil society.	Key focus: Enhancing political accountability and promoting new entry to take maximum advantage of a stronger legacy of state capacity. Challenges: High concentration of power by vested interests. Weak structures for monitoring and accountability. Powerful groups that block further reforms to preserve their advantages. Priorities: Broaden formal channels of access to the state. Deconcentrate economic power through competition and entry. Enhance oversight through participatory strategies.
High Administrative Corruption	Key Focus: Enhancing state capacity to improve the provision of basic public goods. Challenges: Highly underdeveloped public administration. Lack of control and accountability within the state. Nascent civil society. Priorities: Build the capacity of public	Key focus: Breaking the hold of vested interests on the policy-making process. Challenges: Highly concentrated economic interests. Limited implementation capacity of government. Weak anti-corruption constituencies. Restricted channels of access for countervailing interests. Priorities: Deconcentrate economic interests

TABLE 6.1. (*continued*)

Type	Medium State Capture	High State Capture
	administration. Develop instruments for financial management. Encourage civil society development.	through restructuring, competition, and enhanced entry. Build accountability and oversight mechanisms. Promote collective action among countervailing interests. Recognize that stand-alone technocratic reforms have limited impact.

Source: World Bank 2000, 59, 63, 66, 71

expect that the decline in political stability would be particularly significant, as the country would experience the loss of a charismatic leader who held tight reins in the affairs of the state for more than four decades. In contrast, voice and accountability might improve significantly under a regime committed to transparency and one that fosters independent civil society organizations, but it will take time for changes in this dimension to take hold. Government effectiveness is likely to deteriorate in the short term.

In the early stages of a Cuban transition, it is not unreasonable to anticipate the nightmarish conditions of the high administrative corruption / high state capture scenario (see the right bottom corner of the World Bank typology in Table 6.1). This concern arises not only from a behavioral perspective but from an institutional one as well, as Cuba's bureaucracy—with the withering of totalitarianism—will be poorly prepared to manage the transition and potential corruption. The Cuban state currently lacks modern management tools, including training, ethical orientation, motivation, and incentives, to restrain administrative corruption. The political *nomenklatura,* as noted in Chapter 5, appears to be already engaged in or preparing to embark on massive state capture through spontaneous privatization, more than likely in collusion with willing foreign partners seeking positional advantage to tap the wealthy American tourism market after the transition; they also may attempt to assume control of state-owned enterprises.

To make matters worse, the refusal of the top leadership to look to the future and take steps to prepare a soft landing for the transition by accommodating diverse viewpoints further exacerbates the potential for corruption. The leadership does so, for example, when it closes spaces for civil society organizations, a potential deterrent to corruption, as it did in March 2003 by jailing peaceful dissidents. In the hybrid development model Cuba is pursuing at this time, in which a crippled command economy coexists with capitalist enclaves, no room has been created for the small-business sector; such a sector could provide a counterpoint to concentration of economic power and serve as a deterrent for state capture. Finally, there is a void in accountability due to the lack of transparency, the absence of independent civil society organizations, and the lack of independent media.

Given this situation and assuming that those in power today in Cuba initially will guide the transition, what can be done to limit corruption? An important issue to ponder is that implementation of credible anticorruption measures (if possible!) as the transition unfolds could interfere with the goal of completing the transition process. The transition could be derailed if officials with power and authority to facilitate it resist making concessions until their economic well-being is assured. Impeding such officials from preserving a measure of privilege and economic control may be counterproductive, as they may obstruct the transition, creating costly instability.

But a course of action that preserves ill-gotten privileges for members of the former regime may be more damaging in the long term. According to the World Bank, the experience of most transition countries suggests that the odds for political peace and economic progress were considerably improved in countries that sought a definitive break with the past. In this sense, Cuba will face a stark choice: tolerating corruption and allowing members of the ruling elite to gain ownership or retain control over illicitly acquired wealth may be politically expedient in the short term but quite costly in the long run. As in republican Cuba, opting for the easy way out and postponing the day of reckoning may solve the problem of the day but may contribute to mortgaging the country's future for decades to come.

A series of questions are relevant: Will a transition government have the vision and political will necessary to prevent corruption? If not, can other actors take actions capable of averting corruption? More immediately, what capacity will a Cuba in transition have to implement a liberalization reform package that limits corruption over the short term?

As may be recalled, the policy recommendations made by the World Bank to curtail corruption in a high administrative corruption/high state capture situation are intended, in essence, to start a transition through bypassing a corruption-prone state apparatus, as we fear will prevail in

Cuba. The World Bank recommends an approach that seeks to establish the foundation for eventual implementation of a transparency and accountability framework based on the rule of law and development of state institutional capacity. More specifically, and based on the analytical insights from the World Bank framework further enriched by consideration of the Asian experience (Bhargava and Bolongaita 2004, 246), the suggested policy prescriptions include:

- Forging broad anticorruption coalitions to enhance political will for reform from the bottom up;
- Promoting citizen and media involvement in support of the emergence of political will;
- Encouraging fundamental reforms to develop the capacity of independent oversight agencies, despite their initial institutional weaknesses, by seeking and rewarding reform leadership;
- Beginning to build the institutional capacity and independence of prosecutorial agencies and the judiciary, with the strategic objective of building government accountability; and
- Implementing economic reforms capable of reducing opportunities for administrative corruption, to deter corruption before it occurs, given the state's lack of investigational and prosecutorial capacity once it occurs.

In Cuba's case, reforms along these lines should include measures to achieve economic liberalization. Macroeconomic reforms and deregulation will contribute to the expansion of markets and reduction of opportunities for rent seeking. Lowering and eliminating tariffs, quotas, and other barriers to international trade, as well as eliminating exchange-rate restrictions, price controls, and unwarranted permit requirements, will strip government officials of discretion and of the power to extract bribes. Removing such controls would reduce transaction costs, eliminate supply bottlenecks, and foster competition. If unchecked, domestic interests—particularly those that have captured the state—will attempt to slow down or build in exemptions for their industries, resorting to infant-industry arguments and doomsday employment-loss scenarios to protect their status.

In addition to positive effects on economic efficiency, privatization would remove the state from economic activities and reduce opportunities for corruption in sales, procurement, employment, and financing. To ensure the integrity of privatization, transparency measures must be an integral part of such processes. If former *apparatchiks* are in charge of privatization processes, they will conduct the transactions with a great deal of opacity. Regulatory and commercial frameworks must accompany the privatization process to promote competition and protect consumers and investors. In the absence of such frameworks, privatization merely shifts rent seeking from government to the private sector.

During the early stages of the transition, large-scale privatization of state-owned enterprises is not likely to occur, as much work is necessary to prepare the ground for such an action. But as the economic framework is liberalized, many small and medium-size enterprises (SMEs) are likely to emerge, provided there is a stable macroeconomic environment conducive to growth. Based on the experience of the reforming countries in Central and Eastern Europe, among the policies that can promote the creation of SMEs early in the transition are an economic stabilization program that imposes hard budget constraints and minimizes state subsidies, efficient markets that foster competition through deregulation and liberalization of markets and prices, sound and transparent fiscal policies, and fair and effective taxation (Gayoso 1999, 62).

Also important at this stage of the transition would be to establish as streamlined a system of SME licensing as possible in order to accelerate their establishment, encourage their legal status (critical in the longer term for the establishment of a taxation system), and reduce the opportunity for administrative corruption (bribes, "grease" payments) that might be demanded by officials who issue licenses and permits. How effectively administrative corruption could be reduced remains an open question.

Completing the privatization process, including privatization of the largest state-owned enterprises, will be left to the medium term. For it to be effectively accomplished with a minimum of corruption, it will be essential first to put in place a basic institutional framework to make the process transparent and maximize its returns to the nation. In any case, the process is likely to be highly contentious and in many cases difficult to manage. As noted, in the reforming socialist countries, in Nicaragua, and in other nations, former political and military elites were able to safeguard their own interests by effectively retaining control of state-owned enterprises. Regardless of how and when it is accomplished, the privatization process is certain to be accompanied by considerable litigation arising from contesting ownership claims, independent of which privatization approach is pursued.

The extent to which a Cuba in transition will be able to implement economic liberalization measures over the short term will depend on how the country's political and economic environment unfolds as the transition gets under way. In the sections that follow, we consider several hypothetical situations that could have a major bearing on the pace and nature of reform, and hence on corruption. They include: the nature of the transition itself; which political factions would lead it; the economic scenario under which the transition would occur; the transitory legal framework; and the potential for political demagoguery given Cubans' expectations regarding the redistributive state. The interplay of these variables will determine to a large extent how corruption plays out during the early stages of the transition.

Nature of the Transition

This probably will be the crucial factor determining the evolution of corruption in a transitional Cuba. There is a considerable academic literature that has examined, from different perspectives, the manner in which the transition of former socialist states and of former Latin American dictatorships came about. Based on the study of these experiences and careful analysis of the Cuban situation, several analysts have speculated on potential scenarios for Cuba. With few exceptions, they assume that a transition will not begin until after Fidel Castro, who has dominated Cuban politics for close to five decades, passes from the scene (for representative views of transition scenarios see, for example, Amuchástegui 2002; Espinosa and Harding 2002; E. González 2002; and Mujal-León and Busby 2002). Once Castro's physical removal occurs, most analysts believe that the pace and nature of the transition will be controlled by the current military and political elite.

In contrast, other analysts (e.g., Colomer 2002) take the view that the regime eventually will collapse under the sheer weight of its inefficiency and citizen dissatisfaction and its refusal to accommodate popular economic, social, and political expectations. For those few analysts forecasting this outcome, Romania serves as a model, and regime collapse and the start of the transition could occur even while Castro is alive.

Several of these analysts assume that while the onset of the transition may be initially conditioned by the present elite, the decision to embark upon it may be forced by developments (of a diverse nature) inexorably drawing the country toward change. Analysis of this scenario is very messy, as a multiplicity of outcomes could result based on different power-sharing arrangements involving, for example, factions of the elite, the internal dissidence, and, less likely, the émigré community. Regardless of combinations and the dominant presence in the mix, this scenario assumes a measure of power sharing in which officials from the former regime will leverage their influence to protect personal and institutional interests in a setting where the loss of privilege and potential retribution cannot be ruled out. Political and military elites anticipating losing control are sure to pursue efforts to capture the state to maintain privileges or negotiate future terms from a position of strength. Whatever the case, corruption will be at the vortex of the transition, be it because officials from the former regime will attempt to manipulate the process of change to preserve privileges or because the transition process itself—and the structural changes it will bring—will offer innumerable corruption opportunities. Thus, from the outset, the foundations of democratic governance and the market economy will be undermined.

Leading Political and Economic Actors

Assuming that the transition unfolds according to conditions negotiated between the current elite and an opposition of undetermined composition and strength, the first relevant question is, in Castro's absence, which government-aligned force will have the final say in the negotiated terms. Analysts of the Cuban situation tend not to make a distinction between political and military leadership, noting that the two fuse at the highest levels of power. Indeed, most influential leadership figures have been drawn from the military and exercise their authority from the confidence vested upon them by Fidel Castro himself.

Thus, the answer to the question of who will control the course of a negotiated transition from the side of the current Cuban government is unequivocal, as it reflects a consensus regarding the dependence of the socialist regime on the military. This has been reaffirmed since the socialist world collapsed, as Castro increasingly militarized the country, presumably to guard against foreign threats, and began to rely more and more on the military to run the economy. The literature has explored these issues in considerable detail, noting that as the economy began to deteriorate in the late 1980s, the leadership turned to the military to implement efficiency-oriented management reforms (see Chapter 5). Positive assessments of these experiences (within the Cuban context) led to an expanded economic role for the military, managing traditional but troubled economic sectors such as sugar as well as emerging sectors such as tourism on which the government, facing harsh economic times, began to rely to assure regime survival. Thus, the military's influence on the management of the economy grew significantly in the 1990s and 2000s.

The presence of the military in the emerging economic sectors, however, responded to concerns beyond economic efficiency. These are also the sectors in which managers, due to the increased international openness of the economy, come into closer contact with foreign capitalists and their ideological impurities and temptations. The military, as revolutionary Cuba's most loyal institution, would be best equipped to safeguard ideological purity and least likely to become contaminated by capitalist malpractices. The emerging economic sectors also serve as employers of a military in retrenchment, whose ranks were reduced as a result of budget cuts connected with the end of Soviet subsidies and internationalist missions.

The fact that the military controls a large portion of the "privatized" *sociedades anónimas* in operation since the late 1980s suggests that a "spontaneous privatization" process akin to what occurred during the waning days of socialism in Eastern Europe, the former Soviet republics, and Nicaragua is already under way in Cuba. Alternatively (or complementarily), some state-owned enterprises may be kept under the control, although not technically the ownership, of private parties—usually the military and former or current dominant party officials—as has occurred in Nicaragua, China, and other countries. Equally worrisome is that many of the *sociedades anónimas* are closely aligned or in partnership with foreign companies through joint ventures, cooperated production contracts, and so on.

In its assessment of foreign direct investment in transition economies where corruption is pervasive, the World Bank found that the type of foreign investor attracted tends to be of "lower quality," that is, more prone to engage in state capture, particularly when the investor associates with local partners. The opposite is true for large multinational corporations. This differential behavior may in part be influenced by the fact that larger multinational firms place more emphasis on ethical behavior and good business practices, while smaller and less risk-adverse foreign investors have fewer qualms about gaining market advantage by associating themselves with domestic partners prone to unethical business practices (Hellman, Jones, and Kaufmann 2002). Lower-quality investors seem to be overrepresented in contemporary Cuba.

In some cases, state-owned Cuban firms are making investments abroad, generally in association with foreign partners; examples include hotel ventures in partnership with the Spanish firm Sol Meliá in Cancún, Mexico, Lanzarote, Canary Islands, Spain, and the Pudong District of Shanghai, China, and with the Chinese firm Suntime International in Shanghai. Cuban enterprises have also granted commercial licenses to foreign entities for the operation abroad of chains of well-known restaurants such as La Bodeguita del Medio and entered into joint ventures to produce abroad a range of products from vaccines and biotechnology products to the typical Cuban *guayabera* shirts (Collazo 2004, 4–5). The ease of transfer of revenue generated by these investments and licensing ventures to private parties rather than to the Cuban state is obvious.

These business ventures contain all the necessary ingredients for a combustible mixture designed by the ruling elite in due course to launder the acquisition of national assets through the sale to, or nominal exchange of ownership shares with, foreign-based corporate entities. Such procedures might legitimize and/or safeguard the proceeds of illegitimate enrichment behind the smokescreen of foreign ownership, particularly in countries lacking transparency and/or with a high tolerance for shady business transactions.

Thus, state capture on a grand scale appears to be already occurring in Cuba. Not only is the formation of laws and procedures being manipulated to benefit some interests, but also those taking advantage of the situation appear to be doing so in association with actual or potential foreign partners who will be willing to do their bidding when the time comes. While arrangements with foreign traders and investors are often touted in the official media, details surrounding the terms of the transactions usually are treated as state secrets. The fine print regulating these transactions is sure to contain many seeds of corruption that could be fertilized by the connivance of foreign partners or by relying on Cuban-owned firms already established in European and Latin American countries. With fifteen years of experience setting up such business deals, the leadership may not have much reason to worry about the future.

Economic Scenarios

How the Cuban economy evolves during the transition may have a substantial bearing on certain types of corruption. Sluggish economic growth in an environment shaped by economic distortions inherited from socialism would accentuate petty administrative corruption associated with complex and unnecessary regulations. The lack of opportunities for employment in the private sector would encourage public officials to cling to poorly paid positions that could be supplemented with bribes. In contrast, rapid economic growth fostered by macroeconomic reforms (see below) that eliminate market distortions would stimulate demand for private-sector workers, inducing workers to shift away from the state sector. Economic growth would likely result in the movement away from government service of the most able civil servants, whose skills would be more marketable to private-sector firms, as was found to be the case in the Eastern European countries following their transitions (Miller, Grodeland, and Koshechkina 2002, 560). As a consequence, the management capacity of the state will be further eroded, thus opening wider the door to corruption. On the positive side, petty administrative corruption should be reduced as the number of unnecessary rules and regulations is curtailed.

Under either scenario, high-level officials intent on deriving personal benefit from the transition would prefer to retain a discretionary and opaque regulatory framework and to establish rules of the game from which they could benefit. Their incentive to slant procedures in their favor may be greater under sluggish growth, when pickings are slimmer. If rapid growth were to occur during the initial stages of the transition, these same officials might instead benefit by acting as gatekeepers between investors seeking to retain or gain a foothold in the Cuban economy (Corrales 2004). They would also seek—as they are doing already—to place state-owned enterprises they control in positions to gain maximum benefit from emerging economic opportunities. The latter may occur in the tourist sector, where it is widely anticipated that once the transition begins and U.S. travel restrictions are lifted, millions of American visitors would arrive and create an unprecedented boom for the industry. Officials with discretionary power will be able to decide which privatization bids to accept, which natural resource concessions to offer, and under what conditions. They could manipulate the rules to retain partial ownership of state assets within privatization schemes or through spontaneous privatizations or by maintaining control of state-owned enterprises.

The timing of pervasive state capture may also be a significant determinant of economic growth, as it could severely derail foreign investment. This would depend on the behavior of foreign investors and how they evaluate the potential long-term consequences of scheming with corrupt politicians and officials to gain market advantage. Potential investors will surely factor many elements into their decisions, including economic variables, ethics, and corporate responsibility. They will probably also assess the potential for sanctions that could arise under the still-untested legislation of many countries that have banned the payment of bribes in transnational business transactions.

Transitory Legal Framework

The 1976 Cuban Constitution, as amended in 1992 and 2002, does not provide a framework to prevent corruption in a Cuba in transition. In addition to lacking the principle of judicial review, essential to curb abuses of power and enforce the rule of law, Cuba's socialist constitution does not embody the basic separation of powers and system of checks and balances key to encouraging accountability and democratic governance. Instead, the constitution vests all discretionary legal power in the ANPP. This means that all matters of law are subject to its jurisprudence, and there is no countervailing mechanism to balance its decisions.

The ANPP, furthermore, is vested with nearly total authority to amend the constitution and pass judgment on the constitutionality of laws and regulations. Domínguez (2003) has argued that with this extreme concentration of political, economic, social, and military power, the ANPP, under proper circumstances, could exercise a crucial and positive role in the transition, as it would have the authority to modify the country's legal framework to create an orderly process of change. This argument can be extended to corruption-minimizing measures, insofar as the political will is there.

Regardless of what constitutional instrument is ultimately adapted or developed to guide the transition, the reality is that when the transition occurs, the country will lack institutional structures to prevent the misuse of public office for personal gain at a critical time when the nature of the economy, particularly property relations, will be changing. Existing laws and regulations pertaining to *sociedades anónimas,* for example, will have to be carefully scrutinized and modified as appropriate to conform to the market economy. A sound constitutional and legal framework will take time to develop, since it will entail forging a consensus and harmonizing laws and regulations. In the interim will be plenty of scope for mischief.

A related issue is the nature of the regulatory framework that the authorities may adopt as the transition unfolds. Even if institutions of the command economy were to be rapidly dismantled, many questions would remain regarding the regulatory functions of the state. As a general rule, the more complex regulatory processes are, the wider the scope, at one extreme, for petty corruption and, at the other, for high-level administrative corruption. The transformation of the regulatory environment opens the door for state capture as well, as economic interests may attempt to influence the formulation of rules to gain advantage. The nature of the transition will also determine the complexity of the regulatory framework. It is safe to assume that the stronger the influence of officials from the former regime, the more likely it is that the regulatory framework will remain highly intrusive. This will be the case not only because of the benefits that complex rules will confer on these officials, but also because such a regulatory regime is more consistent with the underlying command economy with which they are familiar. Macroeconomic reforms introduced to enhance the efficiency of the economy may be able to counter these tendencies.

The extent of transparency and accountability implicit in the chosen regulatory framework will have a great impact on what traditionally has been one of the government functions most vulnerable to corruption: procurement. Modern state procurement systems demand fairness and impartiality; they also require that the complexity of the bidding process be commensurate with the nature of the goods and services being purchased. The bases for all decisions should be justified and recorded, and throughout the procurement process, transparency should be the standard.

Developing a transparent procurement system is a complicated task: it requires not only the design and implementation of proper procurement rules but also the development of an efficient, trained, well-paid, specialized civil service. Even under the best of circumstances, such a service will not be available to a Cuba in transition, providing still another opportunity for corruption to occur. And as the experience of other transition countries suggests, procurement is extremely vulnerable to corruption, as state purchasing decisions are often shaped more by political institutions than by bureaucratic rules (Gray, Hellman, and Ryterman 2004, 40).

The Redistributive State

The propensity for corruption to persist is buttressed by Cubans' affinity with the redistributive state. Starting in the late 1920s and climaxing during the revolutionary period, Cubans have looked to the state as the ultimate source of economic security (see Chapter 3). Thus, it appears likely that despite the economic catastrophe afflicting the country since the early 1990s, many Cubans will resist attempts to reform the distributional and welfare institutions of the socialist state. For example, of the 1,023 respondents to a survey of recent Cuban émigrés conducted in South Florida in 1998, 89 percent said they were in favor of retaining the free medical care provided by the socialist state (Betancourt and Grenier 1999, 254). Even stronger was the opinion that socialist Cuba's medical system should not be changed, as expressed by 94 percent of the respondents to a survey conducted in September–October 2003 of recent émigrés eighteen years of age or older who had been in the United States for less than six months (Gómez and Rothe 2004, 31). While it may be desirable to retain many links to a safety net, they will have to be reengineered to make them conform to modern practice and to a market economy and place them on sound financial footing. These are complex problems whose solutions will have to be negotiated and only gradually implemented. In the interim, they will remain as overregulated social programs, highly vulnerable to abuse and corruption.

Because of these high expectations, the potential for political demagoguery will also be significant at a time of great uncertainty about the future. Entrenched political factions may wish to play this social card as a means to retain political support while at the same time providing some cover for unsavory conduct, as has occurred in some of the Newly Independent States of the former Soviet Union. Management of large and complicated bureaucratic programs offers ample opportunities for cronyism and the extraction of rents.

TRANSITION STAGES AND CORRUPTION

How the economic transition is effected and in what sequence policy actions are taken can have profound implications for corruption. For purposes of this discussion, we define the short term to coincide with the onset of the transition, that is, the time period (one year to two years) when first-generation (or Type I) reforms are implemented. While primarily enacted to facilitate the emergence of the market economy and promote growth, early reforms also can diminish corruption as they contribute to the dismantling of the systemic underpinnings of socialism that sustained many forms of corruption. Reform measures typically applied during this period include macroeconomic stabilization, price liberalization, encouragement of new firms, and the dismantling of the institutions of the socialist system (including the breakup of state-owned enterprises and selected privatization actions). It is at this stage when the danger is greatest that corrupt officials will begin to illegally acquire national assets through retaining control of state-owned enterprises, spontaneous privatizations, or colluding with unscrupulous businesses to cash in on their insider knowledge.

Mid- and long-term transition coincides roughly with the period when second-generation (or Type II) reforms are put in place. These reforms, some of which will be discussed in Chapter 7, typically involve the development and enforcement of laws, regulations, and institutions that would ensure a successful market-oriented economy. These include completion of the privatization of large and medium-size enterprises; establishment and enforcement of a market-oriented legal system and accompanying institutions; and further in-depth development of a viable commercial banking sector and the appropriate regulatory infrastructure, labor market regulations, and institutions related to public unemployment and retirement systems.

Assuming that the transition to democratic governance proceeds apace, the implementation of second-generation reforms coincides with the development of transparent political institutions (including regulations for political party organization and funding) and corporate governance rules designed to minimize private-sector corruption and the incidence of state capture. This stage, embedded within the goal of establishing the institutional framework for good governance and a market economy, foresees the creation of a transparent, efficient, and customer-oriented public sector grounded in a legal system respectful of human rights, equipped with suitable democratic checks and balances and with appropriate control institutions, and under the oversight of informed citizens and independent and free media vigilant that the government adheres to and enforces relevant accountability and transparency obligations.

CAN CORRUPTION BE MITIGATED IN THE SHORT TERM?

Cuba could potentially benefit from what has been learned in other transition economies regarding the control of corruption, although as we have seen, the history of political and economic transitions is littered with experiences gone awry. Expectations, therefore, should be tempered, as corruption is likely to be widespread during the beginnings of the transition, even if we were to assume that the transition will be guided by enlightened leaders and bureaucrats with Cuba's best interests in mind.

Policy makers are not likely to assign priority to combating corruption during the early stages of the transition—in fact, we assume that many will attempt to do exactly the opposite, to try to obtain personal benefit from their control of the levers of power and the disorganization accompanying the transition. Nonetheless, many transition economic liberalization policies that simplify the regulatory environment and check some of the oligarchs' most egregious attempts at state capture could potentially have the secondary effect of dampening corruption. This could be accomplished by enhanced political and economic competition and by civil society and media oversight over the stewardship of the public patrimony, as suggested by the experience of transition and nontransition countries challenged by state capture and administrative corruption (U.S. Agency for International Development [USAID] 2004, 17–19). Cuba could rely on the international development and business communities to further support policies that enhance the political will to prevent corruption and the capacity of economic liberalization to do so.

International Assistance and Corruption

A transitional Cuba could derive countless benefits from technical assistance and financing from international financial institutions (IFIS)[1] and the bilateral and multilateral donor community. With respect to corruption, a minimum level of transparency and accountability would result from the internal controls imposed by the IFIS and donors to manage disbursement of funds. While positive, these controls are not likely to be sufficient by themselves to prevent corruption due to inadequate institutional and political structures aggravated by an ingrained culture of corruption and the erosion of the totalitarian state. Thus, the international development community initially should adopt a proactive anticorruption strategy heavily weighted toward oversight.

The outlines of such a strategy could begin to take shape if the international donor community, in particular the Washington-based financial and development agencies (the World Bank, International Monetary Fund, Inter-American Development Bank, Organization of American States, and U.S. Agency for International Development), were to establish a task force on transparency/accountability policy issues in a post-transition Cuba. Precedents exist for the establishment of such informal consultation bodies. A relevant example is the Donors' Consultative Group on Accountability/Anticorruption in Latin America and the Caribbean (DCG) sponsored by the U.S. Agency for International Development (USAID).[2] The DCG has been meeting for more than a decade to assess financial management and, increasingly, corruption issues in the Latin America and Caribbean region. A Cuba-focused donors' forum would provide a venue for exchanging information, identifying potential best practices applicable to a transition Cuba, and negotiating a preliminary division of labor among IFIS and bilateral agencies to prevent corruption, particularly with respect to disbursement of emergency assistance and support for initial macroeconomic reforms. This group could also be tasked with working with international business organizations to develop privatization and trade rules capable of ensuring a minimum level of transparency. This cooperation could eventually be expanded under second-generation reforms to encompass implementation of non-overlapping and integrated technical assistance, close collaboration in project design, and provision of compatible and non-redundant training programs.

The Business Community and Corruption

As noted earlier, the danger for large-scale corruption is most severe and immediate in the case of joint ventures, where unscrupulous foreign partners already appear to be conniving with public officials to gain control of state-owned assets at very advantageous terms. Not surprisingly, some of the foreign firms with a presence in Cuba today are based in countries whose commitment to transparency is questionable.

Fortunately for Cuba, the tolerant international environment of the 1990s that condoned wholesale corruption in former Soviet bloc and other transition countries, in Latin America, and elsewhere has changed for the better. Acknowledging the harm to economic and political development caused by corruption and prodded by growing global trade pressures, the international community has endorsed several conventions to curb corruption at home and abroad (for more details see Chapter 7). Enforcement of obligations under these conventions and oversight by signatory nations have the potential to significantly reduce corruption, even in countries where the political will to do so is lacking. There is also a growing movement among corporations themselves to take steps as a group or individually to combat corruption.

An international instrument particularly germane to this discussion is the 1997 OECD Convention on Combating Bribery of Foreign Public Officials in International Business Transactions (OECD 1998). By criminalizing corruption and recognizing that advancing the anticorruption agenda demands national efforts as well as multilateral cooperation, the thirty-five countries—responsible for 75 percent of world trade—that had ratified the convention as of January 2005 created a potentially powerful instrument to minimize corruption. Ratifying countries include many of Cuba's current key trading partners and foreign investors (Canada, Spain, Italy, Mexico, France, the United Kingdom, the Netherlands, Chile, and Argentina).[3] Although the OECD convention explicitly excludes from criminalization "small facilitation payments," it implicitly covers, as do other international conventions, connivance with host-country parties to engage in unethical business transactions, including those that could lead to state capture or the laundering of assets to the benefit of unidentified third parties.

A complementary instrument is the OECD Guidelines for Multinational Enterprises. With a broader anticorruption content, the guidelines ban private-sector bribery, solicitation of bribes, and extortion while encouraging multinational enterprises to extend these provisions to foreign subsidiaries and business partners (OECD 2003a). The guidelines specifically state, "Enterprises should not, directly or indirectly, offer, promise, give, or demand a bribe or other undue advantage to obtain or retain business or other improper advantage . . . [and should] encourage, where practicable, business partners, including suppliers and subcontractors, to apply principles of corporate conduct compatible with the Guidelines." The convention requires that enterprises comply with additional requirements to ensure proper standards of conduct, appropriate disciplinary procedures, rules governing the employment of agents, accounting, internal control, and audit practices, and protections for whistleblowers, among others.

Other anticorruption conventions, such as the Organization of American States' Inter-American Convention Against Corruption and the United Nations Convention Against Corruption (see Chapter 7) explicitly address the obligations of private-sector firms. They do so, as in the case of the Inter-American Convention, by requiring that "publicly held companies and other types of associations maintain books and records which, in reasonable detail, accurately reflect the acquisition and disposition of assets." Meanwhile, the UN convention promotes transparency explicitly calling for states to implement "measures [binding on private entities] regarding the identity of legal and natural persons involved in the establishment and management of corporate entities and of holders of the capital and shares of corporate entities."

Independent instruments that complement these government efforts have been developed by private-sector associations or groups of companies to prevent corruption. Among them are the Rules of Conduct to Combat Extortion and Bribery in International Business Transactions developed by the International Chamber of Commerce (ICC), most recently revised in 1999, and Business Principles for Countering Bribery, jointly developed by Transparency International and Social Accountability International. The latter principles were formulated as "a tool to assist enterprises to develop effective approaches to countering bribery in all their activities . . . and give practical effect to recent [international anticorruption] initiatives" (OECD 2003b, 18). Many multinational corporations have taken matters into their own hands and developed "zero tolerance" policies against paying bribes, and some of them—for example the world's biggest construction and natural resource companies, such as Bechtel and Fluor of the United States and Rio Tinto PLC of England—are considering a coordinated approach to bribery named the "Partnering Against Corruption Initiative" (Simpson 2005).

Although international conventions and guidelines and voluntary initiatives are still at an embryonic stage of implementation, they offer the promise of an avenue at the international level through which private citizens and civil society organizations—and post-transition Cuban governments—could contest dubious property ownership claims and could hold the possibility of recovering proceeds of bribes and illicit transactions. These instruments will also increasingly facilitate the exchange of information, detection of illicit practices, and prosecution of corrupt public officials and private-sector firms engaged in bribery and crimes such as international money laundering and drug and human trafficking that often prosper in settings conducive to corruption.

While it would be naïve to think that these anticorruption instruments could bring an end to corruption—witness the alleged corruption and bribery perpetrated by firms from several signatory countries to the OECD convention and guidelines that participated in the Iraq Oil for Food program managed by the United Nations—they could at least minimize their occurrence. The availability of the international instruments described above suggests that the international development and business communities, working closely with civic-minded individuals and civil society organizations (OECD 2003a), may be able to restrain corruption—even in the presence of uncooperative transition authorities—should former *apparatchiks* attempt to take advantage of their position to capture the national patrimony.

In the event that a transitional government shows the willingness to fight corruption, Cuba could benefit from the practices being developed in other transition countries. Of note is the Anticorruption Network for Transition Economies established under the auspices of the OECD and the Turkish government to support the governments of Armenia, Azerbaijan, Georgia, the Russian Federation, Tajikistan, and Ukraine in adopting a regional anticorruption action plan. The purpose of the action plan is to "reduce opportunities for corruption through more effective oversight of officials with discretionary decision-making powers and action to avoid potential conflicts of interests" (OECD 2003b, 20). Although this initiative arose long after corruption battered the economies of these countries, the cooperative model on which it rests—involving government, civil society, international organizations, financial institutions, and donor agencies—may be applicable to a Cuba in transition since it is consistent with an anticorruption strategy in which institutions outside government provide close oversight. Similar regional instruments have been launched in southeastern Europe, the Asia-Pacific region, the Baltics, and Latin America (ibid.).

Legal Anticorruption Safeguards

Since the odds are modest that a transition Cuban government will be honest and transparent and that international vigilance is unlikely to deter many unsavory deals, further legal actions will be necessary to reverse attempts at state capture. These actions, which may have to be delayed until implementation of second-generation reforms including effective governance, will depend on two basic premises. First, at the start of the Cuban transition, no private parties will own any assets, other than personal property such as homes, vehicles, and small farms. Similarly, farmland held in cooperatives and assets of joint ventures (other than foreign partners' shares) will not be in private hands. Thus, for all practical purposes, when the transition begins, no one in Cuba should be able to claim any significant assets, financial or otherwise.

Second, until substantiated, all ownership claims should be deemed invalid. How to establish legally valid ownership claims will be a challenge. Measures to demonstrate legal ownership could include, for example, a property ownership registry relating current claims against pre-1959 ownership information. Inputs could include pre-Revolution official public records, historical documentation held by claimants in Cuba and abroad, and private property ownership rosters compiled in the United States or elsewhere. The registry should include information on joint-venture properties such as names of foreign entities, valuation of original and current investment, and name of Cuban entity or entities (and individual officers) involving joint ventures.

To prevent misappropriation of state assets, a post-transition government would be advised to take two steps: declare null and void the transfer of state assets to private parties, including foreign persons, that have not gone through a privatization or claims-resolution process with procedures set by the government; and declare null and void all corporations formed under the pretransition government, subject to reinstatement on a case-by-case basis under procedures for a corporate audit to be set up. Operation of the validation system will be made vastly more complicated, of course, if the pretransition government or a corrupt transition government decided to alter or destroy existing records.

Satisfying claims will result in disputes that could take years to resolve, as has happened in other transition countries. This, of course, will be detrimental over the medium and long term for property rights and will adversely affect the national investment climate and economic growth. However, incentives could be built into the claims-resolution process by expediting property certification claims for bona fide owners who satisfactorily document or settle claims.

What we are suggesting should not be construed as a recommendation on whether properties taken over by the Cuban government since 1959 should or should not be returned to their original owners or their descendants. This is a difficult political and economic issue that should be addressed within an overall restitution or compensation framework (Roca 1993). Our concern here is with minimizing spontaneous privatization and other forms of state capture by powerful or well-placed government officials associated with the former regime.

CONCLUSION

It might be possible to minimize corruption in a transition Cuba by relying on available international instruments to prevent corruption in international business transactions and on the financial and policy clout of the international donor community. For this to happen during the early stages of the transition—a time when domestic control mechanisms will be in flux and at their weakest—Cuba's citizens and the international corporate and donor communities must be vigilant. Should preventive measures fail and acts of grand corruption occur absent conniving external actors, redress through the justice system might be possible if in due course Cuba manages to achieve a rule of law and a system of democratic governance.

Seven AVERTING CORRUPTION IN THE LONG TERM

Once the early transition is on its way—and assuming Cuba embarks on a path toward democratic rule and a market economy—the difficult work begins: building a firm economic, institutional, political, and legal foundation to promote good governance and prevent corruption. This will be a complex and time-consuming process. Experiences from many developing and transition countries suggest thatmany policy interventions focusing on institutional reform have fallen short of expectations, and in some cases have failed altogether, where policy makers neglected to take into account how political variables and private-sector agents coalesce to shape the governing environment (Kaufmann 2003).

Results are somewhat more encouraging when the focus is placed exclusively on corruption trends in some of the transition countries. This conclusion is based on analysis of surveys of firms conducted by the World Bank and the European Bank for Reconstruction and Development (EBRD) in 1999 and 2002 in twenty-four countries undergoing reform in Central and Eastern Europe and the Commonwealth of Independent States. When assessing the impact on corruption of reforms in the policy and institutional environment, the World Bank and EBRD found that

> [p]olicy reforms that liberalize the economy generally reduce the power and discretion of public officials and therefore reduce both their opportunities to demand bribes and the benefits that firms derive from bribery. Reforms in public sector management strengthen transparency and accountability and thereby reduce incentives for corrupt behavior. (Gray, Hellman, and Ryterman 2004, 34)

These positive changes were interpreted to have been produced by the joint effect of eight highly interrelated variables whose impacts could not be assessed independently. These are:

- how effectively a country manages inflation and internal and external macroeconomic imbalances;
- the extent to which the trade policy framework and exchange-rate regime promote trade and investment;
- how competitive the private sector environment is;
- how liberalization policies affect factor and product markets;
- how well the public administration designs and implements government policies and delivers public services;
- how effective budgetary and financial management is at setting policy priorities, among other measures, for example in meeting budgeting targets, fiscal reporting and auditing, and implementing budget and revenue allocations at all levels of government;
- whether tax policies work as intended; and
- how effectively private-sector activity is regulated by governments that enforce property and contract rights.

These reforms encompass the gradual establishment and enforcement of market-oriented legal systems and institutions, the development of a viable banking system, enactment of labor market regulations, and creation or modification of institutions related to public employment and retirement systems. They also entail the eventual completion of the privatization process initiated during the early stages of the transition that required a transparent and accountable framework to minimize the potential for abuse.

Furthermore, these economic and management dimensions are complementary to the governance transformations that must be achieved for corruption to be controlled while a national integrity system, as defined by Transparency International, is developed. Through the implementation of such a system, a modern government should attain the goal of promoting "the public interest rather than the private interests of those in control." Pope (2000, 33) finds that the challenge for countries embracing democracy is

> to move away from a system which is essentially top down: one in which an autocratic ruling elite gives orders which are followed, to a greater or lesser degree, by those down the line. The approach

is to move instead to a system of "horizontal accountability"; one in which power is dispersed, where no one has a monopoly, and where each is separately accountable.

Several interconnected and mutually supporting elements are necessary for an integrity system to come into fruition. These embrace the standard separation of powers (executive, legislative, and judicial) that checks the power of rulers in democratic systems, complemented by active citizen involvement and institutions specifically charged with providing oversight and preventing corruption. Included among the latter are a free press and an informed citizenry willing to provide continuous oversight over how public funds are managed and spent. Equally important are an appropriate legal infrastructure to prevent and punish corrupt acts, a civil service capable of effectively and honestly running government operations, and specialized official entities (e.g., comptroller general office, ombudsman, investigation agencies, anticorruption commissions) with a partial or full focus on assessing the management of the state and preventing corruption. No less significant are political institutions (including political parties) willing to curtail abuses and a business environment that rewards rather than punishes firms that play by the rules.

Although the specific components of an integrity system and how they function together may vary from country to country—according to form of government, legal tradition, and so forth—the ultimate goal is to have them operate as part of a coherent whole that, through its combined actions, thwarts the ability of dishonest individuals to exploit corruption opportunities. If they do, the system should be capable of detecting and punishing corrupt acts. Continued vigilance will always be necessary, however. Corruption occurs in the dark, looks for opportunities, and benefits from unrecognized loopholes. Thus, to control corruption, it is essential to be constantly on the lookout for creative new approaches intended to bypass controls, to be prepared to fine-tune preventive mechanisms, and to shine the light of transparency and good governance on potentially corrupt acts.

Rather than focusing on isolated anticorruption instruments, the goal of an integrity system is to build mutually supportive relationships. "As with the pillars of a physical building," the United Nations (2004, 74) notes, "the pillars of integrity are interdependent. A weakening of one pillar will result in an increased load being shifted to the others. The success or failure of the overall structure will thus depend on the ability of each element to support the loads expected of it. If several pillars weaken collectively, or if any one pillar weakens to an extent that cannot be compensated for by the others, the entire structure will fail."

An important insight is that there is no one-size fits-all strategy to combat corruption; the design of a strategy should take into account the type of corruption being targeted and the underlying country-specific causes or "drivers" of dysfunctional governance (Shah and Schacter 2004). Based on studies of Guatemala, Latvia, Pakistan, the Philippines, and Tanzania, the World Bank identified the following corruption drivers: the commitment of national leaders to combat corruption is not strong; the rule of law is weakly embedded; institutions of accountability are ineffective; and the legitimacy of the state as the guardian of the "public interest" is contested.

Where the incidence of corruption is high and the quality of governance poor, the priority of anticorruption efforts should be focused more on the broad underlying features of the governance environment (for example, establishing the rule of law, strengthening institutions of participation and accountability, limiting government intervention, and implementing economic policy reform) and less on tactics that are narrowly targeted at corrupt behavior (such as establishing anticorruption agencies). In societies where the incidence of corruption is low and the quality of governance is good, anticorruption efforts should be focused on strengthening governance capacity, for example by creating anticorruption agencies, strengthening financial accountability, and raising public and official awareness. Our assessment of where Cuba stands with respect to the incidence of corruption and the quality of governance suggests that architects of the Cuban transition should focus on redressing malfeasance in the public sector.

POLITICAL WILL AND POLITICAL INSTITUTIONS

Political will is essential for anticorruption initiatives to succeed. In its absence, reform efforts—no matter how well planned—are condemned to failure. Furthermore, in the presence of a political leadership predisposed to the predation and looting of the state, all imaginable anticorruption measures will fail, as Cuba's own history demonstrates. Political will in a democratic context should not be understood as arising exclusively from the executive, the legislative, or both. Rather, it should be understood as a concerted effort in which the polity as a whole, including the citizenry and the courts, agree to abide by and uphold the rule of law to prevent the use of influence—whether achieved through kinship, political ties, bribery, or friendship—to pervert the decision-making process of public officials (Scott 1969/2002).

This demands the internalization of integrity and accountability values that entail deep attitudinal and normative changes, often in conflict with entrenched cultural values acquired as a result of tradition or historical developments (Heidenheimer and Johnston 2002, 139–140). Internalizing these changes takes time and intensive and sustained civic education effort, coupled with rigorous enforcement mechanisms, as modern forms of political, economic, and administrative procedures consistent with democratic governance are institutionalized (Huntington 1968/2002). In short, an effective anticorruption framework depends on a strong institutional base backed by sufficient political will to make it work.

The departing point, therefore, should be the establishment of transparent and accountable political institutions to safeguard the legitimacy of democratic governance. And in this context, the integrity of political parties is a must. Particularly vulnerable as entry points to corruption are fund-raising for political parties and the financing of election campaigns (see, for example, Whitehead 2002). The history of republican Cuba—and of Latin America more generally—is replete with electoral scandals, the purchase of political influence, and deviation of public resources to favor particular political interests. Seeking to prevent a recurrence of political corruption in a post-transition Cuba must be a top priority. Adequate legal frameworks must be formulated early on to regulate the funding of political parties. These should be based on verifiable requirements for transparency, full disclosure, and campaign contribution funding limits.

Another important element of political will is the readiness to punish corrupt officials who violate the public trust. In fact, some observers believe that punishment is among the most effective deterrents for corruption when used, even if selectively, against high-visibility transgressors (Klitgaard 1988). The jailing of former Nicaraguan President Arnoldo Alemán for grand corruption in 2004, for example, is likely to have a strongly deterrent effect despite continued political instability as the citizens of Nicaragua, a nation with a long history of corruption, come to appreciate that not even a past president is above the law and no one is immune from prosecution for misappropriation of public funds.

Political corruption, to one degree or another, affects all nations, including the United States and other countries with democratic traditions.

Cuba's future rulers will have a great deal to say about how political institutions evolve. A post-transition Cuba should call on European- and U.S.-affiliated governmental, partisan, political, and philanthropic organizations for technical and financial assistance to develop transparent and accountable political institutions that will serve the nation in the long term.

BUILDING PUBLIC AWARENESS

Discounting Cubans' unfamiliarity with democratic governance as a result of the relentless misinformation campaigns carried out during more than four and a half decades of socialist rule could be very costly. Modern concepts of transparency and accountability are unknown to most Cubans, who have only had access to the official media and have been taught that the paternalistic state is not to be questioned. The concepts that public servants are accountable to the citizenry and that citizens have the right to know how government decisions are made are foreign to most Cubans.

While the basic principles of transparency and accountability are second nature to many citizens of democratic societies, they will come as a revelation to many Cubans. Unfortunately, basic rights of access to information and public accountability are not fully exercised in many countries in Latin America and other developing regions. In many countries, national and local budgets and how they are derived continue to be treated as state secrets, programmatic and spending decisions are made in the dark, and public officials act as if they were accountable to no one.

Once the transition is under way, a systematic and long-term effort must be made to educate the citizens of Cuba regarding their right to know how government operates and to assist them in monitoring it. These efforts must begin at a very elementary level and include transparency and accountability as part of a broader national objective to inculcate in the population basic knowledge about civil rights, democratic governance, and the operation of a market economy. Governance education must take into account the awe with which most Cubans regard the state: they must be shown that actions by public officials can and should be challenged when warranted, without fear of retribution. These are obviously difficult topics that will require long-term efforts through many different means including the mass media, school curricula, civic organizations, and government itself.

A COHERENT LEGAL INFRASTRUCTURE TO FOSTER TRANSPARENCY AND ACCOUNTABILITY

It is beyond the scope of this discussion to dwell in detail on the legal infrastructure that will be necessary for a transparent and honest Cuban government. The constitutional and legal foundations of a future Cuba are complex problems whose elucidation will be determined by the country's legal traditions, the nature of the transition, and political leadership.[1] Development of these domestic legal foundations could draw on a body of transnational legal instruments that support national anticorruption initiatives (more on this below).

Domestic legal anticorruption measures generally fall into preventive and curative instruments. As described by Ofosu-Amaah, Soopramanien, and Uprety (1999, 3), the former refer to "a set of upstream rules and norms of good behavior (e.g., codes of conduct, manifestos) conducive to a corruption-free society," and the latter consist of "anticorruption laws proper (general or specific legislative enactment), whose purpose is to provide appropriate remedies, including criminal sanctions and penalties, procedural rules, and institutional mechanisms, as needed, to combat acts of corruption that have already occurred."

A comprehensive legal framework includes organic laws that structure and regulate the public sector and may encompass explicit or implicit transparency/accountability elements, such as civil service laws and associated ethical standards for public servants, and laws regulating how state resources are managed and controlled. Of particular relevance to preventing or reversing state capture are initiatives that promote openness of the state's decision-making processes and the disclosure of interactions that could influence such decisions. Among the specific initiatives to enhance transparency (see, for example, USAID 1999) that might be relevant to a Cuba in transition are:

- Sunshine laws that require government officials to hold certain meetings in public, promoting accountability and transparency in government decision making. Particularly important would be public access to meetings discussing budgetary issues and leading to decisions regarding the use of public property, public hearings to inform citizens about impending public policy issues, and mechanisms to obtain citizen input regarding the development of laws, rules, and regulations.

- Freedom of access to information that would guarantee citizens the right to know how they are governed and consequently would reduce opportunities for mischief. For example, citizens should have a right to know the contents of draft legislation being considered by the government, views put forth by parties regarding legislation, and the voting record of elected officials. When codified as freedom of information requirements, three important issues must be addressed: what government institutions will be covered (as on occasion there are legitimate reasons for governments to withhold information, such as national security); when a covered institution will be justified in withholding information; and what reasonable steps are to be implemented to make freedom-of-information requirements affordable to both government and citizens. These are important criteria, as otherwise the intent of a freedom-of-information system could be thwarted administratively or financially (Roberts 1999).
- Public financial disclosure rules that would require government officials with a certain degree of decision-making power to periodically disclose the extent and nature of their assets, not only to prevent illicit enrichment while holding such positions but also to identify potential conflicts of interest in decision making.
- Whistleblower legislation that would afford employees the right "to challenge workplace corruption and mismanagement," since "secrecy and silence through intimidation and fear are the ultimate objectives and methods underlying organizational reprisal techniques" (Keshet and Devine 2002).
- Ombudsman offices that would allow citizens to raise concerns about governance issues and require government entities to respond to those concerns (Pope 2000, 83–94). Data from surveys conducted under World Bank auspices in many countries suggest that when citizens have ready access to responsive and transparent complaint mechanisms, reductions in corruption in public service delivery follow (Anderson, Kaufmann, and Recanatini 2003, 26).

The domestic legal framework should also devote special attention to issues related to drug trafficking, money laundering, and human trafficking. Following the dismantling of Cuba's police state and the opening of the island to the global economy, these forms of illicit activities are likely to increase significantly and feed corrupt appetites unless effective preventive and curative measures are put in place.

JUDICIAL REFORM

A comprehensive legal framework will not be enough to arrest corruption if judicial institutions are not able to do their part in enforcing the law. A priority task in Cuba will be to dismantle the judicial infrastructure created under socialism and replace it with a judiciary consistent with democratic rule and the separation of powers. This must begin with revamping the country's legal framework and legal educational institutions and must be extended to: recruiting and training new judges and court staff; retraining former judges and court staff who are to be retained; developing prosecutorial and police investigatory capabilities; and creating a judicial career, a judicial service, and defense and legal assistance services. A priority goal should be to put in place measures to ensure judicial independence and prevent political and private business interests from influencing court decisions, in order to limit opportunities for corruption and improve governance overall.

Such an ambitious endeavor will take many years to implement and must be part and parcel of a much broader government reorganization and innovation process. To enhance its effectiveness, the judicial reform effort should rely on the introduction of the latest management and communications technologies to ensure fairness and transparency. In many settings, information technologies have been found to be particularly useful in keeping track of investigations, expediting trials, and limiting corruption in court proceedings by minimizing opportunities for unethical judges and court staff to manipulate assignment of cases and ensure proper court proceedings, such as in filing and tracking evidence. Downstream, the reform effort must be extended to build enforcement and penal capacity, since punishment of those convicted of illegal behavior is among the most effective anticorruption interventions.

INTERNATIONAL LEGAL INSTRUMENTS

The international community has adopted several legal instruments to minimize public sector bribery and other illicit practices, recognizing that "international cooperation can help engender both the will to fight corruption and the capability to do so" (Klitgaard 1998, 5). Since bribery often involves illegal payments by transnational corporations to public officials in the country where the corrupt act occurs, international instruments tend to complement each other by criminalizing bribe payment by foreign firms and/or penalizing bribe acceptance by public officials or politicians. International cooperation is often needed to investigate, prosecute, and punish corrupt individuals or to recover ill-gotten assets even when the offense is committed solely within a country's border and without the involvement of an offender from a second country.

Of particular relevance for a post-transition Cuba are anticorruption conventions developed by the OECD, the OAS, and the UN. Also relevant will be Cuba's eventually more active participation in the World Trade Organization (WTO), as this will require modernizing the island's legal and institutional commercial frameworks and effectively enforcing laws, a development that in due course will contribute to dampening corruption.

The Convention on Combating Bribery of Foreign Public Officials in International Business Transactions adopted by the OECD in 1997 (OECD 1998) is modeled after the U.S. Foreign Corrupt Practices Act (FCPA). It is intended to prevent bribe payments by private entities of signatory countries conducting business abroad. Signatories to the OECD convention agree to the following stipulations, among others:

- Each party shall take measures as necessary to establish that it is a criminal offense under its law for any person intentionally to offer, promise, or give any undue pecuniary or other advantage, whether directly or through intermediaries, to a foreign public official, for that official, or for a third party, to influence the official to act or refrain from acting in relation to the performance of official duties in order to obtain an improper advantage in the conduct of international business;
- Each party shall take any measures necessary to establish that complicity in—including incitement, aiding, and abetting—or authorization of an act of bribery of a foreign public official shall be a criminal offense. Attempt and conspiracy to bribe a foreign public official shall be criminal offenses to the same extent as attempt and conspiracy by that party to bribe a public official.

An important regional instrument, very germane to a post-transition Cuba, is the Inter-American Convention Against Corruption (ICAC) adopted in 1996 under the auspices of the OAS; its focus is on curbing corruption at home. It complements the OECD convention by requiring signatory countries to promote and strengthen the development the mechanisms needed to prevent, detect, punish, and eradicate corruption, as well as to promote, facilitate, and regulate cooperation with fellow signatory states to ensure the effectiveness of these measures and actions in the performance of public functions and acts of corruption specifically related to such performance.

The ICAC requires signatory countries to develop standards of conduct for public officials, strengthen control systems, and promote civil society involvement in the prevention of corruption. Corruption is defined in the convention as an extraditable offense; signatory countries "shall not invoke bank secrecy as a basis for refusal to provide the assistance sought by another state" conducting an investigation. Upon the ICAC's ratification by OAS member states, a follow-up mechanism was established in May 2001 to monitor implementation of national commitments. Civil society plays a leading role in monitoring compliance.

The United Nations Convention Against Corruption (UNCAC) signed in late 2003 is similar in intent to the ICAC but has a global reach. It includes chapters on preventive measures, criminalization and law enforcement, international cooperation, asset recovery, technical assistance and information exchange, and mechanisms for implementation (UN 2003). Like the ICAC, the UNCAC calls for each ratifying state to "take the necessary measures, including legislative and administrative measures, in accordance with fundamental principles of its domestic laws, to ensure the implementation of its obligations under this Convention."

A Cuba in transition should promptly become signatory to the ICAC and the OECD convention (both instruments are open to signature by non-members of the OAS and the OECD, respectively) and to other international agreements to combat corruption. It should also adopt the necessary legal enabling domestic mechanisms to comply with national enforcement and international cooperation obligations embodied in these international instruments.

REINVENTING AND INNOVATING GOVERNMENT

A major revolution in state management, driven by a reassessment of the role of the state in promoting economic growth and social welfare, is occurring around the world (OECD 2000, 2001; Osborne and Gebler 1992). Mostly driven by globalization and technological developments, this reassessment of the role of the state has concluded that what is required is not large and all powerful governments that plan for and control all aspects of economies and societies but competent states that guide and facilitate economic growth, enhance human capacity, mobilize financial and human resources for development, promote and encourage private enterprise, protect economically and socially vulnerable groups, combat poverty, and protect the natural environment and physical resources through democratic, participatory, honest, efficient, effective, and accountable political and administrative systems. (Rondinelli and Cheema 2003, 243)

Governments are seeking more cost-effective and strategic approaches to manage public resources, serve the trust of the people, and accommodate the increasingly complex demands of an interdependent, competitive, and technologically proficient world. A post-transition Cuba must embrace this global trend and adopt government innovations pioneered over the past two decades by the more developed nations. The country is well equipped to join this trend, given the high educational levels of its population and the relative ease with which it should be able to modernize its technological infrastructure once a transition begins.

Government management reform takes maximum advantage of information and communication technologies, whose costs are on a permanent downward sloping trend, to provide more transparent and higher-quality services and improve government efficiency. Current "electronic government" (e-government) programs being implemented in most developed and many developing countries include:

- "government to government" (G2G) services to facilitate interactions and refine management processes within the public administration;
- "citizens to government" (C2G), through which citizens can gain rapid and unimpeded access to public information and conduct numerous transactions with government;
- "employees to government" (E2G), through which employees interact with the bureaucracy, including for recruitment and training activities; and
- "business to government" (B2G) programs intended to open and make transparent the relationship between the public sector and private sector firms that supply goods and services to the government to enhance efficiency and economy and to reduce opportunities for corruption, as modern procurement systems increasingly

rely on e-procurement to simplify government acquisitions procedures and conduct public tenders under the watchful public eye.

In addition to the availability and use of the basic technological infrastructure, effective implementation of e-government procedures demands
a broad-based training component to make public officials aware of their
responsibilities. It also calls for a legal regulatory framework that clearly
delineates e-government functions and rules controlling interactions
among government, the business community, and the citizenry. Finally,
for e-government to take root, it will also be essential to launch a comprehensive public education program to inform citizens about their rights and
how transparency-enhancing technology can be used as an oversight tool.

A PROFESSIONAL CIVIL SERVICE

An essential pillar of a long-term transparency/accountability strategy is a
well-trained, professional civil service capable of efficiently discharging its
obligations to the nation and the public while safeguarding the national
patrimony and complying with international obligations. Developing such
a professional civil service is fraught with difficulties and will require many
years of effort. However, its development should be tackled systematically
and with an eye to what is and is not achievable.

The upper echelons of socialist Cuba's civil service are thoroughly politicized: Communist Party *apparatchiks* and their families and friends control all of the top government positions. Furthermore, Cuba's civil service
is bloated, notorious for its inefficiency, out of tune with modern managerial concepts, enmeshed in a tradition of secrecy and lack of transparency, oblivious to the notion of customer service, and poorly paid. What
is needed is a change in the culture of the civil service, doing away with
an unsavory tradition, dating to before 1959 and aggravated by socialism,
wherein as "corruption becomes the rule, and non corruption the exception, the practice transforms itself into a norm" (Médard 2002, 394).

As conceptualized by the international development community, civil
service reform should begin with a thorough assessment of the country's
governance needs in relation to projected resources and include the development of clear procedures for recruitment, retention, promotion, and
training. From the onset, a civil service reform program must make it a
priority to link objectives with results, that is, to promote accountability.
Advancement and promotions should be contingent on the accomplish-

ment of results within allotted budgets, and hiring strictly should be contingent on merit. To the extent possible, the pitfall of insufficient remuneration should be avoided. The system, finally, must be designed to make the professional civil service impervious to changes in political winds to ensure its long-term sustainability, thus minimizing the chances for establishing a threatening and punitive atmosphere that may be demoralizing for honest and dedicated public servants (Anechiarico and Jacobs 1996/2002).

Current thinking in development circles calls for integrated civil service reforms to be based on results-oriented management and decentralization of decision making, the focus being placed on four particular dimensions of reform. These are, first, to establish a connection among civil service management, financial controls, and incentives management to forge strong links between personnel and budget functions; second, to provide ample room for citizen oversight of public management; third, to establish decentralized and results-oriented management, so that government actions are brought closer to the public and service delivery is improved through civic and business oversight; and fourth, to align central government reforms with sector-level reforms, particularly for important line ministries (such as education and health) to reduce malfeasance through transparency and accountability. An important component of these efforts is the identification of sectors particularly prone to corruption and the implementation of control measures (UN 2004, 110, 112–113).

The end result should be a professional and nonpolitical civil service that operates according to transparent and unambiguous rules and that rewards and advances staff based on merit rather than on political favoritism or nepotism. The United Nations (2004, 114) has observed that developing countries, including Cuba, will be well served if they adopt practices introduced by industrial countries in the 1990s for

> building integrity to curb corruption and improving the timeliness, quality, value for money, and coverage of service delivery. Governments have reshaped rigid, hierarchical, unresponsive, closed, unaccountable, bloated and corrupt bureaucracies into flexible, affordable, evidence-based, impact-oriented, accountable, citizen-responsive organizations with corruption under control.

In practice, the civil service reform process has proved far more difficult than was envisioned by the experts and organizations that designed them. A recent assessment of civil service reform in developing countries concludes that it "has proven among the most difficult of developmental reforms to sustain, and there is little evidence that nationally or donor-inspired reform efforts have met with much success" (Sheperd 2003, 2). The reason, he asserts, is that in most countries, political, economic, and social circumstances have not been conducive to reform.

Since the end of World War II, a stronger state was deemed an instrument for economic growth and a provider of welfare services. The size of the civil service expanded, often beyond the state's financial capacity, with government becoming the de facto employer of last resort. Along the way, civil servants became potent interest groups invested with rights such as tenure enshrined in law that have proven very difficult to reverse. In developing countries, high unemployment aggravated the situation, as even skilled professionals had only limited employment options outside the state sector, raising the political price to pay for attempting to reduce the size of the civil service. One approach may be to seek to separate the management and welfare functions of state employment, thereby simplifying the reform process.

Given this reality, Sheperd (2003) recommends that civil service reform strategies should be reformulated by reassessing the role of patronage systems in state management. He reasons that while in principle professional bureaucracies may be more efficient, they are generally ineffective in providing quality services, as they lack political wherewithal. Paradoxically, argues Sheperd, it may make more sense over the short term to deepen the reach of political appointments into lower layers of the bureaucracy to enhance civil service effectiveness while accommodating patronage demands. This may require reconsidering, over the short term, the value of merit-based reforms and lifetime tenure for civil servants. The history of countries that have implemented lasting and consequential civil service reforms indicates that "it is economic and social development that will improve the pool of human resources, reduce the need to use public sector jobs for welfare policy, and create a demand from the public and business for better public services." When this happens, "merit-based reforms are likely to follow, as they did in today's rich countries" (Sheperd 2003, 16).

Alternative approaches to these dilemmas are being implemented or considered in a number of countries. While they are not perfect, they offer practical means where other models have failed. These alternatives range from the partial introduction of merit-based criteria in agencies being reformed to professionalization of selected segments of the civil service. For example, if the focus is on reducing corruption, the emphasis should be placed on reforming accountability entities (an Office of the Comptroller General), agencies very vulnerable to corruption (Customs), and government functions prone to be corrupted by bribes or state capture (procurement). Another option would be to implement hybrid systems where elements of patronage and merit-based systems are combined such as by assigning applicants to a pool on the basis of qualifications and then selecting candidates for appointments from the pool on the basis of political criteria. Regardless of approach, suspicion and political manipulation could be minimized by consistency of rules and transparency.

In the final analysis, results of empirical studies suggest some basic steps to build effective civil services. These include reliance on meritocratic and clear administrative rules to increase performance; careful attention to the sequencing of reforms; and monitoring by government, the public, and the courts. With respect to reducing corruption, political commitment is paramount, as is the need to align economic incentives to encourage private firms to play by the rules rather than to try to capture the state (World Bank 2003).

The transition away from socialism will eventually lead to a substantial reduction in the number of civil servants as more satisfying and better-remunerated employment opportunities open in the private sector and the role of government in the economy declines. This means that a painful process of retrenchment lies ahead for Cuban civil servants. Political realities and sensitivities will determine which public officials will be retained and which let go, but as much as possible these decisions should be made according to well-specified skill criteria and organizational needs.

A CODE OF ETHICS
FOR PUBLIC OFFICIALS

For codes of ethics to be effective, they must be implemented in national settings characterized by political openness and transparency, two ingredients lacking in Cuba today. They have been found to work reasonably well in countries where the actions of the highest authorities can be discussed and challenged openly. Furthermore, they appear to work best when "an improper act of a professional nature can be questioned by peers, and the professional group may take actions according to the mores of the group" (Ofosu-Amaah, Soopramanien, and Uprety 1999, 16).

On the basis of the conduct of public officials in socialist Cuba, there is ample reason to be pessimistic about the usefulness of codes of ethics for public officials as a means to limit corruption in the near future. But once the institutional, economic, ideological, and political setting changes, there is some room for optimism.

In 1997 Cuba enacted a Código de Ética de los Cuadros del Estado Cubano (Colombié Santana 2001, 7). Reflecting the ideological dogma of the totalitarian state, this code of ethics relies on the same principles that over more than four decades have been unsuccessful in controlling corruption in socialist Cuba; it fails to come to terms with the lack of transparency, lack of individual accountability, and inability of public servants to challenge the upper reaches of political leadership. While calling for honesty and probity in managing public resources by mid- and high-level officials, the code of ethics invalidates accountability requirements by demanding obedience to the dictates of the Communist Party and by formalizing "the inevitable duty of preserving State secrets, regarding all subjects and information, to contribute to safeguarding our interests against enemy action" (ibid.). These requirements place official actions beyond public scrutiny, making a mockery of the accountability and transparency foundations upon which modern government management systems are built.

Once a Cuban transition occurs, code of ethics may play an important role in limiting corruption, particularly if institutional mechanisms and enforceable laws are able to control abuses of power. Public servants should be protected from political pressures; decision-making processes should be made transparent and open to scrutiny; and adequate accounting mechanisms should be adopted (Pope 2000, 175–194).

In market economies, the effectiveness of codes of ethics for public officials hinges on training and enforcement dimensions. Government officials are routinely trained on their application, and there are procedures to make them work. These include conflict-of-interest rules backed up with penalties, asset declaration, antinepotism rules, and post-employment limitations. In their absence, codes of ethics are only pieces of paper with no real impact.

FINANCIAL MANAGEMENT, CONTROL, AND AUDIT

Effective management of the national economy has never been a policy priority of socialist Cuba. Generous Soviet subsidies, which lasted through the end of the 1980s, masked the regime's inefficiency and misuse of resources. During a period in the mid-1960s, as noted earlier, Cuba went so far as to abolish the Ministry of Finance, eliminate the national budget, and set aside accounting systems, doing away with concepts such as cost of goods sold and interest payments; the study of the political economy of socialism, as well as the career of public accountant, disappeared from the university during this period (Batista Odio 1986, 239–240).

In the 1970s some of these radical policies gradually began to be reversed as attempts were made, under Soviet prodding, to regain a modicum of economic efficiency. In 1995 President Fidel Castro, noting that widespread corruption had been an important factor behind the demise of the Soviet Union, put forth measures to improve accounting and auditing procedures, as well as to reduce black-market activities ("Cuba crea" 2001). In May 2001 the Cuban government announced the creation of a new Ministry for Audit and Control ("Creado el Ministerio" 2001). At the same time, the government took action to promote other anticorruption measures, including the referenced code of ethics for public officials, establishment of a national financial control commission, new laws to punish corrupt public officials, and improvements in government accounting practices (Colombié Santana 2001; "Cuba crea" 2001). The government expanded training for accounting and audit personnel to support *perfeccionamiento empresarial,* a new management system for state enterprises intended to enhance their efficiency within the context of state ownership and control. The magnitude of the challenge should not be underestimated. In 2000, for example, in 54 percent of three hundred audited state enterprises, accounting procedures were poor and resources inadequately controlled (Espinosa Chepe 2001). While many of these initiatives are part and parcel of the standard anticorruption tool kit, they are unlikely to have the desired impact under the conditions prevailing in socialist Cuba.

The factors that conspire against the efficacy of current control systems in Cuba should be at the forefront of the thinking of those designing post-transition transparency/accountability initiatives. Perhaps the most significant is that to fulfill its functions adequately and prevent corruption, political and financial independence must be guaranteed for a Supreme Audit Institution (SAI), the functional equivalent of Cuba's current Ministry for Audit and Control and in many countries the domain of the Office of the Comptroller General. This can only be assured if the SAI enjoys "a significant degree of functional independence and separation both from the legislative and from the political elements of executive government" (UN 2004, 86), conditions not present in today's Cuba.

A post-transition Cuba must guard against the temptation to recreate institutions that have failed to control corruption in Cuba and elsewhere and instead have engendered political deals to cover corrupt acts, such as courts of accounts (*tribunales de cuentas*). The principles underlying a court of accounts are in conflict with those of a modern SAI. SAIs typically provide an independent audit function, promote financial control improvements, and disseminate audit findings but do not make legal determinations or prosecute wrongdoing. Courts of accounts, meanwhile, are empowered to render judgments and prosecute wrongdoing, which creates grave conflicts and the opportunity for cover-ups through the political process that appoints its members. Furthermore, the fairness of the courts' decisions are always open to question—their rulings cannot be appealed because their own audit findings are not subject to independent review.

Since the 1980s many Latin American countries, at the urging of the USAID and with financial support from the World Bank and the Inter-American Development Bank, have embarked on complex and ambitious long-term efforts to develop Integrated Financial Management Systems (IFMSs) in Latin America. An IFMS consists of

> an interrelated set of subsystems that plan, process, and report
> on resources, quantifying them in financial terms. The basic sub-
> systems normally are accounting, budgeting, cash management,
> debt management, and their related internal controls. Other sub-
> systems sometimes included in an IFMS are collection and re-
> ceivable management, acquisitions and supply management,
> information management, tax and customs administrations, and
> retirement or social security system administration, together with
> their own internal controls. One of the most important elements
> of internal control is an independent and professional internal audit
> function, which constitutes an integral part of IFMS. (Wesberry
> 2001b, 97)

When working in tandem with other control and oversight mechanisms, an IFMS can contribute significantly to the fight against corruption. The strength of an IFMS in deterring corruption lies in its ability to generate a "common, single, reliable database to and from which all data flows" (ibid.) since all data users must submit information to a shared accounting system. Modern IFMSs, dependent on powerful high-technology tools, help prevent corruption in many ways. They provide multilevel budgetary control, spotlight weaknesses, validate integrity, and enable control over resources. Further, IFMSs promote transparency, require consistent policies, decentralize authority and accountability, provide immediate audit capabilities, can discern patterns of corrupt practices, and facilitate computer-assisted auditing (Wesberry 2001b, 98–99; see also Pope 2000, 221–234).

The importance of effective internal controls in a modern government financial management system should not be underestimated. Internal controls depend on strategic and operational planning approaches to identify corrective actions that can minimize risks. Internal control guidelines developed by the Committee of Sponsoring Organizations of the Treadway Commission (COSO 2004), although originally intended for the private sector, are also being applied to public-sector activities. Their five interrelated components are: control environment, risk assessment, control activities, information and communication, and monitoring. Within government, COSO-based internal control systems seek to achieve impartiality, ethical behavior, efficiency, economy, timeliness, and transparency (Casals and Associates 2004a). When coupled with internal and external audits, modern internal controls encourage efficiency in government agencies, minimize chances for the misuse or misappropriation of resources, and result in increased institutional and individual accountability. Internal controls are not infallible, however, as their intent can always be frustrated by manipulations by unscrupulous individuals. But in association with other control instruments such as internal and external audits, they can act as powerful deterrents to corruption.

Contemporary government audit procedures provide a wide assortment of approaches to boost the efficiency of government operations and promote probity. Audits are intended to provide independent verification of information and analysis, although the degree of independence varies according to requirements: internal audits provide the least independence, as they are generally conducted under the purview of the administrative heads of units being audited, while external audits allow the greatest degree of independence. Audits are intended to pinpoint evidentiary weaknesses; identify strengths and weaknesses of administrative structures; develop baselines against which to assess changes in procedures; provide credible information to the public; and when evidence of administrative deficiencies or wrongdoing is uncovered, make pertinent information accessible to disciplinary or law enforcement agencies (UN 2004, 83–84). The range and scope of public audits (both internal and external) are extensive and encompass diverse objectives, from the more traditional financial audit to the most comprehensive and specialized performance audits. Political will and management commitment are essential if auditors and auditing agencies are to fulfill their functions, including taking action on audit recommendations.

Although the advantage of an IFMS for a post-transition Cuba is beyond dispute, both for efficiency in government and for curbing corruption, it will take a decade or more and tens of millions of dollars to make such a system fully functional. An IFMS that is national in scope requires the development and implementation of accounting and auditing standards, the initial and ongoing training of financial management personnel, and the acquisition and installation of modern computer systems linking all branches of government, from the central government to the municipalities. Fortunately, technological advances, particularly the development of microcomputers, make it feasible to gradually introduce modern financial management practices, perhaps focusing first on key organizations (i.e., line ministries). Also to Cuba's advantage are the considerable experience and knowledge the international financial institutions have accumulated through the technical support and financial assistance they have offered to many countries in the design and introduction of IFMSs.

PUBLIC PROCUREMENT

Few areas of government activity offer more opportunities for corruption than public-sector procurement. Public-sector purchase decisions are vulnerable not only to bureaucratic discretion but also to the misuse of political influence. In pre-Castro Cuba, allegations of corruption in public-sector procurement were common and often the source of political disputes. Since 1959, comparable accusations have become relatively infrequent, mostly due to the centralized nature of the totalitarian state, the absence of domestic private firms, and rigid press censorship. In addition, international public-sector procurement in socialist Cuba is conducted behind closed doors, outside public scrutiny, and according to whatever rules are found expedient to satisfy political or national-security goals or simply the interests of the governing elite.

With a transition to a market-oriented economy, Cuba would do well to adhere to accepted international norms regarding public procurement. There is a growing global movement to reform public procurement procedures to accelerate economic growth, make government more efficient, and rein in public spending. The impetus for change has been the realization that corruption in public sector procurement creates many economic distortions that interfere with the development process. Key remedies relate to greater transparency and clearer rules governing how public contracts are awarded to bidders.

Pope (2000, 206–207) has identified the following basic principles that define a fair and efficient public procurement process:

- It should be economical; that is, through the procurement process the government should acquire those goods and services that offer the best combination of quality and price.
- It should be fair and impartial. Bid winners should be chosen on the basis of qualifications and merit.
- It should be transparent. Bidders should respond to specifications that are announced publicly. The overall process should be transparent so that "institutions, processes, and decisions are made accessible to the public at large or to representatives of the public so that processes and decisions can be monitored, reviewed, commented upon, and influenced by the stakeholders" (Wiehen 2001, 86).
- It should have a complexity commensurate with the nature of the goods or services being purchased and, most importantly, should be accountable to the public.
- It should justify and record the bases for all decisions.

Establishing a market-oriented public sector procurement system in a post-transition Cuba may be facilitated by the adoption of a modern e-procurement system as part of an overall government innovation strategy, as well as by embracing norms recommended by international organizations. Examples are norms embodied in the international competitive bidding (ICB) principles of the World Bank and the Model Law on Procurement of Goods, Construction, and Services of the UN Commission on International Law (UNCITRAL). These recommended norms should not be adopted uncritically, however, but rather tailored to the national context in which they are to operate, seeking within that national context to maximize efficiency, timeliness, and anticorruption objectives. Public procurement reforms that should be carried out in Cuba as elsewhere "highlight the tradeoffs between avoiding corruption and giving officials the flexibility to make decisions in the light of their own knowledge. Discretion increases corrupt incentives, but critics of elaborate procurement codes point to their excessive rigidity" (Rose-Ackerman 1999, 59).

When appropriate, past procurement experience should serve as valid selection criteria, provided sufficient information is available to allow as many bidders as possible to participate in public competitions. Related to the above is the need to prevent firms from using information to collude to rig prices. Rose-Ackerman recommends that, when feasible, procurement officials rely on price benchmarking—comparisons with prices of goods and services offered in the marketplace—to simplify purchases and acquire the best products and services for the lowest prices. A basic principle of procurement systems where integrity is at a premium is that the more accountable and transparent they are, the more discretion they could grant public officials (ibid., 64).

In summary, a post-transition Cuba should design and implement public-sector procurement procedures guided by the principle of transparency and accountability for public officials. Following Wesberry (2001a, 86), bidding competitions should "describe clearly and fairly what is to be purchased; publicize the opportunity to make offers to supply; establish fair criteria for selection of bids; receive offers (bids) from responsible suppliers; compare them and determine which is best, according to the predetermined rules for selection." Contracts should be awarded to winning bidders with no price reduction demands or changes in winning offers (other than those negotiated under pre-established rules for Best and Final Offers, BAFOs). The establishment of modern and transparent procurement procedures should be part and parcel of a broader civil service reform process whose ultimate intent is the development of an efficient and responsive state.

CITIZEN OVERSIGHT

There is broad consensus in the transparency/anticorruption community that without a vibrant and vigilant civil society, legal and technical measures by themselves are insufficient to stem corruption (Kaufmann 2003). Involving civil society in the fight against corruption is at the center of most anticorruption efforts today because doing so is vital to help create or sustain political will for anticorruption reforms, monitor implementation of anticorruption initiatives, and provide oversight of public budgets and procurement. This is the case, for example, with the specialized anticorruption agencies established in various countries with the three-pronged mandate of investigation, prevention, and public education (see below). The rationale behind this mandate is that the three domains are mutually supportive: a well-educated and vigilant public provides crucial input for preventive and investigative functions, while effective prevention and investigation encourage citizen involvement. Other more focused approaches, popular in Latin America, rest on the notion that the citizenry has to be educated and mobilized to provide oversight on how the government sector allocates and uses public resources. Social auditing (also known as social control in Honduras, *veedurías* in Colombia, and scorecard in India) entails mobilizing citizens to provide oversight of particular types of projects, generally but not always at the community level. Puerta (2004) provides general guidelines for the future establishment of social auditing in Cuba.

While citizen oversight initiatives are part and parcel of the right of association citizens enjoy in a democratic society and should rightfully play a role in limiting corruption in a post-transition Cuba, the history of the country dictates that they should be designed cautiously. More than four decades of government-inspired and -controlled mass organizations will surely leave a sour taste among many Cubans.[2] They are likely to react to citizen oversight schemes as they do to the Committees for the Defense of the Revolution and other totalitarian-inspired organizations created by the Castro government as instruments for social and political control. A similar concern has arisen in the former Soviet Union, where the introduction of whistleblower programs advocated in the West has been politically contentious, given the country's totalitarian past. To succeed, future social auditing programs must be given very clear and specific legal mandates and promoted strictly on a voluntary basis.

Current thinking in developing circles is emphatic in the notion that one of the most effective ways to curb corruption is to shift political power and spending authority away from central governments and toward local or municipal governments. Citizens are more aware of and have a more direct stake in how local governments deliver services and manage resources, have a greater ability to influence the decision-making process, and can more closely monitor performance. Thus, governments in the developing world have amended their constitutions and other legal instruments to gradually increase the financial resources and responsibilities flowing from central to local governments, especially municipalities. Aside from efficiency and equity reasons, the goal is to shift power away from highly centralized governments that historically have been responsive to powerful urban-based political constituencies and neglected more marginal segments of the national population.

Although the situation in Cuba over the past several decades has differed in some significant respects from most of the developing world, the centralization of decision-making under the socialist regime has been extreme. A notable exception appears to have been in the management of social services, where municipalities have a significant role (Dilla 2001). A long-term transparency/anticorruption strategy should devolve political and financial management to communities, with the caveat that such communities must have the institutional capacity to manage and monitor public spending. Initiatives of this nature must be accompanied by legal instruments that encourage community participation in decision making and grant unrestricted oversight rights to individuals and citizen groups over how local government decisions are made and financial resources managed. The latter should be facilitated by the introduction of e-government, through which most public documents, including those related to financial affairs, can be made readily available for citizen inspection. It should be obvious that aside from its beneficial effects in controlling corruption, decentralization of financial and management authority will result in deepening democratic governance by encouraging citizen involvement in all facets of political life.

THE BUSINESS COMMUNITY

As a key actor in implementing anticorruption initiatives, the role of the business sector in curbing corruption cannot be minimized. Private-sector firms bear the brunt of public-sector corruption that harms their interests, while perversely, others benefit from it. Most reputable businesses would prefer to operate in a competitive, corruption-free environment, but often they are deterred from doing so by a "prisoner's dilemma": firms unwilling to pay bribes or provide other favors to corrupt officials can lose business to firms not likewise constrained. Firms sometimes also engage in state capture, creating or bending laws and regulations in their favor, which perhaps is the most costly and damaging form of corruption.

The experience of countries in transition suggests that to prosper, they must create conditions whereby citizens and the private sector appreciate the forces that drive a market economy in an environment where business adheres to basic rules to promote commercial success and social welfare. The U.S. Department of Commerce (2004, ix) summarizes this interaction in a publication intended to promote ethical business practices in transition economies:

> Government has an important role in the spread of freedom and democratic capitalism. It provides for the essential market-oriented legal framework and reliable dispute resolution processes that allow businesses to compete fairly on the quality, prices, and delivery of their goods and services alone. It enforces laws, regulations, and judgments to safeguard the social order its citizens value. It cannot,

however, act alone. Businesses and civil society must also be involved in solutions to community problems. They can help in the fight against the corruption that saps national resources. They must reform the unethical business practices that breed cynicism and distrust in communities. . . . Markets become free and remain free if their players are responsible and respect the basic values of honesty, reliability, fairness, and self-discipline.

Firms and business associations that adhere to ethical standards and principles of good corporate governance and corporate social responsibility can have a substantial impact on averting corruption—firms by adhering to ethical standards in their conduct and associations by promoting the wide adoption of ethical standards and by discouraging shady deals. Business associations and companies acting individually or as a group could enact and help enforce business ethics codes, assist individual firms comply with procurement procedures and rules to prevent the payment of bribes, and serve as conduits for transparency-promoting dialogues between the private and public sectors (OECD 1999).

Openness to international trade can also act as an incentive for transparency and accountability in business transactions, as firms and the public sector come under growing pressure to conform to global trade standards. Embracing international trade rules set out by the WTO and embodied in bilateral or regional trade agreements will have important anticorruption ramifications. Although the WTO does not directly address corruption, provisions of WTO agreements that promote transparency, foster nondiscrimination (recall that corrupt practices often involve the differential treatment of potential suppliers), and create dispute settlement mechanisms to allay arbitrary government actions. Clear rules prevent officials from requesting bribes and firms from offering them in exchange for preferential treatment (OECD 2000).

COALITION BUILDING

Citizen oversight is a most effective means of combating corruption, particularly when broad sectors of society join forces to do so. While the efforts of individual citizens can contribute to averting corruption, collective actions instigated or embraced by citizen organizations coalescing around particular goals or professional interests can have multiplier effects that greatly enhance the impact of anticorruption initiatives. Collective actions by professional associations (of accountants, auditors, lawyers, engineers, physicians, educators, and so forth) and by labor unions, media, business associations, and other organizations to curb corruption can be particularly effective. These could include, for example, the adoption of professional or business codes of ethics, the promotion of ethics training, and the creation of peer monitoring and review mechanisms to ensure proper conduct.

Even more significant is the coming together of different social sectors to achieve common goals, as when professional associations lend their technical expertise to civil society organizations to monitor the manner in which public-sector projects are designed, managed, or financed. The cooperative principle is implicit in many social auditing schemes, such as when professional associations provide expertise to citizen watchdog groups or when firms agree to public procurement bidding principles monitored by citizens' organizations. As long as a true commitment exists to adopt ethical and transparent values, the broader the coalition building a framework of integrity, the better.

ANTICORRUPTION ENTITIES

An important policy issue for a post-transition Cuban government will be to decide whether to establish special-purpose anticorruption entities in addition to anticorruption units embedded within government ministries and institutions. In most functioning democracies with transparent and efficient public sectors and routine citizen oversight of government activities, such special-purpose agencies are redundant, as their functions are carried out by other government bodies. However, the need for such agencies seems to be present in countries with a history of authoritarian rule and lacking a transparency tradition. Specialized anticorruption agencies could be provided with a legal mandate to conduct investigations and engage in preventive functions; alternatively, anticorruption commissions could be convened as vehicles for the private and public sectors and civil society to collaborate in developing, implementing, and monitoring a national transparency/accountability strategy.

The formal mandate of existing specialized anticorruption agencies includes investigative and initial prosecution functions, a preventive agenda, and a broad directive to educate and raise awareness about corruption. The best-known and most successful is the Hong Kong Independent Commission Against Corruption instituted under British rule (Johnston 1999). Similar bodies have been created in Singapore, Botswana, Nepal, and Nigeria, among others. Countries facing entrenched corruption have favored the creation of specialized anticorruption agencies because these can rapidly zero in on corruption, given their mandate, and can be effective, given their expertise, autonomy, independence, and public credibility. Important issues that must be assessed when considering establishment of specialized anticorruption agencies include their scope (national, regional) and whether they are intended to be permanent or temporary. Disadvantages of specialized anticorruption agencies include their administrative costs and their tendency to diminish the standing of other oversight and investigatory entities. Clearly, for such agencies to be effective they must be embodied with very specific mandates and related authority, sufficient resources, secure tenure for their leading officers, and considerable political capital and will so that they can meet the often difficult challenges they will face (UN 2004, 79–81).

With a few exceptions (notably Hong Kong), the successes of specialized anticorruption agencies have been limited. An assessment of international experiences indicates that for anticorruption agencies to succeed they must have a clear strategy from the outset; include careful planning and ways to evaluate performance; be realistic in their expectations; and have sufficient political backing to pursue their mandate regardless of consequences. The most successful agencies have been able to "overcome coordination, information, and leadership constraint that a multiple agency approach might not have," although they are "largely incapable of addressing the larger forces driving systemic corruption" as "there is no way [they] can be effective in a situation where essentially every important institution is compromised" (Meagher 2004, 72–73). However, that is likely to be the case in a transitional Cuba. Their disappointing performance has been attributed to lack of political will or institutional capacity to implement findings and recommendations and to the common practice (in executive and legislative branches) of constricting their effectiveness by limiting their funding. Repeated constitutional and legal jurisdictional challenges (as in Nigeria) have also contributed to their perceived lack of effectiveness. Other reasons noted for the lackluster record of specialized anticorruption agencies include political interference, unrealistic expectations, excessive reliance on enforcement, low morale, and even that the entities themselves become corrupt (Pope 2000, 95, citing Bertrand de Speville, former director of the Hong Kong Commission).

Some observers have questioned whether specialized anticorruption agencies can be as effective in performing their duties in larger and more complex countries as they can in city-states such as Hong Kong and

Singapore where they seem to have attained their objectives (Heidenheimer and Johnston 2002, 465). It has also been noted in this connection that the effectiveness of the agencies in these two jurisdictions may be a function of their strong mandates in political environments of restricted democracy and limited civil liberties (Ades and Di Tella 1997, 3, 22).

National anticorruption commissions have been established in several countries to provide fora where representatives of the various sectors can regularly meet to identify, discuss, and make recommendations regarding transparency/anticorruption issues. Advocated by the World Bank Institute, such commissions should serve exclusively as consultative, fact-finding bodies with the capacity to make policy recommendations. They typically provide a tripartite forum where high-level government officials (e.g., representatives from the office of the president, justice department, financial control entities, customs, procurement) can meet with civil society representatives (e.g., nongovernmental organizations, media, academia, clergy, organized labor) and the business community to discuss the causes and consequences of corruption; identify viable mid- to long-term strategies to address corruption, including the formulation of anticorruption legislation; and design appropriate institutional frameworks to combat corruption, such as national integrity systems, if warranted. Their tasks may include monitoring the implementation of a national anticorruption strategy, educating society about the implications of corruption, and mobilizing citizen support for anticorruption initiatives. Essential to viability is full participation by civil society, as commissioners must be perceived as incorruptible individuals not likely to be swayed by political or private-sector pressures. Membership should be diverse enough to reflect the complexity of the society where it is embedded and incorporate sufficient expertise to facilitate its mandate (UN 2004, 131–132).

Changes of administration tend to weaken their effectiveness, as shifts of government representatives serve to derail previous working relationships and commitments. National anticorruption commissions have often been viewed as stalling tactics or cosmetic political gestures to appease domestic and international pressure by ruling elites unwilling to embark on meaningful reform. Commissions' credibility may suffer if some members appear not to be actively engaged or if the commissions raise unrealistic and unattainable expectations, fail to communicate their mandate to the public, or are perceived as having too cozy a relationship with political interests, particularly with the executive branch (UN 2004, 134–135).

Success in implementing the recommendations developed by anticorruption commissions (in Nicaragua and Honduras, for example) remains to be seen. How well they perform will depend on the political commitment, as expressed by the vigor with which their recommendations are followed up, the institutional capabilities they posses, and the extent to which central governments provide funding. Despite these potential pitfalls, the utility of an anticorruption commission for a post-transition Cuba ought not to be underestimated.[3] If vested with the proper mandate, constituted by a respected membership, and provided with adequate funding, it could serve as a highly visible forum for dialogue, citizen education, and development of policy recommendations. It could serve as a confidence-building body for a citizenry unfamiliar with the proper management of the state and how citizens can interact with the government and private-sector business interests. An anticorruption commission could be a beacon shining on corruption and mobilizing public opinion against it.

Equipped with a small but committed and well-qualified staff, and with assured funding from general government revenues (or from international sources, if needed), an anticorruption commission could foster government-business-civil society dialogue and serve as a transmission belt for citizen input. While functionally limited to acting as a consultation and recommendation body, the commission could be legally empowered to review government policies and programs and required to make its findings and recommendations public. In establishing a national anticorruption commission, several critical decisions would need to be made: mandate; objectives; number and composition of membership; criteria and persons responsible for selection of members; members' term of service; process for filling vacancies; and procedural rules.

ROLE OF THE INTERNATIONAL DEVELOPMENT COMMUNITY

The IFIS and bilateral development agencies could potentially play a very important role in averting corruption in a post-transition Cuba. Growing concern about the devastating impact of corruption on social and economic development has galvanized an international consensus about the urgency of taking effective action to limit corruption. This has manifested, as noted above, in the development of several international legal instruments. Furthermore, the IFIS and bilateral development agencies have designed and are aggressively implementing policies to prevent corruption within their own programs. They are financing ever more expansive and sophisticated projects in support of anticorruption initiatives sponsored by government and civil society, including projects to strengthen the rule of law, financial control and accountability mechanisms, and citizen oversight.

The World Bank, for example, has revamped its internal operations to explicitly take corruption into account, treating its curtailment as a critical element of governance. It has set aside long-standing reservations about addressing corruption; these reservations stemmed from, among other constraints, the bank's explicit mandate to focus on economic concerns and not on the political underpinnings impeding development (World Bank 1997, 25). The World Bank's anticorruption strategy is therefore largely predicated on preventing corruption in projects it finances and promoting reforms and sector policies that help curb corruption.

Anticorruption efforts of IFIs and bilateral development agencies are mutually supportive. Bilateral development agencies are not constrained by a narrow economic mandate and are able to work on a range of issues typically set out in bilateral agreements with host nations that broadly outline the assistance to be provided. In fact, institution-strengthening efforts supported by different donors often overlap, inducing funding agencies to turn to formal or informal coordination mechanisms to avoid duplication of efforts. Such is the case, for instance, with many of the ongoing national poverty reduction strategies (NPRSs), in which the elimination of corruption increasingly appears at center stage (Clarke 2001), as in the NPRS for Honduras. While seeking to avoid the pitfalls associated with tackling with a heavy hand the internal politics behind corruption, bilateral development agencies are increasingly supporting programs whose ultimate intent is to weaken institutional features favoring corruption and to encourage transparency in politics. Providing support to civil society organizations that promote transparent and accountable government is among the most obvious such efforts, along with programs designed to improve governance and electoral systems.

In 2000, for example, the United States enacted Public Law 106-309, the International Anticorruption and Good Governance Act. The act mandates that U.S. government international development programs "promote good governance by assisting other countries to combat corruption throughout society and to improve transparency and accountability at all levels of government and throughout the private sector" (Section 202[b]). The act specifically encourages U.S. foreign assistance programs to:

- support responsible independent media to promote oversight of public and private institutions;

- implement financial disclosure among public officials, political parties, candidates for public office, open budget processes, and transparent financial management systems;
- support the establishment of audit offices, inspectors general offices, third-party monitoring of government procurement processes, and anticorruption agencies;
- promote responsive, transparent, and accountable legislatures and local governments that ensure legislative and local oversight and whistleblower protection;
- promote legal and judicial reforms that criminalize corruption and promote law enforcement reforms and development that encourage criminal prosecutions of corruption;
- assist in developing a legal framework for commercial transactions that fosters business practices that promote transparent, ethical, and competitive behavior in the economic sector, such as commercial codes that incorporate international standards and protection of intellectual property rights;
- promote free and fair national, state, and local elections;
- foster public participation in the legislative process and public access to government information; and
- engage civil society in the fight against corruption.

While other nations may not formalize the anticorruption thrust of their foreign assistance to the same extent as the United States, their intent is similar and generally complementary. In Honduras, the major agencies providing international development assistance during the early 2000s regularly met as a group (known as the Group of 13, or G-13, which included USAID and other major binational donors as well as the IFIs) with Honduran government and civil society representatives; their purpose in meeting was to coordinate cross-sector transparency/anticorruption initiatives as reconstruction activities began in the aftermath of Hurricane Mitch. Comparable information-sharing and coordination fora are operating in other countries (see Gabriel and Stapenhurst with Thomas 2001).

CONCLUSION

As Cuba transitions toward a more accommodating political and economic environment, many favorable developments will have to come together to offset the country's ingrained corruption tradition and begin to create a culture of honesty and transparency. How will independent professional and partisan interest groups be organized and operate? Will economic growth be sufficient to allow individuals to earn a decent living without resorting to illegal behavior? Will Cubans gradually adopt shared civic and probity values consistent with generally accepted good governance and market principles? Will the business community embrace ethical standards? Will politicians act as stewards of the common patrimony or, as they did in the past, take advantage of their positions for personal benefit? Will the average citizen overcome the behavioral legacy of stealing from the state resulting from decades of scarcity? Will citizens come to realize that the right to associate freely, without coercion or political manipulation, is a fundamental precondition to ensure Cuba's democratic governance and curb corruption? These are crucial questions indeed. They call attention once again to the priority a post-transition Cuba must assign to promoting equitable economic growth, establishing accountable government institutions, helping develop transparent political processes, and promoting education in civic values.

The challenges are considerable, as the experience of many other countries suggests. And these challenges are not only economic, administrative, social, and cultural, but financial as well. Developing a corruption-resistant environment entails developing governmental institutions that are accountable and transparent as well as responsive, efficient, and agile. To achieve a modern public administration is far from easy. It will require the expenditure of enormous resources and the training of a competent, honest, and proud bureaucracy. It will demand a regulatory framework that is sensitive to the need to minimize corruption but not so overbearing as to compromise the efficiency of government and demoralize public officials (Anechiarico and Jacobs 1996).

Economic growth will be key in determining whether public service functions as an effective administrative vehicle or merely continues as the employment of last resort. Just as significant will be the emergence of a private business sector willing to play by the rules and a citizenry always watchful about how the state is managed. Finally, and perhaps most importantly, curbing corruption in a future Cuba will depend on ethical political leaders committed to the national interest and the welfare of their fellow citizens rather than their own.

NOTES

CHAPTER 1

1. In the parlance of the economist, "rents" are payments to factors of production (capital, labor) in excess of normal returns in competitive markets. Governments that operate monopolistic state-owned enterprises or limit competition through excessive regulation or trade restrictions create economic rents and therefore opportunities for corrupt rent-seeking behavior. Krueger (1974) pioneered the term "rent seeking" to describe the behavior of corrupt officials who take advantage of imperfectly competitive markets to seek bribes.

2. In Nicaragua, the property grab that occurred at the end of the Sandinista government is generally referred to as the *piñata*. A similar process occurred in Cambodia following the Khmer Rouge era and the Vietnamese occupation (Gottesman 2003).

3. Liquidation was not the chosen privatization method of any country but was the default method in some instances where the use of others was not feasible.

4. The early expropriations were related to properties owned by former Batista government officials and allegedly acquired through corrupt practices. The legal bases for confiscating these properties were never validated by standard rule-of-law practices, and conceivably at least some of those expropriations could have been or will be subjected to legal challenge.

CHAPTER 2

1. Since this chapter's objective is to provide an overview of the literature to set the context for the Cuba-specific analysis that follows, we have built our review largely on two comprehensive edited collections (Abed and Gupta 2002; Heidenheimer and Johnston 2002) that aptly highlight some of the most important literature on the topic. We acknowledge our reliance on these two sources and, where appropriate, refer to other sources we have consulted.

CHAPTER 3

1. Broadly, the term "contraband" covered several types of infractions. "Fraud" was said to occur if during the conduct of trade of authorized goods appropriate taxes were not paid; "contraband" specifically took place if goods not approved to be traded were traded; and "illicit commerce" was defined as trade conducted in violation of Spain's monopoly (Marrero 1978, 170–173).

2. Despite serving as a font of corruption, the national lottery served an important social function. Sale of lottery tickets provided a source of income to otherwise indigent citizens in a setting where there was no state-sponsored social welfare system (Arencibia Cardoso 2002, 54). In fact, the lottery collectorships were intended to benefit the widows and relatives of War of Independence veterans (Thomas 1971, 512).

CHAPTER 5

1. Vice President Carlos Lage (1999) stated in June 1999: "All of the policy changes that have occurred and will occur in the future are framed within our socialist system. They are aimed at relating more closely our economy to the world economy while maintaining the dominant role of state ownership. Even though we are seeking foreign capital and are willing to accept a higher participation by foreign capital in our economy, in Cuba there isn't now, and there will not be, a policy of privatization."

2. A window into the activities of one of the departments of Cimex S.A., the Moneda Convertible (convertible currency) or MC Department, headed by Antonio de la Guardia, was opened during the corruption trial in 1989 of Ochoa and de la Guardia. Testimony presented at the trial documents transactions involving ivory, diamonds, oil, and wood from Africa, high-technology products from Western Europe and even from the United States through Panamanian front companies, and narcotrafficking. The Cuban government's position was that some of these activities—particularly the narcotrafficking—were illegal operations carried out by rogue officers (see *Causa 1/89* 1989).

3. Some of them advertise on the World Wide Web; a recent search using the Google search engine with the terms "Cuba" and "room rental" yielded 444 hits. Some of the hits are to websites that offer multiple rooms, which suggests that landlords have organized into networks (see http://www.acrosscuba.com and http://www.casaines.com). Some of the rentals provide services such as cable television, telephone service, laundry services, and minibars. In early 2005 the going rate for a room in a *casa particular* in Havana was US$25 to US$35 per night.

4. Fifty independent economic variables are grouped into the following ten factors: (1) trade policy; (2) fiscal burden of government; (3) government intervention in the economy; (4) monetary policy; (5) capital flows and foreign investment;

(6) banking and finance; (7) wages and prices; (8) property rights; (9) regulation; and (10) informal market activity.

CHAPTER 6

1. The agencies commonly known collectively as the IFIS are the World Bank (WB), the International Monetary Fund (IMF), and the regional multilateral development banks; in the case of Latin America and the Caribbean, the regional bank is the Inter-American Development Bank (IDB).

2. In 2004 it was bringing together twenty-one bilateral and multilateral organizations, including the World Bank, the IDB, the Inter-American Agency for Cooperation and Development, the OAS, OECD, and several UN agencies. It was formerly called the Donors' Consultative Group on Financial Management. Other antecedents are the customary formal and informal roundtables established by donors for the coordination of technical assistance that in some instances today includes anticorruption initiatives.

3. However, two important Cuban trading partners are not signatories to the convention: China and Venezuela.

CHAPTER 7

1. There is an extensive literature on the experiences of transition countries as they have confronted the legal changes resulting from the dismantling of totalitarian, socialized economies and the establishment of democratic institutions and market economies. For an examination of some of these issues and how they may be addressed in a Cuba in transition see Patallo Sánchez (2003a, 2003b).

2. The reference here is to the official mass organizations discussed in Chapter 4, such as the Committees for the Defense of the Revolution (CDR), the Federation of Cuban Women (FMC), the Cuban Workers' Central (CTC), and the Union of Communist Youth (UJC). These mass organizations, among others, are explicitly mentioned in Article 7 of the Socialist Constitution of 1976.

3. Obviously, the National Commission to Fight Corruption and Illegalities created by the PCC in 2004 to impose ideological discipline on party members and root out capitalist practices (see Chapter 5) does not constitute a precedent for an independent anticorruption commission such as those that have been established in other countries.

BIBLIOGRAPHY

Abed, George T., and Sanjeev Gupta, editors. 2002. *Governance, Corruption, and Economic Performance*. Washington, D.C.: International Monetary Fund.

Ackerman, Elise. 1997. "Periodistas libres luchan por quitarse la mordaza." In *Desde Cuba con valor,* 21–41. Madrid: Editorial Pliegos.

Ades, Alberto, and Rafel Di Tella. 1997. "The New Economics of Corruption: A Survey and Some New Results." *Political Studies* 45, no. 3: 496–515.

"Afirman que Cuba sigue atrayendo a los narcos." 2005. EFE. Reproduced in *El Nuevo Herald Digital,* March 5.

Agh, Attila. 1993. "Europeanization Through Privatization and Pluralization in Hungary." *Journal of Public Policy* 13, no. 1: 1–35.

Aguirre, Benigno. 1998. "Culture of Opposition in Cuba." *Cuba in Transition.* Vol. 8: 326–343. Washington, D.C.: Association for the Study of the Cuban Economy.

Alam, M. S. 1990. "Some Economic Costs of Corruption in LDCs." *Journal of Development Studies* 27, no. 1 (October): 89–97.

Alarcón Ramírez, Dariel. 1997. *"Benigno": Memorias de un soldado cubano.* Barcelona: Tusquets Editores.

"Aldana-linked Empresario on Trial." 1993. Reuters. Reproduced in *CubaINFO,* April 30.

Alfonso, Pablo. 1999a. "Destituyen a la esposa de Robaina." *El Nuevo Herald,* June 9.

———. 1999b. "La piñata castrista." *El Nuevo Herald,* June 13.

———. 2002a. "Castro dice que es un hombre pobre." *El Nuevo Herald,* June 5.

———. 2002b. "El cerrado mundo de la familia Castro." *El Nuevo Herald,* June 10.

———. 2002c. "España, un paraíso para la jerarquía castrista." *El Nuevo Herald,* June 9.

———. 2003. "Escandalo sacude a la cúpula del turismo en Cuba." *El Nuevo Herald,* December 5.

———. 2004. "Cambio clave en la dirección del turismo en Cuba." *El Nuevo Herald,* June 15.

————. 2005a. "Corrupción en el sector farmacéutico." *El Nuevo Herald*, June 29.

————. 2005b. "Corrupción y 'Batalla de Ideas.'" *El Nuevo Herald*, March 9.

Álvarez, José. 1999. "Independent Agricultural Cooperatives in Cuba?" *Cuba in Transition*. Vol. 9: 157–164. Washington, D.C.: Association for the Study of the Cuban Economy.

————. 2001. "Rationed Products and Something Else: Food Availability and Distribution in 2000 Cuba." *Cuba in Transition*. Vol. 11: 305–322. Washington, D.C.: Association for the Study of the Cuban Economy.

Álvarez Díaz, José R., editor. 1963. *Un estudio sobre Cuba*. Miami: University of Miami.

Álvarez García, Alberto F. 2003. *Cuban Opposition Organizations*. Canadian Foundation for the Americas (FOCAL) Research Forum on Cuba. Updated April 24. At http://www.cubasource.org/pdf/cuban_organizations_english.pdf.

Ameringer, Charles D. 2000. *The Cuban Democratic Experience: The Auténtico Years, 1944–1954*. Gainesville: University Press of Florida.

Amnesty International (AI). 2004. "Further bans on freedom of expression." Press release, January 12.

Amuchástegui, Domingo. 2000a. "Cuban conglomerates setting the pace for the island's business." *CubaNews*, August.

————. 2000b. "FAR: Mastering Reforms." *Cuba in Transition*. Vol. 10: 433–441. Washington, D.C.: Association for the Study of the Cuban Economy.

————. 2002. "Las FAR: Del poder absoluto al control de las reformas." *Encuentro de la Cultura Cubana* no. 26–27: 133–147.

Anderson, James, Daniel Kaufmann, and Francesca Recanatini. 2003. "Service Delivery, Poverty and Corruption—Common Threads from Diagnostic Surveys." Background paper for the 2004 *World Development Report* (WDR), "Making Services Work for the Poor." Washington, D.C.: World Bank.

Anechiarico, Frank, and James B. Jacobs. 1996. *The Pursuit of Absolute Integrity: How Corruption Control Makes Government Ineffective*. Chicago: University of Chicago Press.

————. 2002. "Corruption Control in New York and Its Discontents." In Arnold J. Heidenheimer and Michael Johnston, editors, *Political Corruption: Concepts and Context*, 665–686. New Brunswick, N.J.: Transaction Publishers. First published in 1996 in Anechiarico and Jacobs, *The Pursuit of Absolute Integrity: How Corruption Control Makes Government Ineffective* (Chicago: University of Chicago Press).

Arencibia Cardoso, Pedro Pablo. 2002. "El gobierno de José Miguel Gómez." *Vitral* 9, no. 52 (November–December): 46–54.

"Arremeten contra la empresa privada." 2000. *El Nuevo Herald*, May 25.

Arroyo, Víctor Rolando. 2002. "Se apoderan funcionarios de vehículos donados para enfermos." *Cubanet*, April 16. At http://cubanet.org.

Aslund, Anders. 2002. *Building Capitalism: The Transformation of the Former Soviet Bloc*. New York: Cambridge University Press.

Azfar, Omar. 2005. "Corruption and the Delivery of Health and Education Services." In Bertram I. Spector, editor, *Fighting Corruption in Developing Countries: Strategies and Analysis,* 181–212. Bloomfield, Conn.: Kumarian Press.

"Bajo el ala de Raúl." 2001. *Tal Cual Digital* (Caracas). *Cubanet,* August 14.

Banfield, Edward. 1958. *The Moral Basis of a Backward Society.* Chicago: Free Press.

Bardach, Ann Louise. 2002. *Cuba Confidential.* New York: Vintage Books.

Bardhan, Pranab. 2002. "Corruption and Development: A Review of Issues." In Arnold J. Heidenheimer and Michael Johnston, editors, *Political Corruption: Concepts and Contexts,* 321–338. New Brunswick, N.J.: Transaction Publishers.

Batista Odio, Carlos Alberto. 1986. "Particularidades más importantes de los presupuestos cubanos en los últimos 30 años." In Academia de Ciencias de Cuba, Instituto de Filosofía, *Jornada Científica Internacional XXX Aniversario del Ataque al Cuartel Moncada.* Havana: Editorial de Ciencias Sociales.

Baxter, Thomas C. 2004. "Risk Management and Regulatory Failures at Riggs Bank and UBS: Lessons Learned." Testimony of Thomas C. Baxter, Executive Vice President, Federal Reserve Bank of New York, before the Subcommittee on Oversight and Investigations, Committee on Financial Services, U.S. House of Representatives. June 2. At http://www.newyorkfed.org/newsevents/speeches.

Betancourt, Ernesto F. 2000. "Cuba's Balance of Payments Gap, the Remittance Scam, Drug Trafficking and Money Laundering." *Cuba in Transition.* Vol. 10: 149–161. Washington, D.C.: Association for the Study of the Cuban Economy.

———. 2004. "Respuesta a 'Granma' sobre el lavado de dinero." *El Nuevo Herald,* June 19.

Betancourt, Ernesto F., and and Guillermo Grenier. 1999. "Measuring Cuban Public Opinion: Economic, Social and Political Issues." *Cuba in Transition.* Vol. 9: 251–269. Washington, D.C.: Association for the Study of the Cuban Economy.

Bhargava, Vinay, and Emil Bolongaita. 2004. *Challenging Corruption in Asia: Case Studies and a Framework for Action.* Washington, D.C.: World Bank.

Blechinger, Verena. 2005. "Political Parties." In Bertram I. Spector, editor, *Fighting Corruption in Developing Countries: Strategies and Analysis,* 27–41. Bloomfield, Conn.: Kumarian Press.

Botello, Santiago, and Mauricio Angulo. 2005. *Conexión Habana: Una peligrosa infiltración en las mafias cubanas.* 2d ed. Madrid: Ediciones Temas de Hoy.

Brandeis, Louis A. 1914/1968. *Other People's Money and How the Bankers Use It.* 1914. Reprint, New York: Harper and Row, 1968.

Brito, Joel, and Christopher Sabatini. 2003. "El movimiento sindical independiente de Cuba: Actualidad y desarrollo." *Cuba in Transition.* Vol. 13: 127–133. Washington, D.C.: Association for the Study of the Cuban Economy.

Campbell, Tim, and Harold Fuha. 2004. *Leadership and Innovation in Subnational Government: Case Studies from Latin America.* Washington, D.C.: World Bank.

Cancio Isla, Wilfredo. 2001. "Artistas recurren al soborno para sobrevivir en la isla." *El Nuevo Herald,* August 8.

————. 2004a. "Corrupción en la cúpula empresarial cubana." *El Nuevo Herald,* February 16.

————. 2004b. "Un chivo expiatorio para la corrupción en Cuba." *El Nuevo Herald,* February 22.

————. 2004c. "Cuba restringe los teléfonos y la internet." *El Nuevo Herald,* May 16.

————. 2004d. "Impera la corrupción en tiendas con dólares." *El Nuevo Herald,* April 11.

Carrasco, Juana. 1991. "¿Hay corrupción en Cuba?" *Bohemia* 83, no. 6 (February 8):26–30.

Casals and Associates. 2004a. *Integrated Internal Control Framework for Latin America.* Alexandria, Va.: Americas' Accountability Anti-Corruption Project, Technical Assistance Module.

————. 2004b. *Political Party Finance in Argentina, Chile, Costa Rica and Mexico: Lessons for Latin America.* Alexandria, Va.: Americas' Accountability Anti-Corruption Project, Technical Assistance Module.

Casas, Kevin. 2005. "El estado del financiamiento de los partidos políticos en América Latina." In *Asociación Civil Transparencia, Foro Latinoaméricano sobre Financiamiento de Partidos Políticos,* 25–36. Lima, Peru.

Castellanos, Dimas. 2002. "Mil razones para no estar seguro." *Encuentro en la red,* March 13. At http://www.cubaencuentro.com.

"Castro angry over Forbes listing." 2005. Reuters. Reproduced at http://www.cnn.com, March 19.

"Castro es cinco veces más rico." *El Nuevo Herald,* March 16.

Castro, Fidel. 1986. *Por el camino correcto. Recopilación de textos.* Havana: Editora Política.

————. 1987. "Discurso en el acto celebrado por el XX Aniversario de la caída en combate del Comandante Ernesto Che Guevara, efectuado en la Ciudad de Pinar del Río, el 8 de octubre de 1987." *Granma,* October 12.

————. 1993a. "Speech by President Fidel Castro at the Closing Session of the Eighth Science and Technology Forum." Broadcast on Havana Cuba Vision, December 17. Translated and reproduced in Foreign Broadcast Information Service *FBIS-LAT-93-244,* December 22.

————. 1993b. "Castro Discusses 'Sabotaged Products, Corruption.'" Broadcast on Havana Radio Progreso, December 17. Translated and reproduced by Foreign Broadcast Information Service *FBIS-LAT-93-242,* December 20.

————. 1997. "Address to a Conference of Latin American and Caribbean Teachers." Cuba On-Line database, February 8. At http://cuba.iccas.miami.edu.

————. 2002a. "Discurso pronunciado en la Escuela Latinoamericana de Ciencias Médicas." December 3. At http://www.cuba.cu/gobierno.

————. 2002b. "La revolución cubana convirtió al pueblo cubano en propietario de su propio país." *Granma,* June 3.

Causa 1/89: Fin de la conexión cubana. 1989. Havana: Editorial José Martí.

Chafuen, Alejandro A., and Eugenio Guzmán. 2000. "Economic Freedom and Corruption." In *2000 Index of Economic Freedom,* 51–63. Washington, D.C.: Heritage Foundation.

Chapman, Charles E. 1927/1969. *A History of the Cuban Republic: A Study of Hispanic American Politics.* 1927. Reprint, New York: Octagon Books, 1969.

Chapman, David. 2005. "Education." In Bertram I. Spector, editor, *Fighting Corruption in Developing Countries: Strategies and Analysis,* 65–78. Bloomfield, Conn.: Kumarian Press.

Chetwynd, Eric, Frances Cheywynd, and Bertram Spector. 2003. *Corruption and Poverty: A Review of Recent Literature.* January. Washington, D.C.: Management Systems International.

Clark, Juan. 1990. *Cuba: Mito y realidad.* Miami: Saeta Ediciones.

———. 1999. "Igualdad y privilegio en la revolución de Castro." In Efrén Córdova, editor, *40 años de revolución: El legado de Castro,* 219–252. Miami: Ediciones Universal.

Clarke, Jeremy. 2001. "Improving Coordination of Anti-corruption Policies and Activities by Donor Agencies." In Lara M. Gabriel and Rick Stapenhurst with Mary Thomas, editors. *The Role of Bilateral Donors in Fighting Corruption.* Washington, D.C.: World Bank Institute.

Código de Ética de los Cuadros del Estado Cubano. 1997. Havana: Comité Ejecutivo del Consejo de Ministros (CECM).

Collazo, Enrique. 2004. "Las tres caras de la moneda." *Encuentro en la red,* April 12. At http://www.cubaencuentro.com.

Colombié Santana, Mariela. 2001. "La ética y los valores en el Sector Público como un imperativo de nuestros pueblos." *Probidad,* July–August. At http://probidad.org.

Colomer, Joseph M. 2002. "Los militares 'duros' y la transición en Cuba." *Encuentro de la Cultura Cubana* no. 26–27: 148–167.

Comisión Económica para América Latina y el Caribe (CEPAL). 2000. *La economía cubana: Reformas estructurales y desempeño en los noventa.* Rev. ed. Mexico City: Fondo de Cultura Económica.

Committee of Sponsoring Organizations of the Treadway Commission (COSO). 2004. *Internal Control—Integrated Framework.* At http://www.coso.org.

Corrales, Javier. 2004. "The Gatekeeper State: Limited Economic Reform and Regime Survival in Cuba, 1989–2002." *Latin America Research Review* 39, no. 2: 35–65.

"La corrupción." 2004. *Vitral* no. 59 (January–February). At http://www2.glauco.it/vitral.

"Corruption Law Goes into Effect." 1997. *Economic Eye on Cuba,* August 25–31.

Cosano Alén, Reinaldo. 2002. "Pobres resultados." *Cubanet,* December 12.

———. 2004. "Agujeros negros de la economía cubana." *Cubanet,* April 7.

"Council of State Removes Tourism Minister." 1999. Havana Granma, August 28. Translated and reproduced in Foreign Broadcast Information Service *FBIS-LAT-1999-0828,* August 28.

"Creado el Ministerio de Auditoría y Control." 2001. *Granma Digital,* May 3.
"Crisis en la salud pública habanera." 2003. *Cubanet,* August 12.
Cruz Lima, Ramón Alberto. 1997. "Tourism in Camagüey." *Cubanet,* May 16.
"Cuba acusa a Bush de endurecer bloqueo para 'arrodillar' al pueblo cubano."
    2004. EFE, June 8. Reproduced in Yupi Internacional, June 9. At http://www.
    yupi.com.
"Cuba cracks down on Internet use." 2004. BBC News, World Edition, January 10.
    At http://www.bbc.co.uk/bbctwo.
"Cuba crea el nuevo ministerio anticorrupción." 2001. Reuters. Reproduced in
    El Nuevo Herald Digital, May 4.
"Cuba creates new anti-corruption ministry." 2001. MSNBC News, May 3. At
    http://msnbc.com.
"Cuba limita los contactos con los extranjeros." 2005. *El Nuevo Herald,* Febru-
    ary 24.
"Cuba ridicules report that it has biological arms." 1999. Reuters online. June 24.
Cuban-American Nacional Foundation. 1983. *Castro's Narcotics Trade,* no. 8.
    Washington, D.C.
"Cuba's Communist Party expels Robaina." 1999. *Miami Herald,* August 1.
"Declaran que crece la lucha contra la droga." 2005. Associated Press. Repro-
    duced in *El Nuevo Herald Digital,* February 24.
"Decreto-Ley 196/99: Sistema de trabajo con los cuadros del Estado y del Go-
    bierno." 1999. *Gaceta Oficial.* http://www.gacetaoficial.cu/dl_196_99.htm.
"Decreto-Ley No. 232: Sobre confiscación por hechos relacionados con las
    drogas, actos de corrupción o con otros comportamientos ilícitos." 2003.
    Cubanet. At http://www.cubanet.org/related/decreto.htm.
de la Rosa Labrada, Amado. 2002. "Panelería Novopal: Nueva opción construc-
    tiva." *Opciones,* July 24.
de Mello, Luiz, and Matias Barenstein. 2002. "Fiscal Decentralization and
    Governance: A Cross-Country Analysis." In George T. Abed and Sanjeev
    Gupta, editors, *Governance, Corruption, and Economic Performance,* 333–368.
    Washington, D.C.: International Monetary Fund.
del Aguila, Juan M. 1988. *Cuba: Dilemmas of a Revolution.* Rev. ed. Boulder,
    Colo.: Westview.
del Castillo, Siro, Mercedes Grandío, Andrés Hernández, and Amaya Altuna de
    Sánchez. 1996. *Lista de organizaciones disidentes, opositoras y de derechos humanos.*
    Comisión de Derechos Humanos, Partido Demócrata Cristiano de Cuba. At
    http://www.pdc-cuba.org/orga.htm.
del Pino, Rafael. 1991. *Proa a la libertad.* Mexico City: Editorial Planeta Mexicana.
Desde Cuba con valor. 1997. Madrid: Editorial Pliegos.
"Desvío." 2002. Carta de Cuba. *El Nuevo Herald,* May 25.
Díaz-Briquets, Sergio, and Jorge Pérez-López. 2000. *Conquering Nature: The Envi-
    ronmental Legacy of Socialism in Cuba.* Pittsburgh: University of Pittsburgh Press.
Díaz-Marzo, Ramón. 2002. "Manual para no ser estafado." *Cubanet,* January 9.

Díaz Vázquez, Julio A. 1998. "Cuba: Ajuste en el Modelo Económico." In Eduardo Cuenca García, editor, *Enfoque Sobre la Reciente Economía Cubana,* 27–40. Madrid: Agualarga.

DiFranceisco, Wayne, and Zvi Gitelman. 1984/2002. "Soviet Political Culture and Modes of Covert Influence." In Arnold J. Heidenheimer and Michael Johnston, editors, *Political Corruption: Concepts and Contexts,* 539–558. New Brunswick, N.J.: Transaction Publishers. First published in 1984.

Dilla, Haroldo. 2001. "Municipios, crisis y reforma económica en Cuba." *Encuentro de la Cultura Cubana* 23: 199–206.

Di Tella, Rafael, and William D. Savedoff, editors. 2001. *Diagnosis Corruption: Fraud in Latin American Hospitals.* Washington, D.C.: Inter-American Development Bank.

Djilas, Milovan. 1957. *The New Class.* New York: Praeger Publishers.

Domínguez, Jorge I. 1978. *Cuba: Order and Revolution.* Cambridge: Harvard University Press.

———. 2002. "Government and Politics." In *Cuba: A Country Study,* 227–281. Washington, D.C.: U.S. Government Printing Office.

———. 2003. *A Constitution for Cuba's Political Transition: The Utility of Retaining (and Amending) the 1992 Constitution.* Coral Gables, Fla.: Cuba Transition Project, University of Miami.

Donate-Armada, Maida. 1997. *Sociedad civil, control social y estructura del poder en Cuba.* At http://www.sigloxxi.org.

Echerri, Vicente. 2004. "Los ecos de la mala fama. Valeriano Weyler y su leyenda negra en Cuba: ¿Qué hay de cierto o inexacto?" *Encuentro en la red,* July 6. At http://www.cubaencuentro.com.

Eiras, Ana I., Aaron Schavey, and Anthony Kim. 2004. "The 2004 Index of Economic Freedom: The Countries." Chapter 6 in *2004 Index of Economic Freedom.* Washington, D.C.: Heritage Foundation.

Elliott, Kimberly Ann. 1997. "Corruption as an International Policy Problem: Overview and Recommendations." In Kimberly Ann Elliott, editor, *Corruption and the Global Economy,* 175–233. Washington, D.C.: Institute for International Economics.

"Empleos." 2001. Carta de Cuba. *El Nuevo Herald,* August 8.

"En auge delitos económicos." 2004. EFE. Reproduced in *El Nuevo Herald,* February 21.

"Escándalo de corrupción en Los Palacios." 2003. *Cubanet,* February 25.

Espinosa, Juan Carlos. 1999. "Civil Society in Cuba: The Logic of Emergence in Comparative Perspective." *Cuba in Transition.* Vol. 9: 346–367. Washington, D.C.: Association for the Study of the Cuban Economy.

———. 2001. "Vanguard of the State: The Cuban Armed Forces in Transition." *Problems of Post-Communism* 48, no. 6 (November–December): 19–30.

Espinosa, Juan Carlos, and Robert C. Harding II. 2002. "Paracaídas verde olivo y piñatas a cámara lenta." *Encuentro de la Cultura Cubana* no. 26–27: 168–183.

Espinosa Chepe, Oscar. 2001. "¿Fin del descontrol?" *Cubanet,* May 15.

————. 2002. "Rebelión de los inconformes." *Cubanet,* September 5.

Feldbrugge, F. J. M. 1989. "The Soviet Second Economy in a Political and Legal Perspective." In Edgar L. Feige, editor, *The Underground Economies,* 297–338. Cambridge, England: Cambridge University Press.

Fernández, Damián J. 1994. "Civil Society in Transition." In *Transition in Cuba: New Challenges for U.S. Policy,* 97–152. Miami: Florida International University.

————. 2000. *Cuba and the Politics of Passion.* Austin: University of Texas Press.

Fernández, G., and M. A. Menéndez. 2001. "GAESA: El poder económico de los hermanos Castro." *(Madrid) Diario 16,* June 24.

Fernández, Jesús M. 1997. "The Commandant's Reserves." *Cuba Monthly Economic Report.* August. DevTech Systems. Reproduced by Center for a Free Cuba at http://www.cubacenter.org/media/archives/1997/winter/comand.php3.

Ferreira, Delia. 2005. "El estado del financiamiento de los partidos políticos en América Latina." In *Asociación Civil Transparencia, Foro Latinoamericano sobre Financiamiento de Partidos Políticos,* 37–53. Lima, Peru.

Fink, Rodney. 2005. "Agriculture." In Bertram I. Spector, editor, *Fighting Corruption in Developing Countries: Strategies and Analysis,* 145–152. Bloomfield, Conn.: Kumarian Press.

"La Fiscalía detectó 16.000 delitos en empresas estatales en los últimos tres años." 2005. *Encuentro en la red,* July 7. At http://www.cubaencuentro.com.

Fogel, Jean-Francois. 2003. "Fidel Castro y su círculo," *(Santiago, Chile) Revista de El Mercurio,* November 28.

Foreign Policy Association. 1935. *Problems of the New Cuba: Report of the Commission on Cuban Affairs.* New York: J. J. Little and Ives Company.

Frank, Marc. 2001. "Destituyen al Ministro de la Pesca." *El Nuevo Herald,* March 25.

————. 2004a. "Cuba's Communists launch crackdown." *Financial Times,* July 6.

————. 2004b. "Raul Castro leads Cuba's crackdown on corrupt capitalists." *(Johannesburg, South Africa) Business Report,* June 27.

Freedom House. 2004. *Freedom in the World 2003.* Washington, D.C.: Freedom House. At http://www.freedomhouse.org/research/index.htm.

Friedl Zapata, José A. 2005. *El gran engaño: Fidel Castro, y su íntima relación con el narcotráfico internacional.* Buenos Aires: Editorial Santiago Apóstol.

Fuentes, Norberto. 2002. *Narcotráfico y tareas revolucionarias: El concepto cubano.* Miami: Ediciones Universal.

Gabriel, Lara M., and Rick Stapenhurst, with Mary Thomas, editors. 2001. *The Role of Bilateral Donors in Fighting Corruption.* Washington, D.C.: World Bank Institute.

Gálvez, Julio César. 2002. "Los delitos y la corrupción en los centros de trabajo 'alarman' al régimen." *Cubanet,* July 28.

Garve, Lucas. 2001. "El pícaro, el gerente y la corrupción." *Cubanet,* June 26.

Gayoso, Antonio. 1999. "The Role of Small and Medium Size Enterprise in Cuba's Future." *Cuba in Transition*. Vol. 9: 60–72. Washington, D.C.: Association for the Study of the Cuban Economy.

Gellman, Irwin F. 1973. *Roosevelt and Batista: Good Neighbor Diplomacy in Cuba, 1933–1945*. Albuquerque: University of New Mexico Press.

Glynn, Patrick, Stephen J. Kobrin, and Moises Naím. 1997. "The Globalization of Corruption." In Kimberly Ann Elliot, editor, *Corruption and the Global Economy*, 7–27. Washington, D.C.: Institute for International Economics.

"El gobierno cubano amenaza a caseros." 2004. Agence France Presse (AFP). Reproduced in *El Nuevo Herald*, July 5.

"El gobierno inicia una campaña para frenar el robo de combustible." 2005. *Encuentro en la red*, October 18. At http://cubaencuentro.com/sociedad/noticias/20051018.

Gómez, Andy S., and Eugenio M. Rothe. 2004. *Value Orientations and Opinions of Recently Arrived Cubans in Miami*. Miami: Institute for Cuban and Cuban-American Studies, University of Miami.

González, Edward. 2002. *After Castro: Alternative Regimes and U.S. Policy*. Coral Gables, Fla.: Cuba Transition Project, University of Miami.

González, Gerardo. 1999. "Los llamados empresarios cubanos y la transición en la isla." *Cuba in Transition*. Vol. 9: 469–477. Washington, D.C.: Association for the Study of the Cuban Economy.

González, Lázaro Raúl. 2002. "El robo a todo galope." *Cubanet*, September 11.

González Gutiérrez, Alfredo. 1997. "La economía sumergida en Cuba." In Dietmar Dirmoser and Jaime Estay, editors, *Economía y reforma económica en Cuba*, 239–256. Caracas: Editorial Nueva Sociedad.

Gottesman, Evan R. 2003. *Cambodia after the Khmer Rouge: Inside the Politics of Nation Building*. New Haven: Yale University Press.

Gray, Cheryl, and Daniel Kaufmann. 1998. "Corruption and Development." *Finance and Development* (March): 7–10. At http://www.imf.org/fandd.

Gray, Cheryl, Joel Hellman, and Randi Ryterman. 2004. *Anticorruption in Transition 2: Corruption in Enterprise-State Interactions in Europe and Central Asia 1999–2002*. Washington, D.C.: World Bank.

Grossman, Gregory. 1979. "Notes on the Illegal Private Economy and Corruption." In Congressional Joint Economic Committee, *The Soviet Economy in a Time of Change*, 834–855. Washington, D.C.: U.S. Government Printing Office.

Gunn, Gillian. 1993. *Cuba in Transition: Options for U.S. Policy*. New York: Twentieth Century Fund.

———. 1995. *Cuba's NGOs: Government Puppets or Seeds of Civil Society?*. Georgetown University Cuba Briefing Series (February). At http://sfswww.georgetown.edu/sfs/programs/clas.

Gupta, Sanjeev, Hamid R. Davoodi, and Erwin R. Tiongson. 2002. "Corruption and the Provision of Health Care and Education Services." In George T. Abed and Sanjeev Gupta, editors, *Governance, Corruption, and Economic Performance*, 245–279. Washington, D.C.: International Monetary Fund.

Gupta, Sanjeev, Luiz de Mello, and Raja Sharan. 2002. "Corruption and Military Spending." In George T. Abed and Sanjeev Gupta, editors, *Governance, Corruption, and Economic Performance*, 300–332. Washington, D.C.: International Monetary Fund.

Hammergren, Linn. 2000. "The Multilateral Development Banks and Corruption." Washington, D.C.: World Bank.

Hao, Yufan, and Michael Johnston. 2002. "Corruption and the Future of Economic Reform in China." In Arnold J. Heidenheimer and Michael Johnston, editors, *Political Corruption: Concepts and Contexts*, 583–604. New Brunswick, N.J.: Transaction Publishers.

Heidenheimer, Arnold J. 1970/2002. "Perspectives on the Perception of Corruption." In Arnold J. Heidenheimer and Michael Johnston, editors, *Political Corruption: Concepts and Context*, 141–154. New Brunswick, N.J.: Transaction Publishers. First published in 1970.

Heidenheimer, Arnold J., and Michael Johnston, editors. 2002. *Political Corruption: Concepts and Context*. New Brunswick, N.J.: Transaction Publishers.

Heidenheimer, Arnold J., Michael Johnston, and Victor J. Levine, editors. 1989. *Political Corruption: A Handbook*. New Brunswick, N.J.: Transaction Publishers.

Hellman, Joel, Geraint Jones, and Daniel Kaufmann. 2002. *Far from Home: Do Foreign Investors Import Higher Standards of Governance in Transition Economies?* Washington, D.C.: World Bank.

Hellman, Joel, and Daniel Kaufmann. 2001. "Confronting the Challenge of State Capture in Transition Economies." *Finance and Development* 38, no. 3 (September). At http://www.imf.org/external/pubs/ft/fandd/2001/09/hellman.htm.

Henken, Ted. 2002a. "Condemned to Informality: Cuba's Experience with Self-Employment during the Special Period (The Case of the Bed and Breakfasts)." *Cuban Studies* 33: 1–29.

———. 2002b. "A Taste of Capitalism: The Rise and Fall of Cuba's Private Restaurants (*Paladares*)." Paper presented at the Twelfth Meeting of the Association for the Study of the Cuban Economy, Coral Gables, Fla., August.

———. 2003. "Santiago vs. Havana: Cuba's Underground Economy in Comparative Perspective." *Cuba in Transition*. Vol. 13: 348–353. Washington, D.C.: Association for the Study of the Cuban Economy.

Heritage Foundation/*Wall Street Journal*. 2001–2004. *Index of Economic Freedom*. Washington, D.C.: Heritage Foundation. At http://www.heritage.org.

Hernández, Normando. 2002. "Funcionario de Las Tunas 'desvía' materiales de construcción para ampliar su casa." *Cubanet*, April 2.

Hidalgo, Alcibíades. 2004. "Solos en el bosque: El Partido Comunista de Cuba despues de Fidel Castro." *Encuentro en la red*, May 28.

Holmes, Leslie. 1993. *The End of Communist Power*. New York: Oxford University Press.

"How Hungary Escaped Transition Failure and Runaway Corruption." 2001. *Transition Newsletter,* October-November-December.

Human Rights Watch. 1999. *Cuba's Repressive Machinery: Human Rights Forty Years After the Revolution.* At http://www.hrw.org/reports/1999/cuba/.

Hungarian Gallup Institute. 1999. *Basic Methodological Aspects of Corruption Measurement: Lessons Learned from the Literature and Pilot Study.* Budapest: Hungarian Gallup Institute.

Huntington, Samuel P. 1968/2002. "Modernization and Corruption." In Arnold J. Heidenheimer and Michael Johnston, editors, *Political Corruption: Concepts and Context,* 253–263. New Brunswick, N.J.: Transaction Publishers. First published in 1968.

Ibarra, Jorge. 1985. *Un análisis psicosocial del cubano: 1898–1925.* Havana: Editorial de Ciencias Sociales.

———. 1998. *Prologue to Revolution.* Boulder, Colo.: Lynne Rienner Publishers.

International Bank for Reconstruction and Development (IBRD). 1951. *Report on Cuba.* Washington, D.C.

International Labor Organization (ILO). 2004. *334th Report of the Committee on Freedom of Association.* Geneva: ILO.

International Monetary Fund (IMF). 1997. "IMF Adopts Guidelines Regarding Governance Issues." IMF *Survey* 26, no. 15 (5 August): 233–238.

Izquierdo, José. 2003. "Desmantelan red de contrabandistas en empresa gastronómica de Güines." *Cubanet,* February 20.

Jatar-Hausmann, Ana Julia. 1999. *The Cuban Way: Capitalism, Communism and Confrontation.* West Hartford, Conn.: Kumarian Press.

Jenks, Leland Hamilton. 1928. *Our Cuban Colony: A Study in Sugar.* New York: Vanguard Press.

Johnston, Michael. 1997. "Public Officials, Private Interests, and Sustainable Democracy: When Politics and Corruption Meet." In Kimberly Ann Elliot, editor, *Corruption and the Global Economy,* 61–82. Washington, D.C.: Institute for International Economics.

———. 1999. "A Brief History of Anticorruption Agencies." In Andreas Schedler, Larry Diamond, and Marc F. Plattner, editors, *The Self-Restraining State: Power and Accountability in New Democracies,* 217–226. Boulder, Colo.: Lynne Rienner Publishers.

Johnston, Michael, and Sahr J. Kpundeh. 2002. "The Measurement Problem: A Focus on Governance." *Forum on Crime and Society* 2, no. 1 (December): 33–44.

Kalathil, Shanti, and Taylor C. Boas. 2001. *The Internet and State Control in Authoritarian Regimes: China, Cuba and the Counterrevolution.* Washington, D.C.: Carnegie Endowment.

Kaufmann, Daniel. 1997. "Corruption: The Facts," *Foreign Policy* 197 (summer): 114–131.

———. 2003. "Rethinking Governance: Empirical Lessons Challenge Orthodoxy." *WBI Themes.* Washington, D.C.: World Bank Institute. At http://www .worldbank.org/wbi/governance/pubs.

Kaufmann, Daniel, Aart Kraay, and Massimo Mastruzzi. 2005. *Governance Matters IV. Governance Indicators for 1996–2004.* At http://www.worldbank.org.

Kaufmann, Daniel, and Paul Siegelbaum. 1997. "Privatization and Corruption in Transition Economies." *Journal of International Affairs* 50, no. 2 (winter): 419–458.

Keshet, Jasmin, and Tom Devine. 2002. "The Significance of Whistleblowers to Challenge Corruption." At www.respondanet.com/english.

Klitgaard, Robert. 1988. *Controlling Corruption.* Berkeley: University of California Press.

———. 1998. "International Cooperation Against Corruption." *Finance and Development* (March): 3–6.

Kornai, Janos. 1992. *The Socialist System.* Princeton, N.J.: Princeton University Press.

Krastev, Ivan. 2004. *Shifting Obsessions: Three Essays on the Politics of Anticorruption.* Budapest: Central European University Press.

Krueger, Anne O. 1974. "The Political Economy of the Rent-Seeking Society." *American Economic Review* 64, no. 3 (June): 291–303.

Lafita, Caridad. 1994. "Decree Laws 150, 151 Explained." *Trabajadores,* July 4. Translated and reproduced in Foreign Broadcast Information Service *FBIS-LAT-94-163,* August 23.

Lage, Carlos. 1999. "En Cuba no habrá privatización," *Opciones en el Web,* 13 June. At http://www.opciones.cubaweb.cu.

Lambsdorff, Johann Graf. 2003. *Framework Document 2003: Background Paper to the 2003 Corruption Perceptions Index.* September. Berlin: Transparency International and University of Passau.

LaPalombara, Joseph. 1994. "Structural and Institutional Aspects of Corruption." *Social Research* 61, no. 2 (summer): 325–350.

La Porta, Rafael, Florencio Lopez-de-Silva, Andrei Shleifer, and Robert Vishny. 1998. *The Quality of Government.* NBER Working Paper 6727. Cambridge, Mass.: National Bureau of Economic Research.

La Rosa, Lesmes. 2002. "Página poco conocida del movimiento juvenil." *Granma Digital,* April 4.

Latell, Brian. 2005. *After Fidel: The Inside Story of Castro's Regime and Cuba's Next Leader.* New York: Palgrave Macmillan.

Lee, Susana. 2003. "Inversión extranjera y colaboración económica en Cuba." *Granma,* 28 January.

Leff, Nathaniel H. 1964/2002. "Economic Development Through Bureaucratic Corruption." In Arnold J. Heidenheimer and Michael Johnston, editors,

Political Corruption: Concepts and Context, 307–320. New Brunswick, N.J.: Transaction Publishers. First published in 1964.

Legarda, Astrid. 2005. *El verdadero Pablo: Sangre, traición y muerte*. Bogota: Ediciones Dipon/Ediciones Gato Azul.

Leite, Carlos, and Jens Weidmann. 2002. "Does Mother Nature Corrupt? Natural Resources, Corruption, and Economic Growth." In George T. Abed and Sanjeev Gupta, editors, *Governance, Corruption, and Economic Performance*, 159–196. Washington, D.C.: International Monetary Fund.

Leiva, Miriam. 2003. "Bibliotecas independientes: Lectura sin censura en Cuba." *Cubanet*, January 15.

"Librarians sentenced to 196 years." 2003. Friends of Cuban Libraries. April 30. At http://www.friendsofcubanlibraries.org.

Linares, Juan Carlos. 2001. "Funcionarios de Turismo estafan miles de dólares en Villa Tortuga Gret." *Cubanet*, September 5.

Linz, Juan, and Alfred Stepan. 1996. *Problems of Democratic Transition and Consolidation*. Baltimore: Johns Hopkins University Press.

Lipset, Seymour Martin, and Gabriel Salman Lenz. 2000. "Corruption, Culture and Markets." In Lawrence E. Harrison and Samuel P. Huntington, editors, *Culture Matters: How Values Shape Human Progress*, 112–124. New York: Basic Books.

Llovio Menéndez, José Luis. 1988. *Insider: My Secret Life as a Revolutionary in Cuba*. New York: Bantam Books.

López, Félix. 2002. "Comprobación Nacional del Control Interno de la Economía." *Granma*, October 10.

———. 2003. "Vigía en el control de gastos y en la disciplina de precios." *Granma*, March 17.

López, Juan J. 1999. "Civil Society in Cuba at the End of the 1990s." Paper presented at the Fourth Annual South Florida Symposium on Cuba, Miami, October.

Lotspeich, Richard. 2003. "Crime and Corruption in Transitional Economies: Lessons for Cuba." *Policy Reform* 6, no. 2 (June): 71–87.

Malia, Martin. 1995. "The Nomenklatura Capitalists." *New Republic*, May 22, 17–24.

Mañach, Jorge. 1928/1969. *Indagación del choteo*. 2d ed. Miami: Mnemosyme Publishing. First published in 1928.

Marin, Mar. 2004. "Vuelta a la centralización este 26 de julio." EFE. Reproduced in *El Nuevo Herald*, July 26.

Márquez Sterling, Carlos. 1969. *Historia de Cuba: Desde Cristóbal Colón a Fidel Castro*. New York: Las Americas.

Marrero, Leví. 1974. *El Siglo XVI, la economía*. Vol. 2 of *Cuba: Economía y sociedad*. Madrid: Editorial Playor.

———. 1975. *El Siglo XVII (II)*. Vol. 4 of *Cuba: Economía y sociedad*. Madrid: Editorial Playor.

————. 1978. *Del monopolio hacia la libertad comercial (1701–1763) (II)*. Vol. 7 of *Cuba: Economía y sociedad*. Madrid: Editorial Playor.

————. 1980. *Del monopolio hacia la libertad comercial (1701–1763) (III)*. Vol. 8 of *Cuba: Economía y sociedad*. Madrid: Editorial Playor.

"Más control estatal sobre el turismo." 2004 *El Nuevo Herald*, October 13.

Maseda, Héctor. 2003a. "Corrupción sobre rieles." *Cubanet*, February 21.

————. 2003b. "Reacción en cadena," *Encuentro en la red*, January 29.

Masó, Calixto C. 1998. *Historia de Cuba*. Miami: Ediciones Universal.

Mastrapa, Armando F. 2000. "Soldiers and Businessmen: The FAR During the Special Period." *Cuba in Transition*. Vol. 10: 428–432. Washington, D.C.: Association for the Study of the Cuban Economy.

Mauro, Paolo. 1995. "Corruption and Growth." *Quarterly Journal of Economics* 110, no. 3 (August): 681–712.

————. 1997. "The Effects of Corruption on Growth, Investment, and Government Expenditure: A Cross-country Analysis." In Kimberly Ann Elliot, editor, *Corruption and the Global Economy*, 81–107. Washington, D.C.: Institute for International Economics.

————. 1998. "Corruption: Causes, Consequences, and Agenda for Future Research." *Finance and Development* (March): 11–14.

Mayoral, María Julia. 2005a. "Empezará el país mayor programa de vivienda de su historia." *Granma*, September 2. At http://www.granma.cu.

————. 2005b. "Lo que se hace es darle más al pueblo y repartirlo mejor." *Granma Internacional Digital*, March 18. At http://www.granma.cu.

McAvoy, Muriel. 2003. *Sugar Baron*. Gainesville: University Press of Florida.

McGaffey, Wyatt, and Clifford R. Barnett. 1965. *Twentieth Century Cuba: The Background of the Castro Revolution*. New York: Anchor Books.

Meagher, Patrick. 2004. "Anti-Corruption Agencies: A Review of Experience." Paper No. 04/02, March. IRIS Discussion Papers on Institutions and Development. Center for Institutional Reform and the Informal Sector. College Park: University of Maryland.

Médard, Jean-Francois. 2002. "Corruption in the Neo-patrimonial States of Sub-Saharan Africa." In Arnold J. Heidenheimer and Michael Johnston, editors, *Political Corruption: Concepts and Context*, 379–402. New Brunswick, N.J.: Transaction Publishers.

Medina, Ramón Guillermo. 2001. "Funcionario del Poder Popular lucra con vehículo del Estado." *Cubanet*, November 21.

Meggison, William L., and Jeffrey M. Netter. 2001. "From State to Market: A Survey of Empirical Studies on Privatization." *Journal of Economic Literature* 39 (June 2001): 321–389.

"Menos empresas con capital foráneo." 2004. AFP. Reproduced in *El Nuevo Herald*, February 4.

Mesa-Lago, Carmelo. 1981. *The Economy of Socialist Cuba: A Two-Decade Appraisal*. Albuquerque: University of New Mexico Press.

————. 1989. "Cuba's Economic Counter-Reform (*Rectificación*): Causes, Policies, and Effects." *Journal of Communist Studies* 5 (December): 98–139.

————. 2000. *Market, Socialist, and Mixed Economies: Comparative Policy and Performance—Chile, Cuba, Costa Rica.* Baltimore: Johns Hopkins University Press.

————. 2004. *Economía y bienestar social en Cuba a comienzos del siglo XXI.* Madrid: Editorial Colibrí.

Messina, William A. 1999. "Agricultural Reform in Cuba: Implications for Agricultural Production, Markets, and Trade." *Cuba in Transition.* Vol. 9: 433–442. Washington, D.C.: Association for the Study of the Cuban Economy.

Miller, William L., Ase B. Grodeland, and Tatyana Koshechkina. 2002. "Bribing and Other Ways of Coping with Officialdom in Post-Communist Eastern Europe." In Arnold J. Heidenheimer and Michael Johnston, editors, *Political Corruption: Concepts and Context,* 559–582. New Brunswick, N.J.: Transaction Publishers.

"El Ministro de Turismo toma el control directo de importantes negocios." 2004. *Encuentro en la red,* October 13.

Montaner, Carlos Alberto. 2000. "Cuba: Fin de Fiesta—Castro da por terminado el *Período Especial* y retoma el socialismo puro y duro." *Cuba in Transition.* Vol. 10: 207–211. Washington, D.C.: Association for the Study of the Cuban Economy.

————. 2001. *Las raíces torcidas de América Latina.* Barcelona: Plaza Janés.

————. 2002. *Cuba: Un siglo de doloroso aprendizaje.* Miami: Brickell Communications Group.

————. 2003. "Mucha paranoia y un nuevo escándalo." *Libertad Digital,* December 21. At http://libertaddigital.com/opiniones/opi_desa_16555.html.

Morán, José. 2002. "Incontrolable el robo de ganado en Camagüey." *Cubanet,* August 23.

Mujal-León, Eusebio, and Joshua W. Busby. 2002. "Las fuerzas armadas en las transiciones: Lecciones para Cuba." *Encuentro de la Cultura Cubana* no. 26–27: 127–132.

Mungiu-Pippidi, Alina. 1997. "Breaking Free: Tales of Corruption from the Post-Communist Balkans." *East European Constitutional Law Review* 16, no. 4 (fall), http://www.nyu.edu.

Murphy, Kevin M., Andrei Shleifer, and Robert W. Vishny. 1991. "The Allocation of Talent: Implications for Growth." *Quarterly Journal of Economics* 106, no. 2 (May): 503–530.

————. 1993. "Why Is Rent Seeking So Costly to Growth?" *American Economic Review* 83, no. 2 (May): 409–414.

Naím, Moisés. 1995. "The Corruption Eruption." *Brown Journal of World Affairs* 2, no. 2 (summer): 245–261.

Nichols, John Spicer. 1982. "The Mass Media: Their Functions in Social Conflict." In Jorge I. Domínguez, editor, *Cuba: Internal and International Affairs,* 71–112. Beverly Hills: Sage Publications.

"Nota Informativa del Ministerio de Turismo." 2003. *Granma,* December 8.

Nova González, Armando. 2000. "El mercado agropecuario." In Hans-Jürgen Burchardt, editor, *La última reforma agraria del siglo,* 143–150. Caracas: Nueva Sociedad.

Nye, Joseph S. 1967/2002. "Corruption and Political Development: A Cost-Benefit Analysis." In Arnold J. Heidenheimer and Michael Johnston, editors, *Political Corruption: Concepts and Context,* 281–230. New Brunswick, N.J.: Transaction Publishers. First published in 1967.

Office of Research and Policy. 1992. *Cuba Annual Report, 1989.* Voice of America, U.S. Information Agency. Washington, D.C.: Radio Marti Program.

Oficina Nacional de Estadísticas (ONE). 1999–2003. *Anuario Estadístico de Cuba 1999 to 2003.* Havana.

Ofosu-Amaah, W. Paatii, Raj Soopramanien, and Kishor Uprety. 1999. *Combating Corruption: A Comparative Review of Selected Legal Aspects of State Practice and Major International Initiatives.* Washington, D.C.: World Bank.

Oppenheimer, Andres. 1992. *Castro's Final Hour: The Secret Story Behind the Coming Downfall of Communist Cuba.* New York: Simon and Schuster.

Organization for Economic Cooperation and Development (OECD). 1998. *Convention on Combating Bribery of Foreign Public Officials in International Business Transaction.* Paris: OECD.

———. 1999. *Fighting Corruption in Developing Countries and Emerging Economies: The Role of the Private Sector, Final Report.* Washington, D.C.: Washington Conference on Corruption.

———. 2000. *Government of the Future.* Paris: OECD.

———. 2001. *Governance in the 21st Century.* Paris: OECD.

———. 2003a. "Anti-corruption Instruments and the OECD Guidelines for Multinational Enterprises." *Annual Report on the OECD Guidelines for Multinational Enterprise: 2003 Edition.* Paris: Directorate for Financial, Fiscal, and Enterprise Affairs, OECD.

———. 2003b. *Fighting Corruption: What Role for Civil Society? The Experience of the OECD.* Paris: OECD.

———. 2003c. "Steps Taken and Planned Future Actions by Participating Countries to Ratify and Implement the Convention on Combating Bribery of Foreign Public Officials in International Business Transaction." December 17. At http://www.oecd.org.

Organization of American States (OAS). 1998. *Inter-American Convention Against Corruption.* OEA/Ser.A STI/2. Washington, D.C.: OAS.

Osborne, David, and Ted Gebler. 1992. *Reinventing Government: How the Entrepreneurial Spirit is Transforming the Public Sector from Schoolhouse to Statehouse, City Hall to the Pentagon.* Reading, Mass.: Addison-Wesley.

Pagés, Raisa. 2003. "Ascienden a 270 contratos de producciones cooperadas." *Granma,* February 3.

Patallo Sánchez, Laura. 2003a. *Establishing the Rule of Law in Cuba.* Coral Gables, Fla.: Cuba Transition Project, University of Miami.

————. 2003b. *The Role of the Judiciary in a Post-Castro Cuba: Recommendations for Change.* Coral Gables, Fla.: Cuba Transition Project, University of Miami.

Pax Christi. 1998. *Report of the Pax Christi Netherlands Delegation to Cuba.* At http://www.paxchristi.nl.

Pedroso, Beatriz del Carmen. 2002. "Crece la corrupción en el Sistema de Salud." *Encuentro en la red,* July 26.

Pepys, Mary Noel. 2005. "Corruption in the Justice System." In Bertram I. Spector, editor, *Fighting Corruption in Developing Countries: Strategies and Analysis,* 13–26. Bloomfield, Conn.: Kumarian Press.

Pérez, Louis A. 1995. *Cuba: Between Reform and Revolution.* New York: Oxford University Press.

Pérez-López, Jorge F. 1995. *Cuba's Second Economy: From Behind the Scenes to Center Stage.* New Brunswick, N.J.: Transaction Publishers.

————. 2001. "Waiting for Godot: Cuba's Stalled Reforms and Continuing Economic Crisis." *Problems of Post-Communism* 48, no. 6 (November–December): 43–55.

Pérez Navarro, Lourdes. 2004. "Fortalece la ONAT su gestión recaudadora y fiscalizadora." *Granma,* February 23.

Pérez-Stable, Marifeli. 1999. *The Cuban Revolution: Origins, Course, and Legacy.* New York: Oxford University Press.

Peters, Philip. 2001. *State Enterprise in Cuba: An Early Snapshot.* Arlington, Va.: Lexington Institute.

Pesant, Aleaga. 2004. "El camello a cinco pesos." *Cubanet,* November 22.

"Piden a España que investigue tráfico de visas." 2002. *El Nuevo Herald,* November 23.

Pope, Jeremy. 2000. *Confronting Corruption: The Elements of a National Integrity System.* Berlin: Transparency International.

Puerta, Ricardo A. 1997. *Sociedad Civil en Cuba.* At http://www.sigloxxi.org.

————. 2004. *Corrupción en Cuba y cómo combatirla: Una propuesta de Auditoría Social.* Buenos Aires: Fundación Cadal.

Pumar, Enrique S. 1996. "Labor Effects of Adjustment Policies in Cuba." *Cuba in Transition.* Vol. 6: 100–108. Washington, D.C.: Association for the Study of the Cuban Economy.

Quiroz, Alfonso W. 2003. "Implicit Cost of Empire: Bureaucratic Corruption in Nineteenth-Century Cuba." *Journal of Latin American Studies* 35, no. 3.

Ratliff, William. 2004. *China's "Lessons" for Cuba's Transition.* Coral Gables, Fla.: Cuba Transition Project, University of Miami.

"Raúl Castro supervisa personalmente el sector del turismo." 2004. *Encuentro en la red,* June 9.

Reporters Without Borders. 2003. "Second World Press Freedom Ranking: Cuba Second from Last, Just Ahead of North Korea." At http://www.rsf.fr/article .php3?id_article=8247.

————. 2004a. *Cuba: Annual Report 2004*. Paris: Reporters Without Borders.

————. 2004b. *Internet Under Surveillance 2004—Cuba*. Paris: Reporters Without Borders.

"Revelan ingeniosas vías para robar ron." 2003. *El Nuevo Herald*, August 29.

Reyes, Gerardo A. 2004a. "Cuba lavó $3,900 millones en el sistema bancario internacional." *El Nuevo Herald*, June 9.

————. 2004b. "Profundizan investigación de $3,900 millones de Cuba." *El Nuevo Herald*, September 16.

Reyes Gutiérrez, Félix. 2005a. "Despiden a obreros por robo en fábrica de cigarrillos." *Cubanet*, January 14.

————. 2005b. "Reubicado el cuerpo de seguridad de la antigua Trinidad y Hermanos." *Cubanet*, January 24.

Rivero, Ana Julia. 2004. "El señor de la mano de hierro." *Encuentro en la red*, June 25.

Rivero, Raúl. 2000. "La vivienda: Otra odisea cubana." *El Nuevo Herald*, May 6.

Roberts, Alasdair. 1999. "Access to Government Information: An Overview of Issues." Working paper. Transparency International. At www.transparency.org/working_papers.

"Robo." 2002. Carta de Cuba. *El Nuevo Herald*, January 2.

Roca, Sergio. 1993. "Cuban Privatization: Potential Path and Implementation." In *Transition in Cuba: New Challenges for U.S. Policy*, 567–600. Miami: Florida International University.

Rondinelli, Dennis A., and Shabbir G. Cheema. 2003. "The Competent State: Governance and Administration in an Era of Globalization." In Dennis A. Rondinelli and G. Shabbir Cheema, editors, *Reinventing Government for the Twenty-First Century: State Capacity in a Globalizing Society*. Bloomfield, Conn.: Kumarian Press.

Ros, Enrique. 2003. *Fidel Castro y el gatillo alegre: Sus años universitarios*. Miami: Ediciones Universal.

Rose-Ackerman, Susan. 1997. "The Political Economy of Corruption." In Kimberly Ann Elliot, editor, *Corruption and the Global Economy*, 31–60. Washington, D.C.: Institute for International Economics.

————. 1999. *Corruption and Government: Causes, Consequences and Reform*. Cambridge, England: Cambridge University Press.

Rousseau, Denis. 1999. "Llueven los 'truenes' debido a la corrupción." *El Nuevo Herald*, June 25.

Ruth, Mathias. 2005. "Energy." In Bertram I. Spector, editor, *Fighting Corruption in Developing Countries: Strategies and Analysis*, 115–125. Bloomfield, Conn.: Kumarian Press.

Sáenz Rovner, Eduardo. 2005. *La conexión cubana: Narcotráfico, contrabando y juego en Cuba entre los años 20 y comienzos de la Revolución*. Bogota: Universidad Nacional de Colombia.

Sánchez, Isabel. 2005. "Castro toma medidas de 'categoría 5.'" *El Nuevo Herald,* November 24.

San Martin, Nancy. 2004a. "Cuba's Tourism Chief Replaced by Army Colonel." *Miami Herald,* February 12.

———. 2004b. "Cuban Offcial Fired, Blamed for Energy Woes." *Miami Herald,* October 15.

Schaeffer, Michael. 2005. "Public Finance." In Bertram I. Spector, editor, *Fighting Corruption in Developing Countries: Strategies and Analysis,* 79–95. Bloomfield, Conn.: Kumarian Press.

Schargrodsky, Ernesto, Jorge Mera, and Federico Weinschelbaum. 2001. "Transparency and Accountability in Argentina's Hospitals." In Rafael Di Tella and William D. Savedoff, editors, *Diagnosis Corruption: Fraud in Latin American Hospitals.* Washington, D.C.: Inter-American Development Bank.

Schloss, Miguel. 2002. "Combating Corruption: From Words to Deeds." *Cuba in Transition.* Vol. 12: 16–37. Washington, D.C.: Association for the Study of the Cuban Economy.

Schuknecht, Ludger. 1990. "Rent-seeking and Perestroika." *Public Choice* 66: 83–88.

Schwartz, Rosalie. 1997. *Pleasure Island: Tourism and Temptation in Cuba.* Lincoln: University of Nebraska Press.

Schwenke, Stephe. 2002. "A Summary of Sectoral Reviews of Corruption in Less Developed and Transitional Countries." In *Sectoral Perspectives on Corruption.* November. Washington, D.C.: Management Systems International.

Scott, James C. 1969/2002. "Corruption, Machine Politics, and Political Change." In Arnold J. Heidenheimer and Michael Johnston, editors. *Political Corruption: Concepts and Context,* 221–231. New Brunswick, N.J.: Transaction Publishers. First published in 1969.

———. 1972/2002. "Handling Historical Comparisons Cross-Nationally." In Arnold J. Heidenheimer and Michael Johnston, editors, *Political Corruption: Concepts and Contexts,* 123–136. New Brunswick, N.J.: Transaction Publishers. First published in *Comparative Political Corruption,* Englewood Cliffs, N.J.: Prentice Hall, 1972.

Scott, Rebecca J. 1985. *Slave Emancipation in Cuba: The Transition to Free Labor, 1860–1899.* Princeton, N.J.: Princeton University Press.

Seligson, Mitchell A. 2002. "The Impact of Corruption on Regime Legitimacy: A Comparative Study of Four Latin American Countries." *Journal of Politics* 64, no. 2 (May): 408–433.

Shah, Anwar, and Mark Schacter. 2004. "Combating Corruption: Look Before You Leap." *Finance and Development* (December): 40–43.

Sheperd, Geoffrey. 2003. "Civil Service Reform in Developing Countries: Why Is It Going Badly." Paper presented at the Eleventh International Anti-Corruption Conference, Seoul, Korea, May 25–28.

Shleifer, Andrei, and Robert W. Vishny. 1993. "Corruption." *Quarterly Journal of Economics* 108, no. 3 (August): 599–617.

———. 1998. *The Grabbing Hand: Government Pathologies and Their Cures.* Cambridge, Mass.: Harvard University Press.

Sik, Endre. 1992. "From the Second to the Informal Economy." *Journal of Public Policy* 12, no. 2: 153–175.

Simis, Konstantin M. 1982. *The Second Economy and Corruption at the District Level.* Washington, D.C.: Kennan Institute for Advanced Russian Studies.

Simpson, Glenn R. 2005. "Multinational Companies Unite to Fight Bribery." *Wall Street Journal,* January 27.

Soler, Armando. 2002. "Los enigmáticos fondos de Cuba." *Cubanet,* July 23.

"Sólo 750 sitios en Internet a finales de 2003." 2004. EFE, La Habana. *(Madrid) El Mundo,* January 13. At http://www.elmundo.es.

Spadoni, Paolo. 2004. "The Current Situation of Foreign Investment in Cuba." *Cuba in Transition.* Vol. 14: 116–138. Washington, D.C.: Association for the Study of the Cuban Economy.

Speck, Mary. 2002. "Let There be Candy for Everyone: Reform, Regulation, and Rent-seeking in the Republic of Cuba, 1902–1952." *Cuba in Transition.* Vol. 12: 116–127. Washington, D.C.: Association for the Study of the Cuban Economy.

Stansbury, Neill. 2005. "Exposing the Foundations of Corruption in Construction." In Transparency International, *Global Corruption Report 2005. Special Focus: Corruption in Construction and Post-conflict Reconstruction,* 36–50. London: Pluto Press.

Stratfor. 2005. "Global Market Brief: February 14, 2005." Report by Strategic Forecasting. At http://stratfor.org.

Svejnar, Jan. 2002. "Transition Economies: Performance and Challenges." *Journal of Economic Perspectives* 16, no. 1 (winter): 3–28.

Swart, Koenraad W. 2002. "The Sale of Public Office." In Arnold J. Heidenheimer and Michael Johnston, editors, *Political Corruption: Concepts and Contexts,* 95–106. New Brunswick, N.J.: Transaction Publishers. First published in 1949.

Tamayo, Juan O. 1999a. "Ofensiva contra la corrupción llega a altos jefes." *El Nuevo Herald,* July 2.

———. 1999b. "Scandal in Cuba's Economy." *Miami Herald,* June 8.

———. 2000. "Cuban defector says Castro holding family." *Miami Herald,* March 30.

———. 2002. "De la Seguridad del Estado al capitalismo." *El Nuevo Herald,* August 20.

Tanzi, Vito. 2002. "Corruption Around the World: Causes, Consequences, Scope, and Cures." In George T. Abed and Sanjeev Gupta, editors, *Governance, Corruption, and Economic Performance,* 19–58. Washington, D.C.: International Monetary Fund.

Tanzi, Vito, and Hamid Davoodi. 2002. "Corruption, Public Investment, and Growth." In George T. Abed and Sanjeev Gupta, editors, *Governance, Corruption, and Economic Performance,* 59–88. Washington, D.C.: International Monetary Fund.

Thomas, Hugh. 1971. *Cuba: The Pursuit of Freedom.* New York: Harper and Row.

———. 1997. *The Slave Trade.* New York: Simon and Schuster.

"Toma control el cartel de la Habana del Ministerio del Turismo." 2004. EFE. Reproduced in *La Nueva Cuba,* February 13.

"Top Cuban tourism officials held." 2003. BBC News, December 4. At http://news.bbc.co.uk.

"Tourists: By the left, march." 2004. *Economist,* July 31.

Transparency International (TI). 2003. "Transparency International Corruption Perceptions Index 2003." Press release, October 7. Berlin: Transparency International.

———. 2004a. "Corruption Is Rampant in 60 Countries, and the Public Sector Is Plagued by Bribery, Says TI." Press release, October 20. London: Transparency International.

———. 2004b. *Global Corruption Report 2004. Special Focus: Political Corruption.* London: Pluto Press.

———. 2005. *Global Corruption Report 2005. Special Focus: Corruption in Construction and Post-conflict Reconstruction.* London: Pluto Press.

Travieso-Díaz, Matías. 1996. *The Laws and Legal System of a Free-Market Cuba: A Prospectus for Business.* Westport, Conn.: Quorum Books.

"Two military officers are accused of corruption." 1997. *Cubanet,* January 9.

United Nations (UN). 2003. *United Nations Convention against Corruption.* New York: United Nations.

———. 2004. *Anti-Corruption Tool Kit.* New York: United Nations. At http://www.unodc.org/unodc/en/corruption_toolkit.html.

United Nations Development Programme (UNDP), United Nations Environment Programme, World Bank, and World Resources Institute. 2003. *World Resources 2002–2004: Decisions for the Earth.* Washington, D.C.: World Resources Institute.

U.S. Agency for International Development (USAID). 1999. *A Handbook on Fighting Corruption.* Washington, D.C.: USAID, Center for Democracy and Governance.

———. 2004. USAID *Anticorruption Strategy: Recommendations for Agency-wide Expansion of Anticorruption Efforts.* Washington, D.C.: USAID.

U.S. Department of Agriculture (USDA). 2003. *How Cubans Survive.* USDA Foreign Agricultural Service, Global Agriculture Information Network (GAIN) Report C13006, May.

U.S. Department of Commerce. 2004. *Business Ethics: A Manual for Managing a Responsible Business Enterprise in Emerging Market Economies.* Washington, D.C.: International Trade Administration.

U.S. Department of State. 2004. *Country Reports on Human Rights Practices: Cuba, 2003.* February. Washington, D.C.: U.S. Department of State. At http://www.state.gov.

"Un señorito de la nueva clase en Cuba." 1999. *El Nuevo Herald,* June 29.

Van Rijckeghem, Caroline, and Beatrice Weder. 2002. "Bureaucratic Corruption and the Rate of Temptation: Do Wages in the Civil Service Affect Corruption and by How Much?" In George T. Abed and Sanjeev Gupta, editors, *Governance, Corruption, and Economic Performance,* 59–88. Washington, D.C.: International Monetary Fund.

"Varios latinoamericanos entre los más ricos del mundo." 2004. *El Nuevo Herald,* February 27.

Vian, Taryn. 2005. "Health Care." In Bertram I. Spector, editor, *Fighting Corruption in Developing Countries: Strategies and Analysis,* 43–63. Bloomfield, Conn.: Kumarian Press.

Vicent, Mauricio. 2001. "Un nuevo ministerio combatirá la 'contaminación' capitalista en Cuba." *(Madrid) El País,* June 6. At http://www.elpais.es.

Vignier, Enrique, and Guillermo Alonso. 1973. *La corrupción política y administrativa en Cuba: 1944–1952.* Havana: Editorial de Ciencias Sociales.

Vincent, A. 2000. "Cuba se cierra." *(Madrid) El País Digital,* June 1.

Vinod, H. D. 1999. "Statistical Analysis of Corruption Data and Using the Internet to Reduce Corruption." *Journal of Asian Economics.* At http://www.fordham.edu/economics/vinod/j-asian-e.pdf.

Voslensky, Michael. 1984. *Nomenklatura: The Soviet Ruling Class.* New York: Doubleday.

Wank, David L. 1995. "Civil Society in Communist China? Private Business and Political Alliances, 1989." In *Civil Society: Theory, History, Comparison.* Cambridge, England: Polity Press.

Webster, Russ. 2002. "Corruption and the Private Sector." In *Sectoral Perspectives on Corruption.* November. Washington, D.C.: Management Systems International.

Wei, Shang-Jin. 1997. *How Taxing is Corruption?.* Working Paper 6030. Cambridge, Mass.: National Bureau of Economic Research.

Wesberry, Jim. 2001a. "Combating Fraud in Procurement and Contracting." In World Bank Institute, *Improving Governance and Controlling Corruption,* 83–90. Washington, D.C.: World Bank.

———. 2001b. "Sound Financial Management to Counteract Corruption." In World Bank Institute, *Improving Governance and Controlling Corruption,* 95–106. Washington, D.C.: World Bank.

Whitehead, Laurence. 2002. "High Level Political Corruption in Latin America: A 'Transitional' Phenomenon?" In Arnold J. Heidenheimer and Michael Johnston, editors, *Political Corruption: Concepts and Contexts,* 801–817. New Brunswick, N.J.: Transaction Publishers.

Whitney, Robert. 2001. *State and Revolution in Cuba: Mass Mobilization and Political Change, 1920–1940.* Chapel Hill: University of North Carolina Press.

Wiehen, Michael H. 2001. "Transparency in Procurement." In Lara M. Gabriel and Rick Stapenhurst (with Mary Thomas), editors, *The Role of Bilateral Donors in Fighting Corruption,* 85–93. Washington, D.C.: World Bank Institute.

Winbourne, Svetlana. 2005. "Environment and Natural Resources." In Bertram I. Spector, editor, *Fighting Corruption in Developing Countries: Strategies and Analysis,* 97–114. Bloomfield, Conn.: Kumarian Press.

World Bank. 1997. *Helping Countries Combat Corruption: The Role of the World Bank.* Washington, D.C.: World Bank, Poverty Reduction and Economic Management Unit.

———. 1999. *World Bank Annual Report 1999.* Washington, D.C.: World Bank.

———. 2000. *Anticorruption in Transition: A Contribution to the Policy Debate.* Washington, D.C.: World Bank.

———. 2002. *Transition—The First Ten Years: Analysis and Lessons for Eastern Europe and the Former Soviet Union.* Washington, D.C.: World Bank.

———. 2003. *Understanding Public Sector Performance in Transition Countries—An Empirical Contribution.* Washington, D.C.: World Bank, Poverty Reduction and Economic Management Unit.

Yáñez, Eugenio. 2005. "Mito y Realidad." *La Nueva Cuba,* August 17. At http://www.lanuevacuba.com/archivo/eugenio-yanez-4.htm.

Zimbalist, Andrew. 1994. "Reforming Cuba's Economic System from Within." In Jorge F. Pérez-López, editor, *Cuba at a Crossroads,* 220–237. Gainesville: University Press of Florida.

INDEX

Abed, George T., 33, 239n1
absenteeism, 43, 47, 127–128, 168
academic organizations and "think
    tanks," 112, 114, 140
accountability: building public awareness
    of, 211; and civil service, 218–219;
    and civil society organizations (CSO),
    109–118; and corruption, 6; as
    governance indicator, 173–175;
    internalization of value of, 210; and
    Internet, 120–121; legal infrastruc-
    ture for, 212–214; and mass media,
    118–120; and political will, 210; in
    republican Cuba, 71; and rule of law,
    107–109; in socialist Cuba, 106–121,
    173–175, 223
accounting practices: in republican
    Cuba, 64, 71, 77, 80; in socialist
    Cuba, 167–169; in transition of Cuba
    from socialism, 18, 222–226
acopio system, 99, 100, 101, 105, 133
action groups (*grupos de acción*), 78, 81
administrative corruption, definition
    of, 13
Afghanistan, 25
Africa, 25–26, 240n2. *See also* specific
    countries
Agh, Attila, 13, 147
Agrarian Reform Laws, 90, 91
agricultural cooperatives, 91, 92, 93,
    94–95, 115, 116

agricultural markets, 93, 95, 97, 165, 169
agriculture: and *acopio* system, 99,
    100, 101, 105, 133; agricultural
    cooperatives, 91, 92, 93, 94–95, 115,
    116; agricultural markets, 93, 95, 164,
    169; black markets in, 39, 101; and
    corruption, 31, 38–39; independent
    nongovernmental organizations in,
    115, 116; in Soviet Union, 94–95;
    state ownership of, in socialist Cuba,
    90–92, 99; sugar industry, 65, 67, 69,
    74, 76–79, 85; and transition of Cuba
    from socialism, 204. *See also* food
Aguirre, Benigno, 110
airlines, 83
Aldana, Carlos, 143, 160
Alemán, Arnoldo, 210
Alemán, José Manuel, 78
Alerta magazine, 81
Alfonso, Pablo, 139, 143–146, 153, 160
Almeida, Juan, 145
Almeida, Juan Antonio, 145
Almeida, Juan Juan, 145–146
Alonso, Guillermo, 77, 80, 81
Álvarez, José, 102, 103, 104–105, 115
Álvarez García, Alberto F., 114
Ameijeiras, Efigenio, 141–142
Ameringer, Charles D., 76, 77, 78, 80,
    81
amnesties and pardons for criminal of-
    fenses, 59, 66, 70–71, 75, 76, 81

productive resources owned by state in, 90–99; public perceptions of corruption in, 124–125, 127–164; rationing in, 99, 101–102, 103, 105, 140; Rectification Process in, 124, 164; reform process frozen in 1996 by, 97–98, 122; reforms of 1990s in, 93–99, 121–122, 164–165; rule of law in, 107–109; self-employment in, 92, 93, 94, 97, 98, 122, 128–129, 169, 176; and Soviet Union, 164–165, 222; spontaneous privatization in, 146–156, 180–181, 193, 240n1; and tourism industry, 18, 98, 121, 122, 132–133, 137–139, 149–151, 153, 159; U.S. trade embargo against, 147, 161; wages of state-sector workers in, 98–99. *See also* Castro, Fidel

Cuban transition from socialism: and agriculture, 38–39; and anticorruption agencies and commissions, 232–235; anticorruption efforts in, 18, 19–20, 199–238; anticorruption laws in, 18, 204–205; and business community, 201–203, 230–231; and citizen oversight, 228–232; and coalition building for anticorruption efforts, 231–232; and code of ethics, 18, 221–222, 232; and corruption, 18–19, 180–205; dollarization process in, 18; and economic policy, 20, 21, 194–195; and environmental corruption, 41; and financial management, control, and audit, 18, 222–226; and government management reform, 216–218; and international assistance, 200–201, 235–237; and judicial reform, 214; legal framework for, 195–197; and legal infrastructure for transparency and accountability, 212–213; long-term anticorruption efforts in, 206–238; National Integrity System for, 19–20; nature of the

transition, 191–192; and opening of economy to foreign investment in 1990s, 18; political and economic actors in, 192–194; and political will and political institutions, 209–211; and privatization, 189–190; and procurement system, 226–228; and professional civil service, 218–221; and property ownership claims, 204–205; and property rights, 38; and public awareness of democratic governance, 211; questions on, 237–238; and redistributive state, 197–198; regulatory framework for, 196–197; scenarios for, 185, 187–198; short-term mitigation of corruption in, 199–205; small and medium-size enterprises (SMEs) in, 190; and spontaneous privatization, 180–181, 193; stages of, and corruption, 198–199; and state capture, 19, 21–22, 187, 194–195; strategy for, and corruption, 20–22; and tourism industry, 19, 187; unpredictable form of, 21

Cuban War of Independence, 61, 63
Cuban Workers' Central (CTC), 110, 111, 112, 241n2
Cubatécnica, 145
cultural determinants of corruption, 24–29, 34
customs department, 80
Czechoslovakia, 93
Czech Republic, 10, 14

Davoodi, Hamid, 31, 44
DCG (Donors' Consultative Group), 200, 241n2
defectors, 125, 140
De la Cruz Ochoa, Ramón, 135
De la Guardia, Antonio, 240n2
De la Guardia, Patricio, 162
del Aguila, Juan M., 113

227; on Supreme Audit Institution
(SAI), 223
United Nations Convention Against
Corruption (UNCAC), 33, 202, 216
United States: anticorruption laws
of, 215, 236–237; corruption in,
28; Cuban émigrés, 197; and drug
trafficking, 160–163; financial investment in Cuba by, 65, 69, 73;
foreign assistance programs of,
236–237; and Gómez administration, 67; Great Depression in, 75;
and Index of Economic Freedom,
176; intervention of, in Cuba
(1906–1909), 63–65; and Machado
administration, 75; and mafia, 10,
76, 78, 83–84; occupation of Cuba
by, 16, 62; Prohibition in, 76; real
estate purchases by Cuban investors
in, 81; and Spanish-American War
of 1898, 69; trade embargo against
Cuba by, 147, 161; trusts in, 19; and
undocumented migrants, 20. *See also*
Commerce Department, U.S.; State
Department, U.S.
Uprety, Kishor, 212, 221
U.S. Agency for International Development (USAID), 200, 212, 224, 237
utilities. *See* electricity
Uzbekistan, 176

Valdés, Ramiro, 146, 154
Vázquez Bello, Clemente, 74
Vega, Juan José, 139
vehicles, government, 133–134, 141, 143
Velásquez Vásquez, Jhon Jairo, 162
Velázquez, Diego, 58
Venezuela, 145, 176, 241n3
Verdeja Act, 74
Vian, Taryn, 44–48
victimization survey, 125–126
Vietnam, 7, 93
Vignier, Enrique, 77, 80, 81

Villanueva Madrid, Mario, 143
visa sales, 145–146
Vishny, Robert W., 30, 32
Voslensky, Michael, 9
voting, 52, 68, 107

wages: of educators and educational
officials, 43; of government employees in republican Cuba, 36, 87; of
health personnel, 47; of professionals in jobs outside of Cuba, 145; in
socialist Cuba, 98–99, 177, 178
Wall Street Journal, 108–109, 126,
176–177
Wank, David L., 96
War of Independence (Cuba), 61, 63
Warren Brothers, 73
WB. *See* World Bank (WB)
wealth: of Castro and his family,
156–161; of Saddam Hussein, 156; of
politicians and government officials in
republican Cuba, 68, 69, 77, 78, 83
Wesberry, Jim, 224–225, 228
Weyler, Valeriano, 61
whistleblower protections, 37, 202, 213,
229
white corruption, 27
wholesale and foreign trade, 90–92, 98,
100
Winbourne, Svetlana, 39–41
work. *See* government employees; labor
force; labor unions and labor organizations; self-employment
Workers' Youth Army (EJT), 104
World Bank (WB): anticorruption
strategy of, 236; assistance for Cuban
transition by, 200, 241nn1–2; on civil
service reform, 221; on civil society
organizations (CSOs), 109–110; on
corruption in transition countries, 10,
13–14, 16, 183–189, 209; and Corruption Perceptions Index (CPI), 172;
on Cuban economy in 1950, 80; on